A HISTORY OF BRITAIN

Book VII

The seventh volume of this evolving series covers the first four decades of the 20th century. Britain started with all the trappings of greatness with the largest empire ever known but all this was soon to change. The USA and Japan rivalled the dominance of Europe, countries within the Empire began to assert their own national identities, and divisions within Europe became increasingly fraught leading to the First World War and then to the outbreak of the Second World War. Ireland continued to be a thorn in Britain's side with self-government gained through violence. There were achievements too during the inter-war years: the working classes became more involved in politics and women secured the right to vote. More people than ever began to enjoy a higher standard of living and the provision of State welfare was widely extended.

EH Carter was Chief Inspector of Schools in the 1930s and '40s. **RAF Mears** taught history at Warwick School between 1923 and 1933.

David Evans, who edits the restored series, is an historian and former Head of History at Eton College.

PUBLICATION SCHEDULE

A HISTORY OF BRITAIN

Liberal England, World War and Slump
♦
1901-1939

by

EH Carter & RAF Mears

edited and updated by

David Evans

STACEY
INTERNATIONAL

A HISTORY OF BRITAIN
Liberal England, World War and Slump, 1901-1939

STACEY INTERNATIONAL
128 Kensington Church Street
London W8 4BH
Tel: +44 (0)20 7221 7166; Fax: +44 (0)20 7792 9288
Email: info@stacey-international.co.uk
www.stacey-international.co.uk

ISBN: 9781906768485

This version © Stacey International 2011

Original edition published in 1937 by The Clarendon Press

1 3 5 7 9 0 8 6 4 2

Printed in the United Kingdom

The Publishers of this edition of *The History of Britain*, revised by David Evans (formerly Head of History, Eton College), give wholehearted acknowledgement to the original work of the late EH Carter (sometime Chief Examiner in History, Board of Education, and HM Inspector of Schools) and RAF Mears (former Senior History Master, Warwick School), who died respectively in 1954 and 1940. The Publishers declare that prolonged endeavours devoted to tracing whether rights to the work of these two distinguished scholars rested with any successors or assigns have been made.

Maps by Amber Sheers

CIP Data: A catalogue record for this book is available from the British Library

Contents

List of Illustrations

List of Maps

Note on Place Names
The maps follows contemporary usage, thus 'Rumania' and not the modern
'Romania' and so on.

Glossary

Anti-semitism	dislike of Jews and persecution resulting from it
Blacklegs	labour brought in by employers to break a strike
Capitalism	economic system in which most industry is run by private firms
Duce	Leader (*Italian*), title assumed by Mussolini
Fascist	connected with Mussolini's regime; often used to describe any authoritarian, non-Communist regime
Führer	Leader (*German*), title assumed by Hitler
Laisser faire	Let [someone] act (*French*), the avoidance of government interference in economic and social matters
Luftwaffe	German airforce
Methodist	someone belonging to a Christian church founded by John Wesley
Nonconformist	someone who does not belong to the Church of England, but to a different Protestant church
Pacifist	someone who rejects war as a method of solving disputes
Proletariat	the working class
Quaker	a Nonconformist group, known for its pacifism
Reich	the German state or Empire
Status quo	the existing state of affairs
Suffrage	the vote
Suffragist	a person seeking the right to vote
U-boat	German submarine
Unitarian	Nonconformist group
Whip	party official who ensures that MPs vote in the Commons as directed by the party leaders

Note on Money

In this period, Britain's currency was not decimalized. There were 12 old pennies to the shilling and 20 shillings to the pound sterling. (Hence there were 240 pence to the pound.) The old penny was abbreviated as *d*, the shilling as *s* and the pound as £.

OUTLINE SUMMARY

INTRODUCTION

At the start of the 20th century, Britain was a world power, possessed of an empire on which the sun never set. It was the chief beneficiary of a long process of technological and economic change which had come to a climax in the 19th century. Europe had become the dominant continent, with command of the seas enabling it to project its power to other continents. All the non-European empires had slid into decay. But by 1900 there were signs that this situation was changing. The USA was a sleeping giant, possessed of economic power equivalent to that of all the European powers put together. Japan was about to stun the world by demonstrating that European technology and industrial organization could be borrowed by peoples of non-European culture and used to devastating effect against European powers, in this case the Russians. For the moment, the British gained from the rise of Japan, which became their ally in 1902. In India, however, the jewel in their imperial crown, the unifying and modernizing impact of their rule was beginning to create an Indian nationalism that boded ill for the long-term future of the Raj.

Worried about Britain's future as the world's premier power, some statesmen, such as Joseph Chamberlain, hoped to call upon the Empire to remedy any deficiencies in the mother country. There were projects to turn the Empire into a single economic unit, to create an Imperial economic union. There were hopes that the countries of the Empire would act together against external threat. Hence in 1904 Arthur Balfour set up the Committee for Imperial Defence. The premiers of the white Dominions each had a seat on it, but hardly ever attended. Given the diverse interests of the different parts of the Empire and the tradition of self-government, there was never much prospect of turning it into a super-state, but Imperial solidarity was to be a significant factor in the first half of the 20th century, chiefly in the two world wars.

In 1901 most British statesmen were less worried about the rise of powers outside Europe than they were about traditional enemies inside it. In 1901 attention was still focused on France and Russia, but with astonishing speed projects of alliance with Germany against Russia were replaced by understandings with the old enemies against what came to be perceived as the German threat. Unification and industrialization in the later 19th century had made Germany into the greatest economic and military power in Europe. First Wilhelm II and later, after 1933, Adolf Hitler sought to consolidate and perpetuate German superiority. In doing so, they came to be viewed by the British much as Napoleon had once been regarded. They were the would-be masters of Europe, who, once in control of it, would have the means to destroy British independence. Britain fought against Germany between 1914 and 1918; by 1939 a second war was imminent.

The great unsolved problem within the British Isles that 20th-century Britain inherited from the past was Ireland. Two possible solutions had been advanced in the last two decades of the 19th century. One, put forward by William Gladstone, was Home Rule. The solution had split the Liberal Party and had therefore not been enacted by Parliament. Shorn of the Liberal Unionists, the party remained strongly committed to the policy. It was certain that it would re-introduce it when it was next returned to office, especially as the Irish Home Rulers could give it the support of around 85 MPs. The House of Lords, however, remained a roadblock, as did the opposition of the Protestant majority in Ulster. The Conservative-Unionist administration had hoped to kill the demand for Home Rule in Ireland by conceding the economic demands of the Irish Catholic population, but there were few signs by 1901 that the policy was likely to work.

One of the themes of 20th-century British history was to be the expansion of state provision for individuals and much-increased state intervention to re-shape the economy and society. In 1901 state expenditure was still at a low level. Individuals were expected to do most things for themselves and what they couldn't do was to be done by private charity or the local community. Even at the start of the 20th century, however, pressure was building up for the state to do more. Surveys revealed the state of the poor, which seemed scandalous in relatively affluent 20th-century Britain. Britain's future seemed to depend on an expansion of education and measures to improve health, particularly that of the young. The essential modesty of 19th-century government was rejected.

Within Britain giant steps had been taken during the 19th century towards a democratic political system, but no one had planned to arrive at this destination and progress towards it had been piecemeal. In many ways, Britain in 1901 still did not look democratic. Presiding over the structure was an elderly widow and then her elderly son Edward VII, who were still members of an international guild of monarchs. The First World War was to change that. It compelled the monarchy to domesticate itself by re-branding itself as the House of Windsor, and it swept away many of the greatest members of the guild, the ruling houses of Prussia, Russia, Austria and so on. The House of Lords, still including many representatives of the great landed families, retained the power to reject measures desired by the elected representatives of the people in the House of Commons. In 1901 the Prime Minister Lord Salisbury sat in the Lords and was descended from the ancient aristocratic House of Cecil, and when he retired in 1902, he was succeeded by his nephew Arthur Balfour. It was questionable how much longer such arrangements could survive in an age when the number even of Conservative landed MPs was slowly dwindling. Arguments were heard too for yet another Reform Act for the House of Commons. There were some calls for universal manhood suffrage, instead of the restriction of the vote to householders, and a proposal for votes for women had already won a majority in the Commons.

In the 19th century, new social groups had been brought into the political process by their inclusion in the two historic political parties, the Tories/Conservatives and the Whigs/Liberals. Both of the parties had succeeded in attracting a working-class following. As the election of 1900 had just shown, patriotism and Empire were Conservative causes to which many members of the working classes would rally. The Liberals had support from the working class organized in the trade unions and their parliamentary strength included a (small) number of Lib-Lab working-class MPs in Parliament. The historic parties had enjoyed success, because elections had not been fought on class lines. It was not certain that this happy state of affairs would continue in the 20th century. Some socialists hoped that the working class would break the old mould of politics and establish a new kind of social and political system. One of the big issues of the first half of the 20th century was what the greater involvement in politics of the working class would do to the British parliamentary system.

DATE SUMMARY

SALISBURY (1895-1902)

1900	Conservative victory in Khaki Election	1899-1902 ✕ BOER WAR	
1900	Labour Representation Committee formed; Ruskin *d*.	1900	Relief of Mafeking
1901	QUEEN VICTORIA *d*.	1901	Commonwealth of Australia created
1901-10	EDWARD VII Treaty of Vereeniging with Boers	1902	Anglo-Japanese Alliance Cecil Rhodes *d*.

BALFOUR (1902-5)

1902	Education Act	1902 Wireless (Marconi) invented
1903	Chamberlain resigned to launch Tariff Reform Campaign	1904 ANGLO-FRENCH ENTENTE 1904-5 Russo-Japanese War
1905	Balfour resigned	1905 First Morocco Crisis

THE LIBERAL REFORMERS (1905-14)

1905-8	Campbell-Bannerman Ministry	1906	Liberal Election victory
1906	Algeciras Conference		
1908-15	First Asquith Ministry	1908	First Bosnian crisis
1909	THE PEOPLE'S BUDGET	1909	Blériot flies Channel
1910	Budget and Lords crisis Two General Elections Edward VII *d*.	1910	Union of South Africa created
1910-36	George V		
1911	PARLIAMENT ACT; National Health Insurance	1911	Agadir crisis in Morocco
1911-14	Home Rule Bill		
1912	Coal Strike	1912	Capt. Scott at South Pole 1912-13 Balkan Wars
1914	Irish crisis	1914	(June) Assassination of Archduke Franz Ferdinand
1914	(August) Outbreak of the First World War		

I

THE WORKING CLASS,
THE TRADE UNIONS AND
THE FOUNDATION OF THE LABOUR PARTY

1. The Economy, 1900-14

THROUGHOUT the period from about 1850 to the mid-1890s, the
amount workers could buy with their wages tended to increase decade
by decade. From the mid-1890s, though wages went on rising, prices
increased faster. This was because the prices of British imports went
up more than the prices of its exports. By about 1908 the gradual
deterioration in the workers' position had become obvious and began
to influence industrial unrest.

Rise in cost of living

The other disquieting feature of the economy in the Edwardian
period was of less recent origin. It was the relative slowness of British
industry to innovate in a rapidly changing world. Before the First
World War, Britain still furnished more than half the world trade in
cotton goods and its shipbuilding yards produced over half the new
tonnage of the world. Coal production was at an all-time high and large
quantities were exported. Britain remained very strong in the industries
in which it had led the world throughout the previous century. In the
newer industries - steel, the manufacture of machinery, chemicals and
electricity - Britain lagged far behind the United States and Germany.

Industrial stagnation

The reasons for Britain's failure to respond to the challenge of
industrial change have been endlessly debated. To some degree, its
earlier success was responsible. Industrial sites were often cramped,
hemmed in by working class housing, and so unsuitable for huge
factories with mechanized mass-production such as were coming to
characterize German and American industry. Much of industry was
dominated by family firms which were averse to raising capital in the
market and preferred to rely on re-investing profits, but this too

limited their capacity for growth. In these circumstances, more British investment went abroad than into British industry in the years just before 1914, mostly to the United States and the white Dominions of the Empire.

The British education system has also been blamed for the British failure to maintain its industrial lead. The prestigious schools were the public schools, and their classical curriculum and stress on Christianity and games-playing was geared to producing imperial officials and military officers rather than captains of industry. The products of public schools did not, however, avoid money-making activities altogether. They often became men who worked in the City of London, supplying banking facilities, insurance and other services to the rest of the world. The rationale of their choice of economic activity made good sense from their individual point of view and also from that of the country. Britain's profits from the City's activities made up for the excess of imports over exports. The country's financial dominance of the world was also a major foundation of its international influence.

Public School system

Some Edwardians were convinced that a significant handicap of the country's industry was the strength of the British trade unions. They pushed wages up, reduced working hours and resisted innovations, thereby making British products less competitive in world markets. Yet trade unions were particularly strong in the very industries where Britain maintained its dominance, such as shipbuilding and mining. British wages were, in any case, lower than American ones, which advanced rapidly in the Edwardian period. This was because of the higher productivity of American workers thanks to far greater mechanization. It can be argued that in Britain labour was too cheap and that therefore British manufacturers lacked sufficient incentive to mechanize and develop mass-production methods. Perhaps too the fact that a large pool of cheap labour existed in Britain helped to fuel the resistance of skilled workers to innovation, since they feared being reduced to the same condition.

Trade unions

The wages of British workers around 1900 were high by historic standards, if low by contemporary American ones. Wages had risen enough to make possible the emergence of the first chain stores from the 1870s onwards. Most of them were in food: the Home and Colonial Stores, the International Tea Company and Lyons corner tea shops. They produced or bought wholesale the commodities in which they dealt and then sold a standard range at their retail outlets. They depended on a mass-market which could come into existence only at a certain level of general prosperity. By 1900 there were also chains of stores selling such items as men's clothing, footwear and pharmaceuticals, but the workers' standard of living was still too low for many products to make the transition from luxury to mass-production. This factor limited also the potential of British industrial development.

Most economic change in early 20th-century Britain was slow, but significant changes were afoot. There were examples of rapid and successful mechanization, like the boot trade. Gas and electricity were becoming generally available and transforming homes and workplaces. New products were appearing, such as sewing machines, gramophones, artificial silk and plastics. There were motor cars on the roads, though they were still luxury products limited to the wealthy classes. The structure of employment was changing too. The proportion of skilled workers was slowly falling as factories made more use of semi-skilled and unskilled labour. The satisfaction to be derived from mastery of a skill was becoming rarer. The numbers employed in domestic service were also in decline. Instead, more women were working as shop assistants, typists and telephonists. They were moving out of personal into mass service. This trend was symptomatic of a long-term transition from a situation where most people knew their employer personally and in many cases identified with him (or her) to a situation where the loyalty required was corporate, as in the post office, the railways or the police. The face-to-face society which most Victorians still knew was giving way to the more impersonal world of the 20th century.

Mechaniz-ation in industry

Decline in domestic service

2. Socialism and Working-Class Politics in the 1880s and 1890s

Socialism came in many different forms, but at its core was a desire to bring about a transformation of society in order to improve the living conditions of the working class. One of the earliest English socialists was the industrialist Robert Owen, who believed that human nature was the product of environment and education and could therefore be re-shaped to become the basis of a fully co-operative society. His efforts to found an ideal society failed and the only lasting effect of his various endeavours was the Co-operative Trading Scheme which later blossomed into the Co-operative Movement. The idea was that shops would be established which belonged to the customer and returned their profits to him or her through payment of a dividend. Such stores could be useful, but Owen despised them, since they did so little to change society.

Co-operative Movement

The most famous 19th-century socialist was Karl Marx, a German who spent his entire life after 1849 in England. He had written his *Communist Manifesto* in 1847 and when in England wrote *Das Kapital*, the first volume of which was published in 1867. He looked forward to the collapse of the society of his time, dominated by the middle classes (or bourgeoisie), and its replacement by a working class (or proletarian) society. In the latter private property would be abolished and the land and factories would be owned by the community. The ideas of Marx had an impact on England in the 1880s, when the thinker's works were read by HM Hyndman, who founded the Social Democratic Federation (SDF) in 1884 and committed it to Marx's ideas. Hyndman, himself an Old Etonian, was more successful in recruiting well-to-do middle-class figures like William Morris of the Arts and Crafts Movement than actual workers, but his group had its hour of fame in 1886-7, when there was a brief economic downturn and its orators stirred up crowds of demonstrators in London.

Fabians

Marx also had some effect on a second significant group which emerged in the 1880s. These were the Fabians, who had no ambition to become a mass party, but instead wished to be a sort of think tank which might provide ideas for professional politicians to take up. This attitude won them the label of 'drawing-room socialists'. They had no desire to bring about a revolution, but expected to bring about evolution in the required direction by 'permeating' existing organizations such as the Liberal Party. The leading members of the group were Sidney and Beatrice Webb, who were close friends of another important member, the playwright George Bernard Shaw.

Sidney and Beatrice Webb

The British working class was much more attuned to Christianity than to Marxism or Owenism. Nonconformist religious bodies such as the Methodists, particularly the Primitive Methodists, and Unitarians retained some working-class appeal, though there was a strong tendency for them to become more 'respectable' and middle class. In the 1890s the Labour Church Movement developed a specifically working-class version of Christianity which had wide appeal for a time. Many of the features of Methodist organization, such as travelling lecturers and conferences of delegates, could usefully be copied by a fledgeling working-class political party. Methodism provided many men with training in the art of public speaking. The man who was to be most important in the early development of working-class politics in Britain emerged from a nonconformist background. This was Keir Hardie, a man with a genuine claim to working-class origins. He was born in 1856, the illegitimate son of a Scottish farm servant and a miner. His education was confined to what he could glean at night school, and he worked from the age of eight as an errand boy and then down a mine. Later he became associated with efforts to establish trade unions for Scottish miners. His oratory had the flavour of a sermon and his meetings might include a hymn and a prayer. At first a Liberal, he came to doubt whether the Liberals would ever sponsor more than the occasional token working man as a parliamentary candidate. He

Keir Hardie

began to think that a new party was necessary to put forward the working man's concerns and that if it was to be effective, it would have to be based in the trade union movement. From the end of the 1880s he worked to realize what he called the 'Labour Alliance'.

Formation of the 'Labour Alliance'

In 1893 a meeting in Bradford founded the Independent Labour Party (ILP). The word 'socialist' was omitted from the name, since many at the meeting were uncomfortable with the idea of transforming society. They preferred to concentrate on specific reforms, such as the eight-hour day, proper provision for the old and ill and a reform of taxation. The new party committed itself to seeking a list of such reforms as well as to a democratization of the political system. Its one bow in the direction of more fundamental change was its adoption of a motion for the collective ownership of 'all the means of production, distribution and exchange'. The new party drew most of its strength from the industrial north. It did not look likely to be a success. It was despised by the SDF and condemned by the Lib-Labs, those who believed that the workers could achieve their goals only under the Liberal umbrella. Its record in the election of 1895 was dispiriting, especially since Hardie lost the seat at West Ham which he had won in 1892. Only the determination of Hardie himself and the dedication of the core members kept the party going at all. In the final years of the 19th century membership declined and the future looked even more uncertain. The party was saved by developments among the trade unions.

Independent Labour Party 1893

Fledgeling party faces difficulties

3. Changes in the Trade Unions after 1889

Trade unions flourished in the mid-Victorian period, but they were largely confined to skilled workmen whose scarcity value gave them an ability to negotiate successfully about wages and conditions with employers. Union subscriptions tended to be high and the unions provided a range of benefits in times of illness and old age. Union members were often nonconformist in religion and Liberal in politics.

Most workers were not unionized: total union membership was around 750,000 in 1888, perhaps 5 per cent of the labour force.

The short period 1889-91 witnessed a sudden doubling of union membership. Conditions were favourable. Unemployment stood at 2 per cent, so that almost all workers had scarcity value. In 1889 organized workers won a couple of high-profile victories which emphasized the potential value of trade unions. Led by Will Thorne, the London gas-workers achieved a reduction of their working day from twelve to eight hours without loss of pay. The London dockers had to stage a five-week strike to gain increased pay, but the daily demonstrations and appeals to public opinion made their struggle and its success very generally known.

The consequent growth spurt in the number of unionized workers in part involved the further unionization of occupations already strongly unionized, coal-mining, for example. But the years 1889-91 were also characterized by the emergence of a 'new unionism'. The 'new' unions were much less exclusive than the old ones. Typically, they charged low fees. They could not offer benefits, but sought to attract members by aggressive tactics designed to win gains from employers. Their leaders were often socialists who stressed working-class solidarity, where earlier union leaders had prided themselves on representing the respectable elements of the working class. In 1890 the 'new' union leader John Burns caricatured the difference of 'old' and 'new' union delegates at the meeting of the TUC as follows:

> Physically, the 'old' unionists were much bigger than the 'new' ... A great number of them looked like respectable city gentlemen, wore very good coats, large watch chains, and high hats ... Amongst the 'new' delegates not a single one wore a tall hat. They looked like workmen; they were workmen.

By 1890 the 'new' unions had begun to change the TUC, which adopted parts of the socialist programme, calling, for example, for an eight-hour day to be enacted by Parliament. Burns himself was elected on to the TUC's Parliamentary Committee.

The successes of 1889-91 proved in many ways a false dawn. Unemployment soon rose again. The employers organized themselves and counter-attacked. Dockers' and shipping unions experienced reverses at many of the ports and several of them folded. Of the 'new' unions that survived, most shed members and were forced to become more like the 'old' unions, ignoring the easily replaceable unskilled workers and drawing back from confrontation with the employers. Notions of class war and working-class solidarity were in practice ignored. Yet the trade union movement held on to the bulk of its new recruits. Technical change had created many semi-skilled workers who could not be readily replaced by blacklegs in a strike and therefore had bargaining power. More expensive machinery and more complex production processes increased the damage that stoppages could do and therefore made employers more inclined to submit to union pressure.

The emergence and survival of 'new' unionism was one factor in changing the political outlook of the trade union movement. Yet the 'new' unions were unable to maintain the influence which they had exercised in the TUC of 1890. In 1894 it was laid down that delegates' voting strength was to be proportional to the number of unionists they represented, a rule-change which much reduced the voting power of the 'new' unionists. By this time, however, the political outlook of the older unions was beginning to change. Their enlargement in 1889-91 often brought in younger men, more willing to accept change. The ILP, founded in 1893, was a much more congenial party to consider working with than the older SDF. Moreover, the working-class parties were already showing that they could achieve benefits for working men at municipal level. Their members secured election to school and Poor Law boards and local government bodies. When in 1898 they gained control of West Ham, they introduced an eight-hour day, a 30 shilling (£1.50) minimum

'New' unions gain parliamentary foothold

Support for 'new unionism' fades

wage and two weeks' holiday for council employees. Some workers wanted some of these innovations to be introduced at national level: for example, the miners' experience of wildly fluctuating wages led their union, the Miners' Federation, to consider favourably socialist demands for a minimum wage.

Union leaders had in the past relied upon the Liberal Party to look after the interests of the working class. In some places the party had sponsored working men as its official candidates. They were known as Lib-Labs. Reliance on the Liberals had always seemed to many working-class leaders a more practical way of achieving what the workers wanted than the lengthy and uncertain business of founding Working a new party. Yet there was growing disillusionment with the Liberals in the 1890s. Local Liberal activists were extremely reluctant to adopt working men as their parliamentary candidates, with the result that there was never more than a handful of Lib-Lab MPs. For most of the years between 1886 and 1905 the Liberals were out of power and unable to do much for the working class. When they did get in, briefly, in 1892, they were so busy with Irish issues that working-class grievances were never addressed. In 1894 the charismatic figure of Gladstone at last bowed out as Liberal leader. His successor Rosebery had little appeal to the working class.

Perhaps Liberal shortcomings would not have mattered if the unions had not come to feel under attack in the 1890s. Foreign competition forced employers to raise productivity by introducing new machines and methods. In 1896 the engineering employers combined on a national scale against the ASE (Amalgamated Society of Engineers) and defeated them. Some trade unionists began to feel that direct political representation might do something to protect workers from employers who seemed on the attack. More precisely, there was a growing realization that trade unions might need legal protection. Legal decisions in the 1890s suggested that the unions' right to picket might not be legally secure and that unions might be liable for damages arising from the action of their officials. Even

Working class disenchantment with the Liberal Party

moderate union leaders began to think that they could not simply wait for the Liberals to act on their behalf.

4. The Foundation of the Labour Party

In 1899 at the TUC there was a majority for a proposal to summon a conference of working-class organizations in order to find ways of increasing the number of workers' representatives in Parliament. The conference met in February 1900. It was not an entirely harmonious affair. Members of the SDF wanted a party committed to doctrinaire socialism. Some trade unionists hoped to bury the whole project. In the end, Hardie got more or less what he wanted. There was to be a distinct Labour group in Parliament with its own whips. Yet co-operation with the Liberals was not ruled out, for the Labour group was to co-operate with any party which promoted legislation in the interests of the workers. The executive committee elected by the conference was strongly under ILP influence and Hardie's henchman, Ramsay MacDonald, was to be secretary of the new organization. The new party was to be called the Labour Representation Committee (LRC).

Labour Presentation Committee (LRC)

The conference of 1900 ended in a victory for those like Hardie who stood for a distinct party to uphold the interests of the working class. It was a total defeat for the ideologues with a blueprint for the reconstruction of society. The working-class movements of the 1880s and '90s had made use of socialists for their energy and commitment, but the socialists' vision was ignored in favour of a pragmatic policy of working within the existing economic, social and political framework to secure the workers' interests and better their lot.

The LRC was hailed in the left-wing press as 'a little cloud, no bigger than a man's hand, which may grow into a United Labour Party'. The new body did not look impressive in 1900. It lacked adequate finance and organization. It sponsored fifteen candidates in the election of 1900, but only two were elected. The trade unions were slow to affiliate with it and some of the biggest ones, such as the Miners' Federation, held aloof. A major factor ensuring its survival was the trade unions' reaction to a legal decision which appeared to undermine them.

The Taff Vale Railway Company in South Wales employed imported labour when the workforce went on strike in 1900. The railway workers' union tried to stop this by means of picketing, whereupon the Company turned to the courts for help. Finally, the House of Lords gave judgment in the Company's favour and established that union funds were liable for any damage done to the business. The union had to pay £23,000 in damages in addition to its own legal costs. The unions regarded the decision as a challenge to trade union rights. It appeared to have created a major obstacle to their future activity on behalf of their workers and to have endangered all their funds. The Unionist government refused to do anything and the Parliamentary Committee of the TUC proved impotent. MacDonald seized on the matter as a propaganda godsend in his campaign to get the unions to affiliate with the LRC. In the two years after the judgment the number of workers represented by affiliated unions more than doubled.

The Taff Vale Railway dispute

With 861,000 workers in affiliated unions and the financial security that stemmed from an increased annual levy on them, by 1903 MacDonald was strong enough to negotiate with the Liberals. Liberal leaders such as Herbert Gladstone and Henry Campbell-Bannerman saw a need to strengthen the ties of the Liberals with the working class if they were to reverse the shattering result of the election of 1900. They could not, of course, foresee that the Liberals would win the next election (of 1906) by a landslide. An electoral pact with the LRC seemed likely to be of considerable benefit to them. MacDonald's funds were sufficient to pay a salary to any Labour MPs who were elected, so that they would not be a drain on Liberal resources. For MacDonald, the attractions of a pact were obvious. Few LRC MPs could be elected against Liberal opposition, but it seemed essential to secure a substantial presence in the Commons if the LRC was to exert enough influence to secure its objectives, such as a guarantee of trade union rights. Given that the LRC was not committed to socialism, there could be no ideological objection to a pact, but both parties preferred to avoid controversy within their ranks by not publicizing it. The pact proved of decisive importance to the LRC. Of its fifty candidates in the election of 1906, twenty-nine were returned, and of these twenty-four had been allowed a clear run in that no Liberal had stood against them.

LRC and Liberal Pact

The election of 1906 was followed by a party conference which changed the party's name to 'The Labour Party'. The MPs had already held a meeting to elect a 'chairman'. The term 'leader' was avoided out of a feeling that there was something undemocratic about the notion of leadership. Certainly, this was what Hardie felt and it was unfortunate that sentiment led to his election as Chairman, a post for which he was to prove unsuitable. He was a prophet rather than an organizer and the work of holding the party together devolved upon David Shackleton, the Vice-Chairman, Ramsay MacDonald, the Secretary, and Arthur Henderson, the Chief Whip. In the party conferences of the next few years determined efforts were made to remove initiative and discretion from the party's MPs and subordinate them to the instructions of the annual party conference. The prime mover was Ben Tillett, who wrote a pamphlet in 1908 entitled *Is the Parliamentary Labour Party a Failure?* The leaders were accused of being 'sheer hypocrites' and 'press flunkeys to Asquith', Liberal Prime Minister from 1908. Assisted by Hardie, the leaders finally beat off the attacks and preserved their freedom of action. They were next to experience a still greater threat from the firebrands in the trade unions.

'The Labour Party' founded

5. Pre-War Industrial Unrest

After a decade of industrial peace, the year 1908 brought a huge increase in the number of days lost to strike action. It was a year of bad trade and high unemployment, when certain employers, mostly in the cotton industry and in shipbuilding, sought to improve matters by decreasing their workers' wages. Another bad year for strikes was 1910. The same industries were affected again, but the railwaymen of the north-east also came out on strike and there was massive unrest in the north-eastern coalfields, where there were disputes over payment for work in 'abnormal places', where hewing the coal was particularly difficult. In the autumn of the same year a great strike began in the Welsh coalfields over similar issues. This strike was long and bitter. Strikers clashed with police and some efforts were made to achieve revolutionary goals.

Industry severely disrupted by strikes

The year 1911 was more alarming still. Unemployment had fallen to 3 per cent and unskilled workers saw an opportunity to better their lot by industrial action. Many joined unions; some went on strike spontaneously. There were clashes with police and blacklegs. In the summer the seamen and dockers stopped work and then the first national railway strike commenced. Riots in Liverpool had to be dealt with by troops and two men were shot dead. The same week troops shot two Welshmen in a crowd attacking a train in Wales. Militant delegates to the TUC in 1911 resolved that 'no effort shall be spared by the forces of organized labour to arouse and maintain the discontent of underpaid workers'. In 1912 over 40 million days were lost to strike action. A national miners' strike had to be ended by government intervention with the grant of minimum-wage legislation. The London dockers came out again, but eventually surrendered unconditionally. Theirs was the last great pre-war strike, though numerous lesser ones kept the numbers of days lost at an abnormally high level till the outbreak of war in 1914.

First national railway strike

The unrest of 1910-14 was an attempt by industrial workers to take advantage of an opportunity presented by falling and then low unemployment, which improved workers' bargaining power. Some of them were aware that the purchasing power of their wages had declined in recent years and sought to make up lost ground. Resentment of the level of wages might well have been increased by greater awareness of inequalities arising from the many surveys of poverty and more conspicuous consumption on the part of the middle and upper classes. The extravagance of the latter was widely commented on in the popular press, as the social elite took its tone from the high-spending King Edward VII (1901-10).

The industrial unrest of the pre-war years was also stimulated by men who were dissatisfied with the way in which working-class politics had developed. To secure the co-operation of a pragmatic and resolutely unideological trade union leadership, all commitment to a transformation of society had been sacrificed. The Labour Party that resulted seemed to have no distinctive policy, while its leaders were extraordinarily lacklustre by comparison with men like David Lloyd George and Winston Churchill in the Liberal government. After the increase in the number of its seats consequent upon the adhesion of the Miners' Federation in 1908, the Labour Party made no further advance, and its lack of crusading zeal and complete failure to appeal to the imagination did not appear to promise any. Perhaps it was not surprising that some men with socialist beliefs lost patience with the Party and sought more immediate progress through industrial action. Some militants were attracted to syndicalism, a creed introduced from abroad, especially by Tom Mann, who had returned from Australia in 1910. He was active in many of the major disputes and was behind the drive to create huge industrial unions and federations. Syndicalists aimed to replace capitalist employers by workers' control of industry. Employers would be weakened by strikes, which would also heighten the workers' sense of solidarity. Ultimately, a general strike would bring about their collapse. Syndicalists were highly critical of the

Syndicalism

existing union structure, which represented the sectional interests of different groups of workers, whereas they wanted to stress the common interest of all workers in the class war. They scorned parliamentary methods as irrelevant to the workers' struggle, which had to be fought out on the factory floor.

The syndicalists helped to make the industrial disputes of 1910-14 longer and more bitter. They encouraged workers to seek immediate redress of grievances through strike action. They strove to prolong disputes and to bring other workers out in sympathy. They enjoyed particular influence among the miners of South Wales and some of the dockers and railwaymen who went on strike in 1911. They had influence too in the creation of the huge unions, the National Union of Railwaymen and the Transport Workers Federation, and in the formation of the Triple Alliance of miners, railwaymen and transport workers in 1914.

Yet the chances of a syndicalist revolution in Britain were not high, and syndicalist zealots did not succeed in making irrelevant the moderate and gradualist approach to reform of the Labour Party. The *Economist* of March 1912, the time of the miners' strike, doubted if even a tenth of the miners understood what syndicalism was. Sympathetic action among British trade unionists remained rare: James Larkin led a strike in Dublin in 1913 and appealed to brother union members in Britain quite in vain. The Triple Alliance, embracing 1.5 million workers, was meant to look impressive to employers, but the separate unions had no obligation to support each other and absolutely no intention of using the Alliance for general political or socially revolutionary purposes. There continued to be every incentive to work with the existing system of government and industrial organization rather than against it. Most employers accepted the existence of trade unions, even if sometimes reluctantly, and were willing to co-operate in collective bargaining. The government was usually conciliatory too. It deliberately involved the unions in the administration of labour affairs and showed increasing

Triple Alliance of miners, railwaymen and transport workers

reluctance to engage in confrontation by providing police or military protection for blackleg labour during strikes.

There can be little doubt that working-class consciousness was more pervasive by 1914 than it had ever been before. As industrial concerns got bigger, fewer workers identified with their employers. As skilled workers became fewer, divisions of status in the workforce became less important. By 1914 over four million workers were organized in trade unions. Yet those same unions were chiefly concerned with the sectional interests of their own members and were unprepared to make sacrifices for the sake of other unions or the working class as a whole. Most workers, even union members, had no interest in politics and did not yet think of the Labour Party as theirs.

Sectarian interests of trade unions

6. Popular Culture and Pre-War Cultural Achievements

In the late 19th century, popular entertainment and social activities still often came under the aegis of churches and chapels and were founded on local self-help and participation. Religious bodies sponsored choral groups whose repertoire included such long-established favourites as Handel's *Messiah* as well as the recently written light operas of Gilbert and Sullivan. Youth clubs were also commonly set up by churches and chapels, but after its foundation by Robert Baden-Powell in 1909, the Scout movement and a little later its sister organization the Guide movement rapidly became very important in offering recreational activities of absorbing interest to huge numbers of young people. Scout groups were still run by local adults and usually linked with local churches, but their foundation marked a reduction of the local, amateur and denominational emphasis of earlier provision for young people.

Sports clubs also often began their lives associated with religious denominations, as in the well-known case of the soccer teams of Glasgow, Protestant Rangers and Irish Catholic Celtic.

By the start of the 20th century, soccer was already established as the game of the working class, though it was one that they generally watched rather than played. The matches were by now contested by teams of professional players, who were watched by legions of local fans, released from work at noon on Saturday in time to be spectators of their local club. The Football League had been founded in 1888 with a membership of twelve northern and Midlands clubs. Within five years it was necessary to institute a second division to accommodate twenty-eight clubs and before the end of the century professional football had arrived in London too. It was already clear that sport had the ability to arouse fierce loyalty and to engage passionate interest which the churches and chapels had formerly possessed, but seemed to be losing in the 20th century.

Soccer becomes the working-class sport

Yet sport did not only mean soccer. In Wales it was rugby football that acquired a mass working-class following in the mining valleys of the south. Between 1900 and 1912 Wales vanquished England, Ireland and Scotland six times in the competition for the 'triple crown'. In 1905 their team even defeated the otherwise invincible New Zealand All Blacks. In England cricket was the national game, played on countless village greens and accepted as a symbol of all that was best in British life. One way of saying that something was morally questionable was to describe it as 'not cricket'. Cricket too had its teams of professionals after the County Championship began in 1873. The governing body of the sport was the Marylebone Cricket Club (MCC), which in 1903 took over the business of sending teams on tour. As yet the only regular destination was Australia, which had beaten England on the latter's home ground in 1882, occasioning the comment in the press that English cricket was dead and that its body would be cremated and the ashes taken to Australia. Ever since, the Ashes have been regularly competed for by the two national teams. Cricket was launched in its role as a unifying force within the Commonwealth.

The Ashes

ROBERT BADEN-POWELL (1857-1941)

Probably the most popular indoor entertainment was music hall. It had developed in the saloon bars of London pubs after the 1850s. While smoking and drinking at tables, the audience was entertained by singing, dancing, stand-up comedy and acrobatic turns. Audience and performers were in close proximity, so that there was plenty of audience participation. By the Edwardian period, official restrictions had tended to turn music hall into variety theatre. The entertainment was similar, but the drinking was banished to a separate bar and the audience became more passive spectators. Theatres such as the Coliseum and London Palladium, still in use today, were built in 1904 and 1910 respectively to accommodate variety shows. One of the greatest heroines of variety theatre was Marie Lloyd (1870-1922),

Music hall and variety

who delighted her audiences with innocent-seeming songs which her winks and gestures suggested had a naughty second meaning. 'I can't help it if people want to turn and twist my meanings,' she said. On one occasion she aroused complaint by singing, 'I sits among the cabbages and peas,' whereupon she changed it to 'I sits among the cabbages and leeks.' She became famous for her versions of songs like 'Oh! Mr. Porter' and 'A little of what you fancy', and when she died, one hundred thousand people attended her funeral. Long before then, variety theatre had received a royal stamp of approval when George V attended the Royal Variety Performance in 1912, though Marie Lloyd was not thought decorous enough for royal ears.

While variety shows amused audiences in the London Palladium, others enjoyed the light operas of Gilbert and Sullivan at the Savoy Theatre. First produced in the second half of Victoria's reign, they remained enormously popular in the early 20th century. Audiences enjoyed their affectionate satire of aspects of British life and society, whether of the law and legal profession in *Trial by Jury* (1874), or of the navy and the British obsession with social status in *HMS Pinafore* (1878), or of bureaucracy in the *Mikado* (1885). Satire of a more challenging nature came from the pen of George Bernard Shaw, a critic and playwright much influenced by his contemporary, the Norwegian dramatist Ibsen. In *Major Barbara* (1905) he satirized every kind of do-gooder, including the well-meaning Major. It turns out that her father, an arms manufacturer and therefore an object of detestation to all good Liberals, achieves more for the poor by providing them with a good wage than his daughter does by her charitable works. In *Pygmalion* (1913-4) he explored in an amusing fashion the relationship between accent, social class and personal worth. Many of his works fell foul of the censor, but they were published with extensive prefaces to make sure that his message was not lost to the world.

George
Bernard
Shaw

Among novelists Thomas Hardy (1840-1928) wrote the last of his Dorset-based novels in the early 1890s, but he continued to be one

PORTRAIT OF EDWARD ELGAR (1857-1934) *c.* 1900

of the greatest English poets. For insight into Edwardian society it is hard to better the *Forsyte Saga* of John Galsworthy (1867-1933), even though it was not published till 1922. Creating more of a stir at the time, however, was the work of HG Wells (1866-1946). He lived at a time when the potential of science for transforming the world was just beginning to be realized. Numbers reading for the Natural Sciences Tripos at Cambridge were increasing rapidly; Imperial College London was founded in 1908 in order to further the progress of scientific studies; and many students were graduating with BSc degrees from the new civic universities. Wells himself had been educated at the Normal School of Science, South Kensington, which played a leading role in the training of science teachers. Many of Wells' best-selling novels were works of science fiction which hinted at the power of science. His *War of the Worlds* (1898), for example, describes an invasion of England by Martians, in which the potential of rocketry, advanced weaponry and germ warfare is made clear.

HG Wells

35

'Land of Hope and Glory'

Even the briefest survey of British cultural achievements around the start of the 20th century has to include reference to Edward Elgar (1857-1934). That is partly because he wrote the *Pomp and Circumstance* marches, which include the music for which the words of 'Land of Hope and Glory'* were written, at Edward VII's suggestion, by schoolmaster AC Benson. The composer may have owed his knighthood of 1904 in part to the marches, but he did not like the jingoistic sentiments of Benson's verse and thought more highly of his own more spiritual works, such as the oratorio *The Dream of Gerontius* (1900), based on Cardinal Newman's meditation on immortality. In 1901-2 *Gerontius* and the *Enigma Variations* were played to great acclaim in Germany. Unusually for an English composer, Elgar had achieved international stature.

---

* This patriotic anthem is still sung annually on the Last Night of the Proms.

II

THE POLITICAL BATTLES, 1901-1914

1. The Eclipse of the Unionists

WHEN Edward VII (1901-10) succeeded his mother to the throne, in his sixtieth year, he inherited a Conservative-Unionist government which had recently been confirmed in power at the 'Khaki Election' of 1900. At a moment when the Boer War seemed about to come to a victorious conclusion, the Unionists had been able to get out the patriotic vote and win a handsome majority of over 100. Robert Cecil, Lord Salisbury, the Prime Minister, retired from politics in 1902. His nephew and successor, Arthur Balfour, was a man of long ministerial experience, a skilful debater in the House and a writer and philosopher of distinction. His cabinet was so full of his aristocratic relatives that it became known as the Hotel Cecil. Yet it also included the Liberal Unionist screw manufacturer from Birmingham, Joseph Chamberlain. He had helped to destroy Liberal unity in 1886. He was soon to destroy the unity of his new party, the Conservative-Unionists.

The 'Khaki Election'

The Balfour Government was responsible for one very important reform, the Education Act of 1902. This Act abolished the School Boards established under the Act of 1870, which were detested by the Conservatives as upholders of Board schools in competition with ones controlled by voluntary bodies (in practice, churches). The Boards in any case lacked the resources to establish and run the system of secondary and technical schools that was now felt to be necessary if Britain was to compete successfully with countries like Germany. The Act of 1902 placed all state-aided education in the hands of the county and borough councils, which were to be helped financially by the central government. The change paved the way for a system of secondary schools for those who stayed on in education beyond the

Education Act abolishes School Boards 1902

age of fourteen, thus providing a route into university education for boys and girls who had not attended fee-paying schools. The Act of 1902 meant that the local authorities henceforth maintained all elementary schools, including those founded and run by the various religious bodies - the Church of England, the Roman Catholics, the Wesleyans. Nonconformists complained that ratepayers were forced to subsidize Church schools, and some people objected altogether to religious instruction in schools. Opposition to Balfour's Education Act was a cause round which all Liberals, badly divided over the Boer War, could unite.

Liberal opposition to Education Act

Liberals could unite too in condemning 'Chinese slavery'. After the Boer War, the goldmines of the Transvaal were short of labour. Black people were more interested in acquiring land, while whites demanded high wages. The Transvaal government therefore agreed to bring in labour from China and eventually over 60,000 labourers were employed on three-year contracts. The workers were efficient and gold production greatly expanded, but horrifying accounts reached Britain of prostitution, opium addiction and sadistic treatment of the Chinese. It was easy for the Liberals to blame the Unionists for conniving at a form of slavery, though the Chinese were paid and were repatriated after their contracts expired. The Liberals were able to hint that the episode typified the Unionist approach to labour: they sought to make it cheap and to exploit it.

Chamberlain launches tariff reform campaign

Even before the Chinese labourers had arrived in South Africa, Joseph Chamberlain had detonated a bomb under the Unionist party. In May 1903, at a meeting in Birmingham Town Hall, Chamberlain launched his campaign for tariff reform. His plan was to exclude foreign goods from the British market by imposing a tariff upon them, but to foster the economic unity of the Empire by waiving the tariff in the case of Imperial products. The first step was to be a tariff upon grain for the benefit of the Canadians. To Liberals this scheme looked like the re-enactment of the discredited Corn Laws, which Peel had repealed in 1846. Yet Chamberlain's proposal was not the same thing at all. He was not proposing to subsidize British farmers, who were unlikely to benefit if Canadian wheat was let in on preferential terms. As his policy developed, the beneficiaries would be British industries threatened in their home market by foreign goods, the metal-bashing industries in and around Birmingham, for example. There were plenty of other economic interests which stood to lose from his plans, however. The cotton industry, for example, did not need the protection of tariffs, but the workers faced the prospect of dearer food if Chamberlain's proposals went through, or, if they secured higher wages, loss of jobs when their products became dearer and sold abroad less well. The City of London too benefited from the free flow of goods and services and stood to lose from any artificial impediments placed in its way. Chamberlain could, however, foresee further benefits from his plans. The income from tariffs could provide the government with the means to make social provision, by paying old age pensions, for example.

Free trade and the Tariff Reform League

These proposals divided the Conservative Cabinet. Some of its members still held that Britain's prosperity depended on the free trade established by Peel and Gladstone in the 19th century. Chamberlain resigned in 1903, in order to take the case for tariff reform to the country. His Tariff Reform League was well funded and professionally organized and Chamberlain tirelessly preached the message that Britain's manufacturing base was being eroded and that only tariff protection could halt the process. Balfour did his best to sit on the fence and maintain the unity of his party, but it was obvious that internal feuding, which had been a Liberal speciality, was now dissipating Unionist energies. In contrast, the Liberals had rediscovered causes round which they could unite: free trade and opposition to 'Chinese slavery' and the Balfour Education Act. The forces of Gladstonian Liberalism were on the march for a final time. At the election of 1906, they were to sweep all before them.

The Conservative-Unionists sustained an overwhelming defeat. Only 157 Conservatives were returned, against 400 Liberals, 83 Irish

Unionists suffer an over-whelming electoral defeat members, and 29 members of the new Labour Party. This surprisingly conclusive result was due in part to the brilliant election campaign fought by Herbert Henry Asquith as the right-hand man of the Liberal Premier Sir Henry Campbell-Bannerman on the issue of free trade, dramatized in the contrast between the 'Big Loaf' secured by free trade and the 'Small Loaf' which tariff reform would bring. Very often large and small loaves were specially baked as visual aids to reinforce the message. Asquith had an easier job than Chamberlain in that the case for tariff reform was less familiar and in apparent contradiction to the short term economic trends. At the very time when Chamberlain was urging radical change to deal with Britain's economic decline, exports were increasing by 50 per cent and unemployment declined from 6 per cent in 1904 to 3.6 per cent in 1906. Chamberlain was hampered too by the evident disarray and disagreement in Unionist ranks. The failed campaign overtaxed the author of tariff reform. In 1906 he suffered a stroke and retired to the political sidelines.

2. New Liberalism

In the election campaign of 1906 the Liberals offered few positive policies, but instead confined themselves largely to attacks on Unionist measures and proposals. Gladstone would have been comfortable with virtually everything that they said. Yet, as would eventually become clear, many Liberals now had aims different from those of their predecessors of the Victorian period. As their label implies, Liberals had always stood for liberty. In Gladstone's time, they stood for the religious rights of Nonconformists, for the extension of democratic political rights to all capable of exercising them responsibly and for freedom of opportunity for all those with talent. The new-style Liberals of the early 20th century believed that Gladstonian definitions of liberty were too narrow. The most important constraints on liberty, they argued, were no longer the ones identified by 19th-century

Liberals, but social and economic conditions. Liberal intellectuals like LT Hobhouse believed that the state must accept responsibility for the welfare of the poorer classes in society, since only if it did so could the individual potential of the poor be fulfilled. Views like these involved the abandonment of two of Gladstone's leading ideas. He had given a high priority to reining in state expenditure, so that people could keep as much as possible of what they earned. New Liberalism implied a raising of the level of government expenditure and therefore a changed attitude to taxation. Nineteenth-century Liberals had also stood for *laisser faire* (leaving things alone). New Liberals remained committed to free trade, but within Britain they proposed to intervene in order to assist those who suffered from social and economic disadvantages.

> Divergence of 'New Liberalism' from 'Old Liberalism'

The mid-Victorians had been optimistic about the future of their society. They tended to assume that technological progress and economic expansion would in time solve most problems. Long before the end of the century this optimism had faded. Canon Samuel and Henrietta Barnett had in 1884 founded Toynbee Hall in the East End of London, so that privileged young men with a social conscience, many of them from Balliol College, Oxford, could stay and study at close quarters the poor and deprived area in which it stood. Many left determined to do something to improve the conditions they had witnessed. By 1900 the state of the East End was well known. In 1890 William Booth, founder of the Salvation Army, wrote *In Darkest England and the Way Out*, in which he suggested that the conditions of people living in the East End were scarcely better than those of African tribesmen. From 1886 to 1903 the industrialist Charles Booth (not related to William) produced 17 volumes minutely detailing conditions in the capital. He did not have a theory to prove, but certain conclusions did seem to emerge from the mass of details: that around 30 per cent of Londoners lived below the poverty line and that the resources of charities were insufficient to cope with the problem.

> Toynbee Hall

Meanwhile, in the north, Seebohm Rowntree, of the chocolate-manufacturing family, began his study of poverty in York. The results were published in a book of 1901 as *Poverty, A Study of Town Life*. Rowntree's work exposed poverty as a problem not confined solely to London's East End. His conclusion that about 28 per cent of the people of York lived in poverty was not so very different from Booth's figure for London. Rowntree showed that the poor were not all idle wastrels: according to him, 52 per cent of families lived in poverty because wages were so low. He showed too that poverty was connected less with individuals' moral qualities than with their stage of life. People were particularly likely to live in poverty when they were very young children who earned no money to relieve the financial strain on their parents, when they became parents of several non-earning children and when they were too old to work. It seemed to follow from the studies of Booth and Rowntree that for the most part the poor could not escape from their poverty. New Liberals went on to argue that it was the job of the state to assist them and that those best able to pay must make a contribution through taxation for this purpose.

The label 'New Liberal' began to be applied to various groups and individuals in the Liberal Party from the 1890s. Their ideas were spread in the Liberal press by editors of newspapers such as the *Manchester Guardian*, *Daily News* and *Daily Chronicle*. Some of the wealthy backers of the Party could not tolerate these new ideas and deserted it, but the members of the Rowntree and Cadbury families remained loyal and such industrialists as William Lever, the soap manufacturer, and Sir John Brunner, of the chemical industry, provided funds.

3. The Earlier Liberal Measures, 1906-8

Campbell-Bannerman's Liberal government took up many of the traditional causes of Liberal governments. In response to the Education Act of 1902, Anglican schools were attacked in a bill of

1906, and in 1908 the government attacked the drink trade by attempting to reduce the number of public houses. Both measures fell foul of the House of Lords, but the government felt that it could not appeal to the electorate on issues of marginal concern to many people.

On other issues the Liberals were more successful. In order to please their allies in the Labour party, the Taff Vale decision was reversed by an act granting the trade unions immunity from prosecution. A Workman's Compensation Act provided compensation for industrial diseases. An uncontroversial start was made on social reform. Ever since the rejection on health grounds of so many army recruits at the time of the Boer War, there had been anxiety about the physical deterioration of the urban population. Several Liberal measures were intended to improve 'national efficiency' by attending to the health of children. Local authorities were enabled to provide meals for needy schoolchildren. Provision was made for setting up school clinics and for the medical inspection of schoolchildren. A Children's Act offered protection to children from such sources of harm as negligent baby-minders and drunken parents. *Workman's Compensation Act*

As early as 1907 Asquith, the Chancellor of the Exchequer, introduced novelties in taxation. He began to differentiate between earned (wages) and unearned (profits from investments, rents, etc.) income for tax purposes, imposing a higher rate on the latter, and made personal declarations of income compulsory. What above all made traditional finance inadequate, however, was the combination of the naval race with Germany and Asquith's scheme for old age pensions. *Asquith introduces taxation reforms*

The Victorians had assumed that workers would be able to avoid poverty in old age if they worked hard and practised thrift during their working lives. The prospect of ending their days in the workhouse was to act as an incentive to work and save hard. These assumptions looked over-optimistic in the early 20th century. Many working-class incomes provided too small a surplus over essential current expenditure to allow for saving for old age. People were living longer and tending to exhaust their savings. Many artisans had accumulated

Pension Act - 1908

pension rights with friendly societies, but the societies too were in difficulties as their liabilities to their unexpectedly long-lived clients mounted up. The case for doing something about poverty in old age thus looked overwhelming. In 1908 an Act provided a non-contributory pension of five shillings a week, about a quarter of a labourer's wage, for each old person over seventy, with 7s 6d for a married couple. The cost turned out to be about £9 million a year.

(iv) *The Struggle between the Liberals and the Lords, 1909-11*

Asquith becomes Prime Minister 1908

In 1908 Asquith became Prime Minister. He was a self-made lawyer of great intellectual gifts who dominated a cabinet which contained such forceful personalities as Winston Churchill, who became President of the Board of Trade, and David Lloyd George, who took Asquith's place as Chancellor of the Exchequer. The latter was a Welsh lawyer from Caernarfonshire with a vein of oratory ultimately derived from the Nonconformist chapels of North Wales. His forte was articulating the grievances of the disadvantaged.

Lloyd George implements People's Budget

Lloyd George in 1909 had to balance a budget unbalanced by naval and social spending. He proposed to raise revenue of £200 million (a larger sum than had ever been contemplated before, even in time of war) and to devote some of this sum to social services, such as pensions. In a word, he proposed to carry much farther the tendency of the previous hundred years not only towards state interference, but towards state aid to the poorer sections of the community. 'This is a war budget,' he announced in his budget speech. 'It is for raising money to wage implacable warfare against poverty and squalidness.' Lloyd George called his measure the People's Budget; to raise the necessary revenue, he intended to tax the rich as they had never been taxed before. In addition to the ordinary income tax, a special super tax was imposed on incomes over £3,000 a year. The rate of tax on unearned income was further increased. A duty was imposed on land values which increased when the land was developed for such purposes as building. Death duties, payable when estates changed hands, were increased on estates

44

of between £5,000 and £1 million. The drink trade was also heavily taxed. Lloyd George was also anxious to set aside money for systematic development of the country's resources and of transport: it was in this budget that Lloyd George created the Road Fund to finance future road-building, made necessary by the advent of the motor car.

The Road Fund

The budget proposals raised a storm of indignation among the well-to-do, whose protests were voiced by the Unionist opposition in the Commons, and by the majority in the Lords. The author of the budget was by no means dismayed by this criticism. On the contrary, it made him appear the champion of the disadvantaged and drew attention away from the fact that the proposed pension was far from generous. He toured the country speaking in defence of his proposals. He attacked the landlords and wealthy classes with a virulence not even exceeded by Joseph Chamberlain in his Radical days. In his Newcastle speech of October 1909, he warned the Lords that they were 'forcing revolution'.

Lloyd George as 'champion of the disadvantaged'

'If they begin issues will be raised that they little dream of, questions will be asked that are now whispered in humble voices. The question will be asked: Should 500 men, ordinary men, chosen accidentally from among the unemployed [Lloyd George's description of the House of Lords], over-ride the judgment - the deliberate judgment - of millions of people who are engaged in the industry which makes the wealth of the country? ... Another question will be: Who ordained that a few should have the land of Britain as a perquisite, who made 10,000 people owners of the soil, and the rest of us trespassers in the land of our birth? ... These are the questions that will be asked. The answers are charged with peril for the order of things the Peers represent; but they are fraught with rare and refreshing fruit for the parched lips of the multitude who have been treading the dusty road along which the people have marched through the dark ages, which are now emerging into the light.'

One of Lloyd George's most telling points was made against the landlords' objection to the state valuation of land. He cited many instances where landlords had made huge profits out of the increase in land value; and he now proposed that in such cases the state should take 20 per cent of the increase. If the landlords objected to this, he held them up to ridicule in his speeches. Here is one example, out of many:

Some mining investors (said Lloyd George) bought some property in Yorkshire. 'Will you allow us to build a few cottages?' they asked the landlord. 'Certainly,' he replied, 'I shall want a small return - £6 or £10 an acre.' 'Quite moderate' (commented Lloyd George), 'he is really a most moderate landlord. The land was at 15s. 6d., and he charges £10. That is only 18 times the value of the land. I can give you cases where landlords have charged 30, 40 or 100 times the value of the land.'

Excitement was at its height when the budget was sent up to the House of Lords. Would the Lords break with the tradition that they should not interfere with financial measures and throw out the national budget which had passed the Commons? They did so, claiming that the measure was not an ordinary financial measure, but an attack on the rights of property. They also maintained that the measure went far beyond the mandate that the government had won at the election of 1906. In effect, they dared Asquith to call another election. By-election results had given them the idea that the Liberals would lose. The budget, however, had revived the popularity of the government, particularly with the working class. The House of Lords could easily be presented as a body of rich men acting in their own selfish interests. They claimed to be guardians of the constitution against Asquith's elective dictatorship, but this claim rang hollow: a glance at their record since 1906 seemed to show that they were nothing but 'Mr Balfour's poodle', used by the Conservatives to thwart the democratically elected Liberal government at every turn. When a fresh election was held in January 1910, the Liberals lost

House of Lords rejects the People's Budget

Liberal majority at 1910 elections

some of their middle-class votes, but extended their lead among the working class. In terms of seats held, the Liberals and Conservatives were more or less equal, but with Labour and Irish Nationalist support the Liberals commanded a handsome majority.

The government's priority was to cut the House of Lords down to size, thus clearing the way for social reform and the taxation to finance it, as well as for Irish Home Rule, which the Lords had blocked. It therefore brought in a Parliament Bill, making it illegal for the Lords to throw out money bills in any circumstances. Besides this, the power of the Upper House was further to be limited. Their veto on all legislation - other than financial - was made suspensive; that is to say, they could hold up a bill passed by the Commons in two sessions, but if it passed the Commons a third time, it would become law in spite of their veto. To provide a safeguard against the possibility that a government with a Commons majority might become dictatorial, the maximum period between general elections was fixed at five instead of seven years. Conservative newspapers raged, and complained that the Constitution was being destroyed. Even the death of Edward VII in May, and the accession of a new King - George V (1910-36) - scarcely turned people's thoughts from the political storm. A second general election in December confirmed the government in power, and in 1911 the Parliament Act was passed. The King agreed to use his powers to create 500 Liberal peers if necessary and this threat ensured the passage of the Act through the Lords. Many Conservative peers abstained from voting; some voted with the government. Thus, amid public excitement not paralleled since the First Reform Bill, and in strangely similar circumstances, the Parliament Act became law. The power of the Upper House to thwart the national will was gone for ever; the way lay open for social reform, and more Lloyd Georgian budgets. The taxes imposed in 1909 now came into operation.

House of Lords' authority reduced

Parliament Act 1911

5. The Liberal Record, 1909-14

The years from 1909 onwards saw the passage of a number of acts

designed to improve conditions for the workforce. At the Board of Trade after 1908, Churchill was chiefly concerned with the scourge of

unemployment, one of the principal causes of hardship among the working class. In 1909 he implemented an idea worked out by one of his advisers, William Beveridge, setting up labour exchanges. These were designed to acquaint the unemployed with available vacancies and thus facilitate their re-employment. In 1911 a scheme of unemployment insurance was established. It covered those industries such as construction, shipbuilding and engineering which were particularly affected by the cyclical upswings and downturns of the economy. Altogether two and a quarter million workers were covered, few of whom had previously enjoyed any protection from economic downturns. Benefits were to be paid from a fund into which employees, employers and the state would all make contributions: the benefits amounted to 7s 6d per week for up to 15 weeks. Churchill introduced his scheme at a time of low unemployment and it was not seriously tested before the war. Whether his fund could have coped with a major slump is questionable.

Much more controversial was Lloyd George's attempt to remove

another major cause of poverty among the working class, the ill-health of the breadwinner. This was his National Health Insurance Act of 1911. Health insurance was to cover all workers earning less than £160 a year, around fourteen million of them. Contributions of a few pence per week were to be paid into an insurance fund by the worker, by his employer and by the state. From the fund a worker unable to work because of illness would receive ten shillings per week. There were provisions too for payment of a permanent disability benefit and for maternity benefit. Insured workers were also entitled to free medical treatment from one of a panel of doctors. Lloyd George's proposals aroused furious opposition from the British Medical Association,

DAVID LLOYD GEORGE (1863-1945)
IN A *PUNCH* CARTOON C. 1910

which envisaged that doctors might be reduced to a species of slavery,
but in the end 14,000 doctors accepted membership of the panels and
many of those from poorer areas found that their income became more
secure. The vested interests of friendly societies and insurance
companies, which had previously helped workers in bad health, led
them to object, but they were mollified by being involved in the
administration of the scheme. Even many workers were none too keen
on a scheme which involved their paying for medical eventualities
which might never happen and some elements in the Labour Party

protested on their behalf. With great political skill Lloyd George piloted his proposals past innumerable obstacles and finally they were carried into law. If Liberal social reform seems in retrospect a little timid, unsystematic and ungenerous, the story of the Health Insurance Act serves as reminder of the difficulties which reforming ministers had to overcome.

Ireland Home Rule Bill rejected by the Lords

The Liberal government had been unable to do anything for its Irish allies while the Lords' veto remained absolute, but after 1911 it had no excuse for further delay. Moreover, it had, since the elections of 1910, depended on Irish Nationalist votes. The Home Rule issue, which had lain dormant since 1894, became the question of the hour. A bill giving Home Rule to Ireland was introduced and passed the Commons in 1912. It was rejected by the Lords but, under the operation of the Parliament Act, was likely to become law in 1914. During the intervening time, political passions rose to heights surpassing even the storms over the People's Budget and the Parliament Act.

Irish dispute over Home Rule escalates

Ulster, with its Protestant majority, would not contemplate the prospect of being ruled by a Dublin parliament; all the religious and racial strife of centuries was behind its refusal. Led by Sir Edward Carson, a Dublin lawyer, and James Craig, son of a whisky millionaire, and backed financially by the Ulster business community, the Ulster Unionist Council planned resistance. In September 1912 the Ulster Solemn League and Covenant was signed by almost 240,000 men and nearly as many women: they pledged themselves to resist Home Rule. Before the end of the year, the Ulster Volunteer Force (UVF) had been set up and had acquired a commander in Sir George Richardson, a distinguished British Army officer. At first, the volunteers merely drilled, often with wooden rifles, but at the start of 1914 it was decided to defy a ban on the importation of arms and smuggle weapons in through the good offices of Major Crawford, a Belfast businessman. In April 35,000 rifles and five million rounds of ammunition were landed by ship and distributed throughout the province. The southern

Irish determined to restore the balance by importing arms too. Thus, in the summer of 1914, there were two armed volunteer forces in Ireland, one resolved to preserve the Union of Britain and Ireland, one bent on Home Rule. When the Liberal government tried to strengthen its authority in the north, 58 army officers stationed at the Curragh camp declared that they would rather accept dismissal than comply with orders to coerce the Ulster Protestants. Men with Irish connections were numerous in the army and it began to look as if the government could not rely on the army to carry out its orders in Ulster. Civil war in Ireland looked imminent.

Civil war in Ireland imminent

The Ulster Volunteers were hoping not to fight. They did their utmost to avoid any disorder which might have forced the British government to intervene against them. Their aim was to convince British opinion of their determination to defy Home Rule and thereby to extract concessions. They were encouraged by Unionist supporters in Britain. One of these was Andrew Bonar Law, promoted to the leadership of the Conservative Party when Balfour was replaced at the end of 1911. 'There are things stronger than parliamentary majorities', he declared in public in 1912. It has been very rare for senior British politicians to express disrespect for constitutional forms in such a way and that Law did so indicates how deep were the passions aroused by the issue of Ireland.

Andrew Bonar Law, Conservative Party leader

Asquith's government could not abandon Home Rule but it did increasingly feel that something would have to be done about Ulster. A conference summoned by George V discussed the issue of which areas might be excluded from the operation of the Home Rule Bill, but no agreement could be reached. The Bill granting Home Rule finally received the Royal Assent in September 1914. Meanwhile, the First World War had broken out and it was agreed to suspend the operation of the new Act until the war was over. At that point, provision would be made for Ulster.

Home Rule Bill 1914

6. The Liberals and Labour

Asquith's government

Achievements of Liberal Reform

The energies of Asquith's government in the final years of peace had to be devoted in large measure to Irish and Welsh issues. In Wales its Nonconformist supporters had long demanded the removal of the special position of the Anglican Church, which seemed unjustified to the chapel-going majority. Disestablishment of the Welsh Church, as it was called, was signed into law in the summer of 1914, though it too was to take effect only when peace returned. The problem for the Liberals was that the outcome of the next election, due in 1915, would be determined primarily in England, where most of their potential supporters were not especially interested in Welsh and Irish issues.

Despite some working-class resentment of the charges imposed on workers by the National Insurance Act, the record of the government since 1908 had done much to consolidate its support among the workers. In piecemeal fashion, it had begun to alleviate the hardship arising from three of the principal causes of poverty, old age, unemployment and ill-health. In other ways too, it had shown itself sensitive to worker grievances. In 1912 a national coal strike was ended by the intervention of the government and an agreement that District Boards should be established to impose minimum wages for the

The Land Campaign

miners. The Land Campaign launched in 1913 aimed to tackle the problem of rural poverty. Lloyd George's Rural Land Enquiry had revealed how low rural wages were and what squalid conditions many workers lived in. The Liberals proposed to build 90,000 houses with up to an acre of land to give rural labourers a degree of independence in bargaining over wages with their employers. The principle of a minimum standard already adopted for the miners was to be adopted for farm labourers too. The idea was to squeeze landowners, not tenant farmers: the latter could appeal to tribunals for review of their rent. In this way, the Liberals hoped to gain support from the poorest country people without forfeiting the votes of the middling groups.

The Liberals hoped to achieve something similar in the towns. Their plan was to tax land values and use the sums that were raised to relieve local rates of some of the burden of the costs of education, the roads and the poor. In this way, small businessmen and small property-owners would be helped and the Liberal coalition between the working class and significant elements of the middle class would be able to survive. Though the matter was never to be put to the test, it seems likely that the Liberals were laying a strong foundation for yet another election victory in 1915. Their Unionist opponents had by now given up the policy of tariff reform, leaving opposition to Home Rule as their main distinctive policy. It probably lacked sufficient appeal to win them a general election.

Bankrupt of ideas and probably facing a fourth election defeat in a row, the Conservative-Unionist party might well have met with a crisis soon after 1914. The outbreak of war was to rescue it and bring it back into government as early as 1915. In 1914, the Liberals, on the other hand, had only one more year left in the entire 20th century in which they would form a government on their own. In well under a decade, they were to be replaced as the main opposition to the Conservatives by the Labour Party.

Conservative-Unionist party rescued by outbreak of war

Yet in 1914 there were remarkably few signs of the great future that lay ahead of the Labour Party. After the election of December 1910 Labour had 42 seats in Parliament, but the great bulk of them depended on the pact with the Liberals, which had been renewed for the elections of 1910. In three-cornered contests Labour won not a single seat and was usually bottom of the poll. The pact did not apply in the by-elections held between 1910 and 1914. In those years Labour contested 14 industrial seats and came bottom of the poll in all of them, including the four seats which it had previously held. If an election had been held in 1915, the Labour Party could hardly have avoided a new pact with the Liberals if it hoped to hold on to its seats.

Labour dependent on Liberal pact

Increasingly, it was unclear what the Labour Party was for. Ever since the Liberal government had turned towards social reform in

Labour Party lacking in policy and identity

1908, Labour had done little but applaud and vote for the government's measures. After the elections of 1910 left the Liberals dependent on Labour and Irish Nationalist votes, Labour had been compelled to cling even more closely to the Liberals, for a show of independence could conceivably have turned the government out and put the Unionists in. Labour had no distinctive policies. MacDonald, who became permanent Party Chairman in 1911, sometimes talked about 'socialism', but he meant only the vision of a co-operative society which would one day come into existence: for him the concept did not imply any specific policies. Though MacDonald thought it vital that his party should have a working-class base in the trade unions, he did not intend to fight a class war, but encouraged middle-class people too to join his party. In contrast, the New Liberals began from a base in the middle class and hoped to recruit working men. Whether this difference was enough to sustain Labour as a separate party seemed doubtful in 1914. Labour's future seemed likely to be as part of a Liberal-led progressive alliance, for which the working of local politics in London provided a model. The Liberals still possessed most of the political talent, in contrast with the dull trade-union worthies on the Labour benches, and the habitual loyalty of large parts of the electorate, which Labour had not yet created for itself.

> **MacDonald Labour Party Chairman**

At the start of 1914 the Liberals seemed to have adapted successfully to the conditions of 20th-century politics, in which social issues would prove so important. They had established their dominance over their ancient rivals, the Conservatives, whilst the new Labour Party had yet to set itself up as a truly independent force in British politics. The war that broke out in the summer of 1914, however, was to transform the British political scene.

III

WOMEN AND THE STRUGGLE FOR THE VOTE

1. Changes in the Lives of Middle-Class Women at the Turn of the 19th Century

IN Edwardian England one in ten married women had paid work and most of those belonged to the poorer social classes. For upper- and middle-class girls, paid employment was not thought suitable. As a child, Lady Violet Bonham-Carter asked her governess 'how I was going to spend my life... Her answer came without a moment's hesitation. "Until you are eighteen, you will do lessons." "And afterwards?" "And afterwards you will do nothing."... The deep river, the Rubicon which flowed between, was called "Coming Out"... One day one had a pigtail down one's back short and skirts which barely covered the knees. The next day, hair piled high on top of one's head. It used to be a sin to be vain - but now it became a sin to be plain... Lessons were of course thrown to the winds...In fact I remember being warned by a well-wisher to conceal any knowledge I had managed to acquire... Men are afraid of clever girls.'

Women in paid work

Lady Violet's reminiscences make clear the assumptions of the age. The chief purpose of a woman's life was to marry and bring up children. Hence, once she was 18, she should become an adornment to society, devoting herself to dining and dancing until she attracted a suitable man. Then she would marry him and spend the rest of her life in child-bearing, child-rearing, caring for her husband and running the household. Yet there were difficulties in proposing this lifestyle as the only suitable one for all well-to-do women and the difficulties were growing. Perhaps the most obvious was the fact that some women did not marry. In 1901 the minority of women unmarried at 45 constituted 14 per cent of all women. Many of these women were probably not averse to marriage, but simply unable to find a husband of suitable

The doctrine of 'separate spheres'

rank in society. The category of those deemed suitable seems to have become more tightly defined in the course of the 19th century. It was regarded as very important that a woman should not marry beneath her. This is why her relations with men were strictly policed and she was not allowed to consort with men except in the presence of a chaperone. Yet unmarried women of the well-off classes were condemned to a life on the margin of their father's or brother's household, or to a very restricted range of permissible jobs, such as governess or ladies' companion.

Decline in the birth rate

The lives of married women were changing in significant respects in the later 19th and early 20th centuries. The birth rate was in decline from the 1880s and by 1901 had dropped by about 25 per cent since its peak in the 1870s. This national average probably conceals a disproportionate and earlier shift to fewer children among the better-off classes. We know that by 1911 middle-class families averaged only 2.8 children. Middle-class lifestyles were becoming more costly: boys went to expensive public schools, servants' wages increased, bathrooms became a necessity, and so on. It would have seemed desirable to reduce spending on numerous children in order to have enough money for what had come to seem other necessary expenses. This trend meant that child-bearing and rearing took up much less of women's lives.

Middle-class women were also in many cases seeing less of their husbands. The rise of commuting meant that men's work and their homes were widely separated. Wives often knew little of their husbands' work. Florence Nightingale wrote in *Cassandra* in 1852:

It is not surprising that husbands and wives seem so little part of one another. It is surprising that there is so much love as there is. For there is no food for it. What does it live upon - what nourishes it? Husbands and wives never seem to have anything to say to one another.

Nightingale thought that the cause of this lack of stimulating conversation between man and wife lay in women's deficient education, but we may suspect that it lay rather in the fact that they lived so much apart. Certainly, so much separation meant that women had to find other purposes in life than looking after a husband who was usually absent.

In Victorian and Edwardian England most well-to-do women satisfied much of their need for a purpose in life in voluntary work. Social services were supplied not, for the most part, by the state and its employees, but by the churches and their volunteers. The churches and the charities were led by men, for the clergy of the Established and Roman Catholic churches and the ministers of the Nonconformist denominations were exclusively male. The rank-and-file volunteers whom they led were largely female. The visiting, raising and distribution of money and other activities involved took thousands of women out of the house and brought them into contact with a wide spectrum of society. In the late 19th century women began to undertake political work too. In 1883 the 'Primrose Tory League', named after Disraeli's favourite flower, was founded in order to promote Tory principles such as the maintenance of religion and the imperial ascendancy of Great Britain. From the start women were welcomed as members and undertook much of the work of deluging the constituencies with propaganda and offering a series of social events to keep the organization alive between elections. Dances, evening entertainments, patriotic history put across in magic-lantern shows helped to make politics fun, to the disgust of serious-minded Radicals, but probably very effectively. The Primrose League was welcomed by Conservative politicians because it offered help at elections, but never attempted to dispute their leadership.

Not all women, however, were satisfied with doing voluntary work under the direction of men. Women had some causes of their own, involving the righting of injustices to which women were subjected. In 1857 women were allowed to sue for divorce on grounds of their

Voluntary work

Primrose Tory League 1883

Divorce

husband's adultery in a newly established Divorce Court. A series of Married Women's Property Acts allowed a divorced woman access to the property she had brought to her marriage, so making separation and bringing up children apart from the ex-husband practicable. A cause which aroused a great deal of passion was the campaign led by Josephine Butler to repeal the Contagious Diseases Acts. Stemming from concern for the health of seamen and soldiers, these provided for the arrest, medical examination and, if necessary, detention of women suspected of carrying sexually transmitted diseases in ports and garrison towns. The Acts imposed humiliating treatment on women and appeared unjust, in that no such procedures were applied to men. In 1886 Butler secured their repeal.

Married Women's Porperty Acts

Repeal of Contagious Diseases Acts

Some women also took action to expand the opportunities available to women. Important in this regard was the Langham Place Group, named after the place where the *English Woman's Journal* was produced. One of the group, Emily Davies, was determined to offer higher education to women. In 1869 she founded what ultimately became Girton College at Cambridge. In the next few years Newnham Hall at Cambridge and Somerville College and Lady Margaret Hall at Oxford also made their appearance. The obstacles in the path of those anxious to extend higher education to women were formidable. When Frances Cobbe gave a paper in 1862 entitled University Degrees for Women, she recalled: 'Every daily paper in London laughed at my demand, and for a week or two I was the butt of universal ridicule.' Medical opinion insisted that a condition it named anorexia scholastica resulted if women pursued a study regime similar to that of men. The presidential address to the British Medical Association in 1886 called for protective legislation to safeguard female students. Even Sara Burstall, Head Mistress of Manchester High School for Girls said; 'We ought to recognize that the average girl has a natural disability for Mathematics (Burstall's own subject). One cause may be that she has less vital energy to spare.' Burstall's argument was rather undermined when Millicent Fawcett's daughter

Langham Place Group

Extension of higher education to women

Philippa decisively beat the best male maths student of her year at Cambridge. The biggest obstacle of all to female entry into higher education was ingrained conservatism. University exams and lectures were opened to women at Oxford and Cambridge in the 1880s, but it was not till 1948 that women at Cambridge were admitted to degrees on the same terms as men. Predictably, the University of London had proved less hidebound and admitted them in 1900.

Promoters of university education for women did not necessarily wish to alter women's role in society. Elizabeth Reid, founder of Bedford College for Women in London, wanted to elevate 'the moral and intellectual character of women, as a means to an improved state of society...We shall never have better Men till Men have better Mothers.' There were women, however, who valued increased educational opportunities as a means to a career. Elizabeth Anderson became the first British licensed female doctor. She had attended lectures at the Middlesex Hospital, but had to get her degree from the University of Paris. In 1874 the London School of Medicine for women was established. Even then the numbers of female medical practitioners remained small: by 1902 there were 212. Female would-be lawyers made still slower progress. On the eve of the First World War, it was ruled in a legal case that no woman could practise law or sit as a magistrate or juror and it took the Sex Disqualification (Removal) Act of 1919 to remove this barrier.

Few women even aspired to join the professions, but for large numbers of lower-middle-class girls new opportunities were opening up in the late Victorian and Edwardian period. By 1901 there were 172,000 women schoolteachers. In 1881, 3 per cent of office-workers were women; by 1901, 25 per cent were. What made the difference was the advent of the typewriter and the telephone. The male clerk and his copperplate handwriting were replaced by the invariably female shorthand typist, while the telephone exchanges were manned by legions of girls. The popular journals and magazines were soon full of articles about 'new women'. They went about on bicycles, which

Elizabeth Anderson - first female doctor

Sex Disqual-ification (Removal) Act

gave them independent mobility and enabled them to escape from chaperones. They smoked in defiance of gender stereotypes. They spoke up for themselves and looked down on men. Probably, the stereotypical 'new woman' was mostly a projection of the fears of men, but the changes affecting women were harbingers of the gradual transformation wrought by the 20th century.

'New woman'

2. The Lives of Working-Class Women at the Start of the 20th Century

Paid work for middle-class girls may have been a novelty of the late 19th century, but except for those who had to work unpaid, looking after a member of the family such as a widowed father, young women of the working class always had been expected to do remunerative work in the years until they got married. As workers, they could not hope to earn as much as their brothers. The best-paid occupations were all closed to them: there were no female engine-drivers, boilermakers or engineers, and the trade unions were anxious to keep women out. Numerically, women were dominant in the cotton-spinning industry, but the industry was hierarchically organized, with men as the well paid mule-spinners in charge of the machines organizing the ancillary workforce of women and adolescents. This arrangement was not surprising. The men were in the job for life, but for the women factory jobs usually filled the interval between school and marriage. Married women formed a small proportion of female cotton workers (under a quarter) and most of them had either not started or had finished bringing up a family. At all levels of society child-bearing and rearing were women's primary roles. Often working-class mothers did have to contribute to the family income, but much more often than not, their work was done at home: taking in washing, for instance.

Unequal pay

Gender-stereotyping of jobs had become more prevalent in the 19th century than it had been before. Legislation reflected the trend. After

1842 women were not allowed to work underground in coalmines, though the girls who continued to work at the pithead in Lancashire proved that women were as capable of heavy work as men. Factory inspectors tried to ensure that so far as possible men and women were segregated at work, lest the women be contaminated by men's uncouth company. Many families encouraged their daughters to take clean and relatively genteel work, even if it was not well paid. This was one reason why so many girls went into domestic service, which accounted for more than a third of all female employment. The job was also likely to provide training for their life's work of keeping house for a husband and children. When after 1870 education for girls became first universally available and then compulsory, the segregation of the two sexes was usual, as the separate entrances to schools for girls and boys made clear, and the curriculum for the girls included such activities as cookery and needlework designed to prepare them for their prescribed future roles as wives, mothers and carers.

Compulsory Education for girls

Yet the lives of many working-class women were beginning to change before the turn of the 19th century. They too were beginning to have fewer children. The spread of education and its costs (fees before it became free in 1891, the need for presentable clothes and shoes) were probably one factor producing a falling birth rate among almost all groups from the 1870s. Especially in the towns, there was more to spend money on: more varied clothing, commercial entertainment, items for the home such as pianos, organized excursions, for example. Parents might prefer to spend their money on these rather than on more children. It is interesting that the birth rate remained highest in the isolated mining villages, where the luxuries mentioned were not available.

3. The Argument over Extending the Vote to Women

Before the final third of the 19th century extension of the vote to women was not a live issue. Prior to the Reform Act of 1867 only one adult male in five had the vote. The theory was that the voters cast their votes on behalf of the community which they represented: hence, voting was a public function and there was no secret ballot. Women, like four fifths of men, could be held to be included in the community represented by those who had the vote. But if most men, not just a few community leaders, were to be given the vote, as happened with respect to the towns in 1867, then it could be asked why no women were allowed to be voting representatives of their community. By the 1860s some women wished to challenge the exclusion of women from the franchise. The debates over parliamentary reform in 1866-7 made the issue pertinent and the philosopher and MP John Stuart Mill presented an amendment to the Reform Bill of 1867 proposing that the vote be given to women on the same terms as men. The amendment was defeated by 196 votes to 73. The votes in favour showed that the amendment had attracted sufficient support to make the issue a serious one and a series of petitions through the 1870s and early '80s occasioned 13 debates in the Commons about it.

John Stuart Mill proposes votes for women

From the 1870s onwards, then, arguments for and against extending the vote to women were thoroughly aired by both sides. Those against granting voting rights to women (anti-suffragists) argued that women's interests were already sufficiently represented and upheld by men, as the passage of the Married Women's Property Acts showed. For that reason, they claimed, most women were quite apathetic about the issue. By contrast, most suffragists were convinced that MPs would act more quickly on women's grievances, such as subjection to domestic violence which went unpunished by the courts, if women were voters. Arguments concerning female apathy about politics became less convincing over time as both major parties came to be dependent on voluntary female labour, organized in the Primrose League and Women's Liberal Federation.

Both sides in the debate took it for granted that men and women were characterized by different moral and intellectual qualities, but they differed about the implications of this assumption. Women were supposed to be less open to reason and more easily swayed by emotion than men and for anti-suffragists these qualities ought to debar them from any role in politics. The suffragists often countered by citing the example of Queen Victoria, who discharged her political duties adequately, but was also, according to suffragist leader Millicent Fawcett, 'every inch a woman'. Women were also supposed to possess a more highly developed moral sense than men, which stemmed essentially from unselfishness necessitated by their life of marriage, motherhood and domesticity. They had to develop skills in financial management and knowledge about health and education. Such knowledge and skills were coming to be seen as relevant in politics both by Conservatives anxious about 'national efficiency' and Liberals keen to promote social reform. The changing political agenda by the later 1890s greatly strengthened the suffragists' case.

It could hardly be gainsaid, however, that British governments were much concerned with rivalry with other states, with employment of military force and with imperial rule. Anti-suffragists assumed that any involvement by women in these matters was certain to be disastrous. Yet from the turn of the century suffragists were able to use Australasian experience to counter this assumption. In New Zealand adult women had been granted the vote in 1893; in Australia individual states began to enfranchise women in the 1890s and in 1902 women received the vote at federal level. Suffragists could point out the patriotism of New Zealand women, who supported military training and the sending of troops to South Africa in the Boer War. The women of Australasia were said to be a force for imperial unity. Suffragists agreed with their opponents that women could not fight for their country, but the other demands on its citizens of a state at war, such as the financial, women could and would meet.

Women granted the vote New Zealand and Australia

One of the tap-roots of anti-suffragism was the fear that to give women the vote might accelerate trends in society that were already causing alarm. By 1900 it was clear that there had been a decrease in the rate of marriage for women in their twenties and political emancipation might provide further encouragement to avoid the domestic life. There was disquiet too over the declining birth rate. In the era of enormous conscript armies and fears of foreign invasion, it was alarming to think that Britain's population might be diminishing in relation to that of its potential enemies. The appeal of motherhood needed to be strengthened, whereas granting the vote to women might weaken it. This was especially the case because many schemes for extending the vote to women envisaged single women as the main beneficiaries. To enfranchise married women raised another problem, that of marital discord over political issues.

Anti-suffragists were free to imagine all sorts of dire consequences from allowing women to vote, because their predictions could not be tested against experience. Their opponents did cite foreign experience, mainly of Australasia, but had to admit that those were different societies. What the suffragists required was home-grown experience which might disprove gloomy forecasts of disaster. Increasingly in the late 19th and early 20th centuries this was what they had. The late 19th century saw a massive extension of elective local government.

Female ratepayers included in municpal elections

When in 1869 an act extended the vote in municipal elections, female ratepayers were included. To include them seemed quite natural, for town councils dealt with matters such as poverty, health and education, which were thought of as belonging to women's sphere. In 1870, when school boards were set up by the Education Act, women were allowed to vote for and to be elected to them. In 1894 women were admitted to the electorate for parish, urban district and rural district councils. It was in the 1890s that female representatives began to be elected to office in large numbers. Evidently, their contribution was considered valuable, since women began to be chosen as mayors, and when county councils had to set up education committees under the Education Act of 1902, it was laid down that one of the members had to be a woman.

The debate about extending the vote to women did not take place in an unchanging context. Some other countries allowed women to vote; women entered local government and made a success of their role; and the agenda of national government began to include matters hitherto attended to by local government and traditionally thought of as belonging to women's sphere. The arguments of the anti-suffragists therefore came to seem less convincing and opinion began to shift. This was apparent whenever there was a vote on the issue in the Commons. In 1892 female suffrage was defeated by only twenty-three votes (out of nearly four hundred cast). In 1897, for the first time, the suffragists won by 71 votes a motion favouring the principle of female suffrage. The suffragists won a majority in all parties apart from the Liberal Unionists. In the votes which took place in the first decade of the new century the suffragist majority climbed even higher, to well over a hundred.

Female suffrage defeated by slim margin 1892

4. The Suffragette Campaign, 1903-14

A favourable vote in the Commons for the principle that women should be enfranchised did not mean that the suffragists had virtually achieved their object. Given governmental control of parliamentary time, only a government bill stood much chance of success. A favourable government had to be willing to give priority to the issue in a period when there were other urgent matters, such as social reform and Ireland. Questions of cabinet and party unity might well get in the way: the Liberal governments after 1905 contained important anti-suffragists, especially Asquith, Prime Minister from 1908. Much would depend on framing a bill which would not damage the electoral interests of the party in power.

The parliamentary successes of the 1890s encouraged the suffragists to unify their movement and establish the National Union of Women's Suffrage Societies (NUWSS) under the presidency of Millicent Fawcett. Their aim was to secure the vote for women on the same terms as men. They hoped to achieve it by establishing a presence in every constituency in order to secure the adoption of

National Union of Women's Suffrage Societies (NUWSS)

favourable new candidates and pledges of support from existing ones. In the election of 1906, 415 candidates promised their support for the women's cause.

In 1903, however, a new pressure group was founded by Emmeline Pankhurst and her eldest daughter Christabel. They called it the Women's Social and Political Union (WSPU); the press distinguished its members from the suffragists of the NUWSS by labelling them 'suffragettes'. The strategy that the WSPU developed involved pressurizing the government of the day, which after late 1905 meant the Liberal government, in two ways: first, they aimed to embarrass it for failing to be truly liberal; second, they hoped to mobilize the mass of the people against it. Militant, even violent, tactics they believed to be justifiable after more than thirty years of fruitless agitation by suffragists.

In the early years the suffragettes' favourite tactic was interrupting the speeches of ministers at public meetings. There was a tradition of heckling in English election campaigns and action taken against the women was often seen as highly illiberal. These tactics brought favourable publicity for the suffragette cause and even suffragists such as Millicent Fawcett were impressed. Yet inevitably, the novelty of these tactics wore off and the publicity they attracted declined. The WSPU was compelled to win notice in other ways. By 1908 it had acquired the resources and organization to stage a series of great public displays, the most impressive of which was a huge gathering in Hyde Park. According to the hostile *Times* there were between a quarter and half a million people there. Yet Asquith refused to be impressed and declined to meet a suffragette deputation. In frustration, Mary Leigh and Edith New made the first use of 'the practical argument of the stone' (in the words of Christabel Pankhurst) by smashing the windows of 10 Downing Street. The two women had crossed the boundary into illegal action.

In the next phase of agitation, the space reserved for males in and around the Houses of Parliament came under attack. In 1908-9 there

Margin notes:
Women's Social and Political Union (WSPU)

Hyde Park Rally 1908

was an attempt to rush the House of Commons, many episodes when women chained themselves to railings outside the House or government buildings, and a great demonstration in Parliament Square when the police barred Mrs Pankhurst from Parliament Yard. Arrests followed, contributing to the unease of many who were not persuaded that the women offered a real threat to law and order. From the middle of 1909, arrested women began to resort to hunger strikes in prison in order to step up the moral pressure on the government. In response, the authorities resorted to forcibly feeding the prisoners, judging that the dangerous and degrading procedures involved would be deemed excusable by the clear intention to save the prisoners' lives. Graphic and verbal descriptions of the women's treatment and sufferings undoubtedly harmed the government's image in some quarters, while the suffragettes appeared as noble martyrs for their cause. Yet still the WSPU had failed to produce an overwhelming tide of favourable opinion which Asquith would not be able to ignore.

Hunger strikes

Asquith was, however, induced to allow the supporters of female suffrage in Parliament to produce a Conciliation Bill, which proposed to give the vote to a million female heads of households. The measure was accepted by the Commons in 1911 by 255 votes to 88, but the Liberals became worried that the reform might work to their electoral disadvantage and the government withdrew its support. At once the WSPU, which had declared a truce while the measure was under consideration, resumed its militant campaign. In the spring of 1912 this took the form of a wave of attacks on West End shops, of which *The Times* wrote, 'No one surely can have imagined destruction on this scale in London. Since the Conciliation bill had not yet failed, the violence was hard to justify.' As *The Times* continued, 'Until recently the suffragist militant section have at least been able to urge that only violent methods would secure from Parliament what they desire. But now not even that excuse remains.' In the remaining two years before the First World War, the suffragette campaign reached a violent climax. Windows were broken, letter boxes were attacked and there

Conciliation Bill

Suffragette violence

was a campaign of arson, for example against Lloyd George's house at Walton Heath. One suffragette, Miss Gilliat, even seemed to recommend killing a cabinet minister. Mary Richardson slashed Velazquez's *Rokeby Venus* in the National Gallery and Emily Davison died by throwing herself under the King's horse in the Derby of 1913. These dramatic events certainly brought publicity to the WSPU, but it seems to have been publicity of the wrong kind. The WSPU lost public sympathy to the point where its public speakers attracted hostile crowds armed with eggs, fruit and bags of flour. The Home Secretary Reginald McKenna was able to proceed with a policy that amounted to the suppression of the suffragettes. He ended the policy of force-feeding suffragette prisoners: by the Cat and Mouse Act they could be released if their health deteriorated because of hunger strike and then re-arrested to finish their sentence. This treatment proved demoralizing for the women, but did not win them sympathy.

Death of Emily Davison

Cat and Mouse Act

In 1913 Lloyd George said, 'For the moment, the militants have created a situation which is the worst I have seen for women's suffrage in Parliament.' No doubt, he was excusing the failure of the government to resolve the issue of female suffrage, but he was surely right in implying that WSPU tactics had become counter-productive. Since the women lacked the power to intimidate the government, their only weapon was public sympathy which might threaten the Liberals with loss of votes, but their actions had come to alienate the public. More and more, the suffragettes became an isolated group racked by internal quarrels as other leading figures rebelled against the dictatorship of the Pankhursts.

The Pankhursts had not succeeded in finding a speedy route to female suffrage, as they had promised in 1903. Yet the passion and willingness for self-sacrifice which the suffragettes brought to the women's campaign for the vote and the drama with which they invested it made the women's cause impossible to overlook or to dismiss as merely a fad. The issue had been placed high on the political agenda.

The Suffragettes isolated

THE FUNERAL PROCESSION OF EMILY DAVISON (1872-1913)
Courtesy of the Imperial War Museum

5. The Achievement of the Vote, 1918

The years before 1914 saw a great expansion among women of
interest in the issue of the vote. Very probably, their interest had in
many cases been aroused by the exploits of the suffragettes, but,
especially as militant tactics appeared to lead nowhere, the advantage
accrued to the non-militant NUWSS. In 1908 its affiliated societies
had a total membership of only about 8,000, but by 1914 numbers
had shot up to over 54,000. The women's movement strove to reach
out to working-class women and to men who supported their cause.
It was starting to look like a mass movement. As such, it was of
growing interest to the politicians. Relations with the Labour Party
were especially close, but it is possible that all three parties might
have gone into the 1915 election campaign pledged to legislate for
female suffrage.

Women's
movement
and the
Labour Party

In the event, the election of 1915 was never held because the First World War broke out. Mrs Pankhurst at once suspended her campaign as she made clear her fervent support for the War. Soon she was agitating on behalf of women's right to serve. It was necessity rather than Mrs Pankhurst's pressure which gave women this opportunity. Many took over jobs left vacant when men went to the front and not far short of a million, mostly younger women were employed making munitions. The job could be dangerous: there were some horrifying incidents, including one in the East End of London in which twelve women were killed. Short of copy because of censorship of war news, the newspapers showed a keen interest in women's contribution to the war effort. Old notions that the nation's defence depended solely on men were exploded and anti-suffragist newspapers, such as The *Observer* and the *Daily Mail*, announced their conversion to the cause of votes for women. Politicians showed themselves appreciative of women's efforts: 'Without women victory will tarry', Lloyd George said to a procession of women organized by Christabel Pankhurst in 1915.

Women's role in the Great War

Newspapers support women's war contribution

Yet when women were given the vote in 1918, it is doubtful if they were being rewarded for their war work. Most of the women in the munitions factories or replacing men who had gone to the trenches were young, but it was women over thirty who gained the vote. Insofar as women's contribution during the war was recognized and recompensed, it was the contribution of married women in their traditional roles as wives and mothers that was appreciated. They were the ones who had enabled society to continue to function in difficult circumstances. They were also the women whom it seemed safest to enfranchise.

Women over 30 achieve the vote

The war made it necessary to make some change in the electoral system. Since eligibility for the vote depended on residence, all those serving abroad would, under the pre-war rules, lose their votes. This was not regarded as acceptable, and there was also a strong feeling that all who had fought for their country, householders or not, should be given a vote. The NUWSS made it clear in 1916 that they would not accept any Bill which widened the franchise for men, but ignored women. A conference was therefore set up under the Speaker to produce a solution to all the problems connected with the voting system. When it reported in January, it included a majority recommendation that women above a specified age should henceforth be allowed a vote. By now the Prime Minister was Lloyd George, who had long favoured the suffragist cause, and the coalition government was less concerned with narrow questions of party advantage than politicians had been before the war. Hence it could be agreed by a huge majority that there should be universal adult suffrage for men and that women over thirty should also have the vote. The Representation of the People Act of 1918 raised the male electorate from 7 to 13 million, and there were now 8.5 million female voters. Thanks to their higher age qualification, women did not constitute a majority of the electorate and flighty young women, feared by some politicians, were excluded.

Representation of the People Act - 1918

The large majorities by which female suffrage had been accepted indicated perhaps that the special age qualification for women would not long survive. Experience soon proved that women were unlikely to swamp the political system any time soon, for the number of female MPs remained tiny. There was no significant opposition when all women who had attained the age of 21 were given the vote in 1928, even though they now formed 52 per cent of the electorate.

Women over 21 achieve the vote

IV

THE FAILURE TO TRANSFORM THE EMPIRE

1. The Conservatives and the Empire before 1906

IN the last twenty years of the 19th century there had been intense competition among the European powers to acquire colonial empires. Africa, South-East Asia and the Pacific island groups were all parcelled out among the powers. Britain had felt compelled to join in the scramble for colonies in order to counter possible threats to its strategic interests and to safeguard its economic interests, even though the threats were often very indirect and the economic interests were often small, at least for the present. The result of the many annexations and extensions of frontiers of the later 19th century, when added to the territories already under British control, was an Empire which covered one fifth of the land surface of the globe and a similar proportion of its population, four hundred millions or so.

Scramble for Colonies

In the era of Lord Palmerston, no one had thought much about the Empire. Except for India, no great value was set upon it and much of it, Australia, New Zealand and Canada; for example, was considered likely to become independent one day. Such ideas about the future were convincing enough when most of the Empire consisted of white-dominated colonies, but to the late Victorians or Edwardians the prospect of independence for most of the other places which belonged to the Empire was quite another matter. Lord Salisbury's daughter explained why self-government was thought impossible for Africans. That generation had contemporary knowledge of what 'Africa for the Africans' stood for before civilization entered - the dead, effortless degradation which it represented, broken only by interludes of blood-lust, slaughter, slavery, and unspeakable suffering. It was impossible for them to feel doubt - far less scruple - as to replacing it, wherever occasion served, by white dominion.

White Dominions

THE FAILURE TO TRANSFORM THE EMPIRE

In many areas of the continent, Africans lacked any of what the Edwardians considered the hallmarks of civilization, even clothes, and it is not surprising that they were regarded as backward and primitive. Yet Lord Curzon, Viceroy of India from 1898 to 1905, did not consider the Indians fit for self-government either. The highest ranks of the civil service, he said, must be held by Englishmen for the reason that they possess…the habits of mind and the vigour of character which are essential to the task. Curzon did admire Indian culture and set about preserving and restoring the literature and relics of India's past, but he was convinced that though India would one day be 'the greatest partner of the Empire', it must remain a subordinate partner.

Men like Curzon were not crude racists. Towards the end of her life, Victoria wrote to Curzon: We shall never really be liked in India, if we keep up this racial feeling, and some day real danger may result from it. Curzon fully agreed with the Empress that racial intolerance and unnecessary humiliation of the indigenous inhabitants of India were to be prevented. Other great proconsuls of the period, such as Lord Cromer in Egypt, expressed similar sentiments. Curzon and Cromer did not meet with total defeat in protecting the people they ruled from racial intolerance, as the British did in South Africa, but then India and Egypt would have been ungovernable if they had, given the tiny white element in both countries. India, for example, a country of 250 millions, was ruled through 900 civil servants and 70,000 British soldiers. Yet the proconsuls depended on their officials and soldiers and could not take decisive action against their entrenched racism. Nor could they empower public opinion in Egypt or India, since that too would have endangered British rule. Both Cromer and Curzon had some trouble with nationalists. The Indian National Congress had been founded in 1885 to represent and voice the political opinions of the new professional classes together with some of the businessmen and landowners. The criticisms of congressmen inevitably seemed seditious to the officials whom they criticized and both sides came to feel bitter about each other. To Curzon, congressmen were not representative

Lord Curzon
Viceroy
of India
1898-1905

Indian
National
Congress
1885

Indians, but middle class agitators who wanted to dominate the masses for their own ends. The 'oriental mind', which the proconsuls prided themselves on understanding, had no desire for western-style freedoms or constitutional arrangements.

According to the proconsuls at the turn of the century, what the oriental masses needed, and deep down wished for, was enlightened autocratic government, and it was this that Cromer and Curzon set out Egyptian to provide. Cromer was certain that nationalism would wither away if nationalism he attended to the material interests of the Egyptians. By 1907, when he left Egypt, he had brought state finances under control, introduced a fairer tax system and improved irrigation. Incomprehensibly to him, however, unrest in the country had not disappeared. Meanwhile, in India Curzon overhauled the bureaucracy to reduce delays. He closely studied land questions and lightened the assessment falling on the cultivator. A department of agriculture was set up, and a research institute was founded. Another 6000 miles of railway were built, a 25 per cent increase, and irrigation schemes were extended to six million more acres. The police were reformed, as was the city government of Calcutta. Curzon's romantic streak emerged as he planned the Delhi ceremonies of the Delhi Durbar of 1903, which celebrated the Durbar 1903 coronation of the King-Emperor Edward VII. A great tented city was created as the site for the most elaborate festivities in the entire history of British India. The Duke of Connaught represented his brother the King and Indian princes came riding in on elephants. This was an attempt at government by spectacle. The British Raj was presented as a new edition of the kind of regime which India had experienced under the Mughal Emperors. Unfortunately for Curzon, spectacle was insufficient to banish controversy. Some of his reforms became mired in dispute. Thus his university reforms were attacked because, while extending further education, they also tightened government control. Division His division of the over-large province of Bengal was even more of Bengal controversial: it was interpreted as an attempt to silence the political voice of the Bengali people. Rapidly, a popular political movement developed, spawning a boycott of British goods and even a terrorist movement. Curzon was taken entirely by surprise. He had never thought to consult Indian opinion on either the universities or the Bengal issue. Just about the one thing that the Colonial Office insisted on was the maintenance of order, which Curzon had endangered by his policies. Not only Curzon himself, but his entire style of rule was discredited.

Boycott of British goods

Had Curzon read the works of the poet of empire, Rudyard Kipling, perhaps he would not have been surprised by his failure. In 1899 Kipling had addressed a poem to the Americans, who had just conquered the Philippines in a war with Spain.

Rudyard Kipling

> Take up the White Man's burden
> And reap his old reward -
> The blame of those ye better
> The hate of those ye serve -
> The cry of hosts ye humour
> (Ah slowly!) towards the light:
> Why brought ye us from bondage
> Our loved Egyptian night.

The process of civilizing the non-white inhabitants of the Empire, Kipling believed, was a duty laid on white people, but they would no more be thanked for what they did than Moses was when his liberation of the Israelites from Egypt involved them in hardships. The 'new caught sullen peoples' were, according to Kipling, 'half devil and half child' and could not be expected to know what was good for them or to like it when it was given to them.

If the non-white people of the Empire had so little appreciation of the benefits of civilization, then, some people argued, perhaps it was a mistake to try to westernize them. In northern Nigeria in the 1880s and '90s, Sir George Goldie attempted to rule on African principles through African rulers. In 1900 the policy was continued by Sir

Sir Frederick
Lugard's
'indirect rule'

Frederick Lugard, who developed it into the influential theory of 'indirect rule'. There was nothing very novel about it. Most past empires had been content to utilize the existing institutions of conquered peoples, because, like the British, they found that change was more likely to produce unrest and because they simply lacked the resources and personnel that direct rule would have required. In much of India, for example, the British, like the Mughals before them, could not dispense with the native princes who continued to rule much of the country. No doubt, 'indirect rule' appealed because it was expedient, but it could also appear as humane and founded upon a proper respect for the culture and traditions of subject peoples.

Joseph
Chamberlain
'constructive
imperialism'

The activism of Curzon and Cromer had its counterpart in London in the 'constructive imperialism' of Joseph Chamberlain, Colonial Secretary in Salisbury's ministry after 1895. In origin a Birmingham businessman, he was determined to make the Empire profitable. The Empire had, he believed, enormous economic potential which Britain had barely begun to exploit. All the foodstuffs and raw materials which Britain could possibly need could be produced within the Empire, if only modern production methods were introduced and the necessary means of transport and communication constructed. Enriched by Britain's purchases, the colonies would then have the means to buy British industrial goods. Hence everyone, the colonists and British industrial workers and businessmen, would benefit. Chamberlain saw his schemes as not only desirable, but also necessary, if Britain were to retain its premier position in the world in the face of the challenges from such powers as Germany and the USA. Britain on its own could not perhaps hope to remain the world's leading power, but Britain with its Empire could. Yet Britain with its Empire would have to be treated in many ways like a single huge state. A crucial first step towards that happy state of affairs was tariff reform. Free trade would have to be sacrificed and tariffs imposed on imports from abroad, much to the benefit, Chamberlain supposed, of British industry, which had been hurt by foreigners' duties on their imports, while foreign

JOSEPH CHAMBERLAIN (1836-1914), Cartoon by 'Spy', *Vanity Fair*

goods were let into Britain free. The second step was to bring in imperial preference: imports from the Empire would be let in duty-free or at a lower rate of duty. In this way, British trade would be re-orientated towards the Empire, so that colonies and mother country could grow together as an economic unity. It was true that British workers might have to pay more for their food, but Chamberlain believed that they would gain overall: from increased employment as orders flowed in from the Empire for British manufactures, and from extra spending on social benefits with the proceeds of tariffs.

Chamberlain achieved vastly less than he hoped. A major handicap was the cheese-paring attitude of the Treasury. Some projects, such as taking over Rhodesia for the Crown and developing it, he did not dare even to propose. Only pittances were available for such worthy projects as the establishment of schools of tropical medicine (tropical diseases were a handicap to development in tropical countries) and institutes for research into better agricultural methods. Chamberlain's attempts to interest capitalists in developing the resources of the Empire were not at first all that successful either. It took world shortages of various primary products after about 1900 to cause the production of rubber to take off in Malaya, and the commercial farming of palm trees (for palm oil) and cotton to start up in Africa. In 1902 Chamberlain resigned as Colonial Secretary in order to devote himself to promoting tariff reform and imperial preference. He was successful in winning over the bulk of the Conservative Party, but in the general election of 1906 the Liberals won by a landslide, in part at least because the electorate was too attached to free trade, which was given the credit for Victorian prosperity.

It is doubtful if Chamberlain's vision of imperial unity was ever realistic. Canada, Australia and New Zealand had never, like the American colonies, sought independence, because their ties to the Empire restricted them so little. A tighter embrace such as Chamberlain proposed was not likely to be welcome. Rapid capitalist development was also likely to break down the traditional social

Establish-ment of Schools of Tropical Medicine

Liberals landslide victory on back of Free Trade agenda

structures in the colonies. Yet it was the traditional structures that supported 'indirect rule', which made imperial rule workable in many places. By its very nature the British Empire could not be converted into a dynamic super-state.

2. The Roots of Imperialist Sentiment

Despite Chamberlain's failure to convert Britain to his 'constructive imperialism', there is little doubt that the Empire was taken as a given by most Edwardians and aroused positive enthusiasm among many. Zeal for the imperial cause helped the Conservatives to victory in the 'Khaki Election' of 1900, though when the war dragged on, the sacrifices which the public was prepared to make for the cause were shown to be finite. There was, however, a consensus in Britain about the utility of the Empire to Britain and its essential benevolence towards its indigenous inhabitants.

Conservatives victory in the 'Khaki Election' 1900

Britain was a country which lived on the profits of foreign trade and investment. In the early years of the 20th century the economic difficulties of the late 19th century seemed to recede. Exports grew a little faster than imports and once the profits from shipping and insurance were taken into account, Britain's trade account was in balance. Britain was also investing larger amounts of money abroad than ever and these investments produced a growing stream of income, admittedly mostly for wealthy bankers and investors. Britain's largest trading partner was Europe, if taken as a whole, while the USA attracted more of its investment capital than anywhere else. Yet the share of the Empire was very large. On the eve of the First World War 35 per cent of British exports went to the countries of the Empire, and 42 per cent of Britain's foreign investment was destined for them. In some areas British trade was growing rapidly: trade with Africa doubled between 1900 and 1913. Increasingly, Britain depended upon Malaya for rubber, Egypt for cotton and West Africa for cocoa. It seemed unthinkable to put the British

Britain's trade account in balance

British trade with Africa doubles

economy at risk by getting rid of the Empire. Britain was doing far too well economically for radical experiments to be tried, as Chamberlain found to his cost.

Investment in the Empire was not only financial. There was a huge human investment too. Ten million people emigrated from the British Isles between 1870 and 1914. In the earlier years their favourite destination was still the USA, but more and more they chose the Empire: two and a half million of the three million who emigrated between 1900 and 1910 went to a country within the Empire, mostly to Canada, Australia or New Zealand. Beside settlers, there were many Britons employed as colonial administrators (20,000) and as troops (146,000), not to mention policemen, doctors, engineers, education officers, agricultural advisers and so on. Other than the rank and file soldiers, these people were mostly from an upper or middle class background. For them the Empire provided career opportunities and the public schools expanded mightily in the 19th century to produce men capable of profiting from them.

Many who never went near a colony had relatives who emigrated or who served abroad, but even those who lacked these ties often identified with the cause of Empire. It proved a source of excitement to the millions who read the novels of GA Henty, who extolled the qualities needed by empire-builders in novels such as *By Sheer Pluck* and used recent colonial military campaigns as the settings for his stories. They had titles such as *With Buller in Natal* and *With Kitchener in the Soudan*. The successors to the Great Exhibition of 1851 often had an imperial theme, like The Imperial International of 1909. In the Greater Britain exhibition of 1899, it was possible to experience the excitement of meeting a Zulu warrior in the flesh. The popular press was not slow to exploit the Empire to sell newspapers. The *Daily Mail* was described by one of its employees as 'the voice of the Empire in London journalism'. According to Lord Northcliffe, proprietor of the *Daily Mail*, 'The British people relish a good hero and a good hate.' Stories of the Empire provided plenty of heroes and hate objects. Like

Ten million emigrants from the British Isles

G. A. Henty's popular imperialist fiction

Henty's novels, the popular press fed off existing interest in the Empire, but as it did so, it further heightened consciousness of Empire and attachment to it.

The imperialist cause won its recruits young. The *Boys' Own Paper* was founded in 1879 and soon acquired a sister, the *Girls' Own Paper*. Their circulation was half a million and the staple literary diet on offer consisted of stirring stories in exotic settings on the frontiers of the Empire. The heroes of these stories tended to be the products of the public schools, but the audience for them was clearly far wider. It turned out that many boys wanted a taste of the skills and thrills engendered by life on the colonial frontier. When the Boer War hero of Mafeking, Baden-Powell, wrote a book about scouting in war, it was so popular, even among the young, that he re-wrote it as *Scouting for Boys*. It became the fourth best-selling book of the 20th century. B-P went on to found the boy scout and girl guide movements, perhaps the most impressive and longest-lasting spin-off of Edwardian imperialism.

Imperialism and the growing passion for organized team games were closely associated. Games-playing was supposed to be an ideal preparation for military life in the colonies, not so much because it promoted physical fitness as because it inculcated important moral qualities. In 1897 Henry Newbolt wrote 'Vitaï Lampada (The Torch of Life)'. The first stanza introduces the thrilling finale of a school cricket match. There is enormous pressure on the last man in, who will win the match or throw it away. He is kept steady because:

> ... his Captain's hand on his shoulder smote
> 'Play up! Play up! And play the game!'

The second stanza cuts to a scene in the Sudan campaign to relieve Gordon in 1885.

Marginal notes:
Imperialist cause

Baden-Powell and the scout and guides movement

Imperialism and sport

The sand of the desert is sodden red,--
Red with the wreck of a square that broke;--
The Gatling's jammed and the colonel dead,
And the regiment blind with dust and smoke.
The river of death has brimmed his banks,
And England's far, and Honour a name.
But the voice of a schoolboy rallies the ranks,
'Play up! Play up! And play the game!'

Military encounters in the colonies are presented as having all the excitement of a close fought cricket match and as the fulfilment of a life spent 'playing the game'. In a yet more direct way the passion for watching sport was made to serve the cause of Empire. Sporting fixtures began to be arranged between the various countries of the Empire. Rugby football spread through all the white colonies. In 1905 it was hard to be unaware of Britain's imperial ties as the New Zealand All Blacks beat every opponent but Wales. Cricket brought the nations of the Empire together even more successfully, since the game was adopted by the Indian sub-continent and the West Indies as well as the white colonies. Institutions such as the Imperial Cricket Conference, which first met in 1909 to harmonize the rules of the game, promoted a sense of imperial unity perhaps more successfully than a meeting of politicians like the Colonial Conference of 1907.

Imperial Cricket Conference

Positive enthusiasm for the Empire was not ubiquitous in Britain. A section of the working class was indifferent or hostile. Some were affected by socialist or nonconformist pacifism; others were simply too preoccupied by the difficult business of getting a living to care about the Empire. There were a few intellectual critics, such as JA Hobson, who argued in a book published in 1902 that the Empire was entirely for the benefit of a few plutocrats. In general, though, it was taken for granted that the Empire was a good thing and debate was confined largely to questions about how to manage it.

3. The Liberals and the Empire, 1905-14

In the election campaign which preceded their heavy defeat in 1906, some Conservatives recalled past Liberal failures to avenge the murder of Gordon in the Sudan or the British defeat at the hands of the Boers in 1881 and their advocacy of Home Rule for Ireland and accused the Liberals of wanting to destroy the Empire. In fact, almost all Liberals shared the consensus view that the Empire was good for the British and for the colonial peoples. Some members of the party had grown uneasy and critical about some of the methods used to fight the war in South Africa. The rising radical Lloyd George said:

Lloyd George and Liberal imperialism

> A war of annexation...against a proud people must be a war of extermination, and that is unfortunately what it seems we are now committing ourselves to - burning homesteads and turning women and children out of their homes...The savagery which must necessarily follow will stain the name of the century.

Others were reluctant to go this far. About one third of the parliamentary party consisted of Liberal imperialists who were nearly as enthusiastic about the Empire as most Conservatives. This wing of the party included very influential figures who acquired seats in the Liberal Cabinet of December 1905, such as Asquith, Haldane and Sir Edward Grey.

In 1903 the Liberal leader Sir Henry Campbell-Bannerman wrote to a fellow Liberal:

Sir Henry Campbell-Bannerman

> The truth is, we cannot provide for a fighting Empire, and nothing will give us the power...A peaceful Empire of the old type we are quite fit for.

What he meant was that the Conservative government had decided in South Africa to rely on naked force as the foundation of British

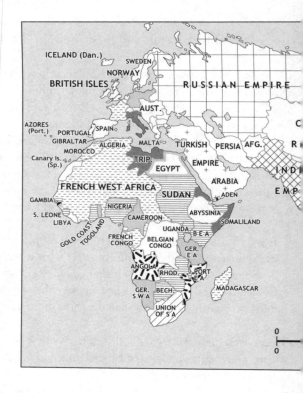

rule there, but the course of the Boer War had proved that Britain did not possess adequate force to rule in this way. Britain's imperial future could be secured only if it could go back to ruling largely by consent. This is what the Liberals had done in Canada, with the result that the country was still a contented member of the Empire. Here was the blueprint according to which the imperial edifice should be constructed in other places too.

If imperial rule was going to be in large part by consent, then the ambitious schemes of a Curzon or a Cromer would have to be given up wherever they seemed likely to run into controversy. Chamberlain's plans for imperial consolidation would have to be

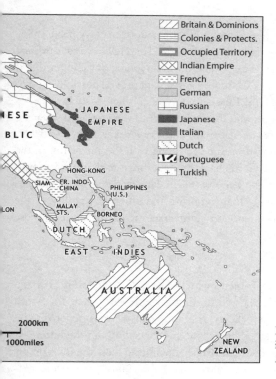

EUROPEAN POSSESSIONS
in Asia, Africa and
Australasia: 1914

dropped, as they were after a series of Colonial Conferences showed how lacking in enthusiasm for an Imperial Council, a Defence League, or a customs union the self-governing components of the Empire were. They were reluctant, in fact, to agree with anything that would limit their freedom of action. Men like Chamberlain believed that to acquiesce in this state of affairs was to court disaster. As he read the signs of the times, Britain was under relentless pressure from rivals and needed to adapt to survive. Colonial Conferences

The Liberals were less certain that disaster and decline were staring Britain in the face. In part, this was because the situation in the world outside Europe seemed less threatening after 1905 than it had done when the Conservatives were in office for most of the period 1886-1905. The great Russian colossus stumbled and fell in its catastrophic war against Japan in 1904-5. There was no longer any danger that it would grab the bulk of China and agreement proved possible in other areas where British and Russian interests conflicted, such as Persia (Iran). All the disputes with France over Africa were resolved when the Entente Cordiale between Britain and France was signed in 1903. The main problem had become relations with Germany, but in the short run at least the Germans were not a threat to the Empire. But, Liberals felt, even if the Empire was in danger, nothing was likely to wreck it more quickly than ignoring the inherent fragility of the Empire and its dependence on a large measure of consent from those within it.

War against Japan 1904-5

Entente Cordiale 1903

(i) *South Africa*
The most urgent problem which faced the incoming Liberal government after 1905 was finding a viable settlement for South Africa. The Liberals believed that only conspicuous generosity on the part of Britain stood any chance of cancelling out the bitterness among the Afrikaners which British attempts to force them to comply with British plans by war had created. In 1906-7, therefore, self-government was restored to the Transvaal and the Orange Free State. The reward which the Liberals sought for this act of generosity was that elusive goal of British policy for the preceding thirty years or more, a federation of the two Boer Republics and the two British colonies of the Cape Province and Natal. The federation was at last achieved in May 1910.

Self-government restored

Despite the Boer defeat in war, the constitution of the new federal state was the product of negotiation. It was not dictated by the British and indeed in important respects did not correspond to their wishes. The Boer leaders were determined to avoid an electoral system such as obtained in the Cape, where the blacks had 5 per cent of the vote and the Indians 10 per cent and rising prosperity made it certain that the number of non-whites satisfying the property qualifications for the vote would increase over time. Even the system in Natal, which produced a total of six black voters in 1907, together with 190 or so Indians, was not acceptable to the Afrikaners. They were adamant that racial inequality should be written into the constitution of South Africa, and that non-whites should be excluded from the vote and seats in Parliament. As the Afrikaner leader Botha declared: 'On one point there must be no manner of doubt - they could only have Europeans in Parliament.' Blacks and coloureds sent a delegation to England to try to get the constitution altered, but their cause was hopeless. There were plenty of Liberals who foresaw that denying political rights to three quarters of the population was likely to be a recipe for disaster in the long run. In the shorter run, discrimination against the numerous Indian population in South Africa embarrassed the British in India, where what was going on in South Africa was widely reported. Gandhi first emerged as an agitator of genius in South Africa, where he first tried his famous tactics of passive resistance, which meant refusal to obey unjust laws, but avoidance of violence. Yet despite these drawbacks to their policy, the Liberals had decided, in Churchill's words, that 'if British dominion is to endure in South Africa, it must endure with the assent of the Dutch'. If the price of their assent was the sacrifice of the rights of the black majority, it would just have to be paid. Given the priorities of the time, the Liberals received far more praise for their magnanimity towards the Boers than they did blame for betraying the blacks. Britain, which had been lampooned internationally as the bully of the Boers, began to recover its good reputation.

Exclusion of non-whites by Botha

Gandhi in South Africa

There is no doubt that the Liberals' policy in South Africa served Britain's short term interests well. The Conservative leader Balfour considered the policy 'a reckless experiment', but it reconciled most of the Boer leaders, who were loyal enough to put down an Afrikaner rebellion at the start of the First World War. Most of the Afrikaners were not in favour of joining in the war, but Botha and Smuts took South Africa in anyway. Smuts was to end up in the Imperial War

Afrikaners join the War

Cabinet. British and Boer were able to co-operate in taking over German South-West Africa (present-day Namibia). British interests in the gold mines and the route round the Cape were better safeguarded than they had ever been by Chamberlain's policy of confrontation. Few Britons lost much sleep over the Natives' Land Act of 1913, an early fruit of white supremacy, whereby blacks were driven off the land, except for the woefully inadequate amount set aside in reserves, and forced to join a huge labour pool designed to keep wages low.

Native's Land Act of 1913

(ii) *Egypt and India*

Egypt and India were both countries with large numbers of educated people and a relatively highly developed political consciousness. In both, therefore, British rulers encountered problems with growing nationalism. There was a big difference, though, in that the British had been in India for a long time and their position under international law was wholly secure, whereas in Egypt they were supposed to be in temporary occupation while they sorted out the Egyptian finances. The Liberal approach to both countries was similar. They would break with the highhandedness of Curzon and Cromer and rule in collaboration with moderate nationalists.

The Liberals had difficulty in conciliating Egyptian opinion. It was highly inflamed when Cromer left in 1907, for effective as he had been in improving the material condition of Egypt, political progress had been negligible and his administration had sometimes been insensitive. Cromer's successor Gorst increased Egyptian participation in local government and allowed more power to the Khedive (King). He successfully won over the Khedive, but the latter's collaboration with the British further eroded his credit with his people. A further concession followed in the form of an enlargement of the powers and representative nature of the Legislative Assembly, but the nationalists simply used it to advertise their grievances more widely. The key Liberal assumption, that generous concessions would

Cromer leaves Egypt 1907

invariably evoke a conciliatory response, was proved wrong in the case of Egypt, where the only measures that seemed to work were repressive ones, such as press censorship and the introduction of imprisonment without trial.

Among the Liberals' priorities, India was much higher up the list than Egypt. The task of governing it was entrusted to John Morley, Indian Secretary in London, and Lord Minto, Viceroy in India. They rightly believed that Curzon had left a difficult situation, but also appreciated that there were deeper forces at work than a simple reaction against Curzon's measures. They believed that Britain was likely in time to face in India the same sort of problems that it had already encountered in Ireland. The nationalist movement they faced was composed of men of very different tendencies. On the one hand, there was Tilak, an admirer of the Indian past, stimulated by the revival of Hindu literature and supported by the strong forces of popular Hindu conservatism. Since he was largely indifferent or opposed to Western ideas, co-operation with the British had little to offer. On the other hand, Gokhale believed that a glorious future for India could be achieved only through the adoption of Western ideas. As importers of those ideas and a force for the transformation of society, the British had a vital part to play in India's history. Co-operation with the British was possible and necessary. Gokhale had great hopes of Morley, seeing in him an exponent of Gladstone's Liberalism, for which Gokhale had the greatest respect.

Governing of India by John Morley and Lord Minto

Morley was not, at this stage of his life at least, a doctrinaire Liberal, but he was sure that repression without concession would simply call forth resistance. 'Reforms may not save the Raj', Morley wrote to Minto in 1908, 'but if they don't nothing else will.' Yet Morley and Minto had to be careful about conciliating Indian opinion. The Indian Civil Service was inclined to recommend repression and its views could not be ignored, since government had to be carried on through it. The initial decision to uphold the partition of Bengal was probably a mistake. Certainly, it produced a wave of assassinations and bomb-throwing which forced the government to adopt repressive measures. Nonetheless, Morley was determined to end the vicious cycle of violence and repression and in 1909 he announced the Morley-Minto reforms. An Indian was to be appointed to the Viceroy's executive council in India and two to the Secretary of State for India's council in London. At every level of government in India more Indians, mostly elected, were added to the legislative councils and the powers of these bodies were extended to include budgetary matters. The reforms left government firmly in British hands, but much wider opportunities were given for the government to hear Indian opinion (though it did not have to act upon what it heard) and for influential Indians to understand government policy and its justification.

Morley-Minto reforms 1909

By and large, the Morley-Minto reforms were a success. Gokhale and his moderate nationalists welcomed them and even men like Tilak now had more confidence in the government's goodwill. Repressive measures such as curbs on the press were still necessary, but violence did die down. Perhaps the only really contentious aspect of the reforms was the provision for separate representation for Muslims, a response to the formation of the Muslim League in 1906. Some Indians believed that this was an attempt to split the national movement on religious lines. Despite such doubts, Britain's problems in India seemed resolved, for the moment at least. The reign of the next Viceroy, Lord Hardinge, from 1910 to 1916 was a relatively harmonious period in the history of British rule in India. Hardinge won acclaim by reversing the partition of Bengal, while his transfer of the capital from Calcutta to Delhi was widely interpreted as a move towards the Indianization of the regime. Another great display of imperial pomp marked the accession of George V. In 1911 he and Queen Mary attended the Delhi Durbar in person.

The Muslim League 1906

Lord Hardinge 1910-1916

(iii) *The Tropical Colonies*

In the colonies in tropical Africa, the Caribbean and south-east Asia there was as yet no clamorous public opinion to be taken into account. Hence Liberal ideas about conciliating it did not seem relevant. The main issues which arose concerned the development of the colonies. Everyone took it for granted that colonies should be developed, but there was plenty of room for debate over how it should be done. Doubts about leaving it to private capitalists had accumulated since Rhodes' highly questionable conduct in the Zambesi area in the 1890s, and methods of colonial exploitation continued to be a hot topic in the early 20th century because of revelations about happenings in the Congo Free State. Entrusted by the Berlin Conference of 1884 to King Leopold of the Belgians, it had been 'developed' by the capitalists of the International Association on the basis of slave labour, which built and operated the railways and rubber plantations established there. Every humane consideration had been set aside. The cost in human life of the murder, starvation and disease involved has been estimated at ten million, half of the existing population. The novelist Joseph Conrad's *Heart of Darkness*, published in 1902, was based on what he learnt as captain of a steamer on the River Congo and portrayed the horror of what was going on there.

Slavery in the Congo Free State

Conrad's Heart of Darkness

The Liberals were little disposed to trust capitalists, but they were not keen either to provide large amounts of capital from government funds. They preferred simply to provide a little help and encouragement to native enterprise. This is what happened in West Africa. There peasant proprietors were already responding to the demands of the European market as represented by European merchants. The colonial governments facilitated that response by research into tropical agriculture and by improving transport links. The results were impressive: a fourteenfold increase in cocoa exports between 1905 and 1915, by which date the British West African colonies produced nearly a quarter of the world's output. This was achieved without any of the

1905-1915 Cocoa exports rocketed

social upheaval which handing large parts of the economy over to foreign capitalists would have been likely to produce.

In West Africa the Liberals relied on peasant proprietorship and 'indirect government'. Yet this was not a formula to be applied everywhere. In truth, the Liberals had no blueprint, which meant that policy was often determined by short term considerations or noisy lobbies. In Southern Rhodesia and Kenya, such factors allowed their development into countries dominated by small minorities of white settlers. The Liberals did not care for the white Rhodesians, but the British South Africa Association was willing to pay the costs of government itself and so it was allowed to follow a policy of settling white farmers on the best land, which seemed its only hope of profit. These farmers might also be useful as a counterweight to the Boers of South Africa. In any case, the white farmers were already installed in some numbers and the government did not care enough to swim against the tide. In Kenya the tide was less obviously flowing in the settlers' direction. There were fewer of them and the British government clearly had responsibility for ruling the colony. The problem was that the basis for a West African solution did not exist. The peasants of East Africa did not produce for the market, but for subsistence. If the colony was to pay its way, then people who would produce for the international market had to be brought in. The establishment of foreign-owned coffee plantations seemed a promising route to profits. Unfortunately, that involved dispossessing the Masai tribesmen of the fertile Laikipia plateau and moving them to the drier Ngong hills. The Kikuyu tribe complained too that some of their ancestral lands had been taken for the benefit of the whites. Meanwhile, the whites secured representation on the Legislative Council, from which all non-whites were excluded. Inadvertently, the Liberals were presiding over the creation of another country dominated economically and politically by a small white minority.

Their record in governing the colonies in the tropics makes it clear that the Liberals had no vision of Britain's imperial future. They

British South Africa Association

Displacement of indigenous peoples and white settlers

preferred conciliation to confrontation and they hoped to rule by consent and not by force, but for the most part they muddled along, reacting to circumstances as they arose and usually taking the line of least resistance given the various pressures they were under. There was nothing heroic about Liberal leadership of the Empire, as committed imperialists complained. The novelist John Buchan, for example, dreamt of 'a world-wide brotherhood with the background of a common race and creed'. The Liberal government seemed bereft of such idealism and Buchan began to fear that 'the Empire might decay at the heart'.

John Buchan

The astonishing expansion of the Empire in the late 19th century and the irresistible force which Europeans appeared to possess in the era of the machine gun led some people to suppose that Britain could transform the world, or at least the fifth of it that was within the British Empire. The Liberals were under no such illusion. They appreciated that in reality the British Empire was a fragile edifice, dependent on compromises with the peoples who composed it and with foreign powers, such as France, Russia and the United States.

The unheroic Liberals made a very good job of keeping the imperial show on the road. They completed the job, already begun by the Conservatives, of appeasing the principal powers that had at times shown resentment of British power, Germany only excepted. By 1914 nowhere in the Empire did opposition to British rule seem dangerous. The adequacy of Liberal solutions to imperial problems was to be tested to the utmost during the First World War. That Britain had serious problems in only one of its possessions at a time when it was fighting for its life is a ringing endorsement of Liberal imperial policies. The one exception was Ireland, the very place where Conservative opposition had prevented the Liberals from implementing their conciliatory policies.

V

BRITISH FOREIGN POLICY AND THE ROAD TO THE FIRST WORLD WAR

1. The Great Powers and the Alliance System

THE German Empire, as founded by Bismarck under Kaiser Wilhelm I (1871-88), was the strongest military power in Europe. The efficiency of its armies had been demonstrated in its successful war of 1870 with France, which till then had been regarded for centuries as the foremost military power. German military might was sustained by a rapidly increasing population of over 50 million in the 1890s and 67 million by 1914. It was also underpinned by a strong economy, which was growing far more rapidly than Britain's. In 1880 the German share of world manufacturing was 8.5 per cent; by 1913 it was 14.8 per cent, somewhat higher than Britain's. In the relatively new industries of steel, chemicals and electrical engineering German advances in the thirty years before the First World War were especially impressive.

German military might

Bismarck, Chancellor of united Germany from 1871 to 1888, was always afraid that the powers which had lost by the unification of Germany might attempt to reverse it. He was acutely aware of the weakness of the German position in Europe: it was sandwiched between other great powers which might force Germany into an unwinnable war on two fronts. His top priority was to guard against a war of revenge by defeated France. He based his plans on a Dual Alliance between Germany and Austria-Hungary, made in secret in 1879, and published to the world in 1888. The Alliance rendered Austria unavailable as a friend for France and Bismarck hoped to influence Austrian policy in the Balkans to prevent any crisis there. Yet he had hitched dynamic Germany to the weakest of the European great powers. Austrian military and economic potential was limited.

The secret Dual Alliance 1879

94

Above all, Austria-Hungary was a state held together by loyalty to a dynasty in an age of nationalism. In particular, the Empire contained large numbers of people who spoke Slav languages: Czechs, Croats and Serbs, for example. Some of them were restless under the rule of the Habsburg Emperor Franz Josef (1848-1916).

The Dual Alliance was supplemented by the Triple Alliance, when Italy joined in 1882. Italy was a recent arrival as a power. The product, like Germany, of recent unification, it owed its independence in large measure to others, to the French in 1859 and to Prussia in 1866. Viewing itself as the heir of ancient Rome, Italy had great ambitions, but wholly lacked the means of realizing them. It did not possess the crucial raw materials of 19th century industry, such as coal, and large parts of the country were mired in desperate poverty. Even so, it hoped to expand in Africa and was mortified when France took over Tunisia, next door to Sicily, in 1881. Bismarck seized the opportunity to bring the state into his alliance system. He expected that this would reassure his ally Austria, which feared that Italy might try to annex Italian-speaking areas such as the South Tirol, which were still part of the Habsburg Empire.

The Triple Alliance

The territories of the Triple Alliance powers formed a solid block bisecting Europe from north to south, a combination so strong that it seemed unlikely that humbled France could ever stand up against it. Still Bismarck was not satisfied; he tried to keep on friendly terms with Russia, and made another secret treaty with the Tsar in 1887. This treaty was designed to make war between the European powers impossible and thus assure Germany's security. Bismarck was, as his successor told him, like a rider on a horse who tossed five balls in the air at once and caught them as they fell. But even for Bismarck the juggling act was very difficult. It was hard to remain friendly with Austria-Hungary and Russia at the same time, since these powers were rivals in the Balkans. Russia had long patronized Balkan nationalisms. It was the leading Slav and Orthodox power and it also saw patronage of Balkan nationalism as a means to improve its position

Bismarck's secret treaty with Russia 1887

against Turkey at the Straits between the Black and Mediterranean Seas. Austria, by contrast, saw Balkan nationalism as its mortal enemy. If Germany was committed to the support of Austria, Russia would have to find another friend.

Kaiser
Wilhelm II
1888-1918

Soon after his succession, Kaiser Wilhelm II (1888-1918) dismissed Bismarck, or 'dropped the pilot', as *Punch* said in a famous cartoon. The young Emperor, anxious to direct affairs himself, appointed a succession of advisers who were not content with the security which Bismarck's policies had brought. In their view, Germany needed to untie itself from Bismarck's entangling alliance with Russia, so that it could play the world role to which its increasing strength entitled it. The Kaiser himself had many wide and visionary schemes. He wanted a larger colonial empire for Germany, 'a place in the sun'. He visited Constantinople in 1889 and declared that he had taken the Muslims of the world under his protection. The opening of a railway across Asiatic Turkey, joining up with the lines through the Balkans to Austria, was a significant step; it made a Berlin to Baghdad railway a possibility in peace – or in war.

Germany's spurning of Russia was France's opportunity. In 1893 the long-projected alliance with Russia was concluded. It has left a permanent memorial in Paris in the form of the Pont (bridge) Alexandre III. In some ways the Alliance was an improbable one. A state proud of its republicanism and its revolutionary tradition had linked up with the only remaining absolute monarchy among the great powers of Europe. Yet the French were desperate to escape from their

Disputed
provinces of
Alsace and
Lorraine

isolation. The war of 1870 had left them with a permanent grudge against Germany in that the latter had taken the provinces of Alsace and Lorraine. A Russian alliance would not help them to recover their lost territory, but it would find them an ally and thereby make it much harder for Britain to thwart them at every turn, as it had done over Egypt. Despite its huge colonial empire, much of which was worthless desert, France was no longer a European colossus. Its population had grown only slowly in the 19th century: Germany and even Britain had overtaken it. Its industrial output was not remotely comparable to that of Britain or Germany. It could hold its own in international affairs only with the support of an ally.

Russia too needed assistance. Its population and resources were enormous, but it needed to industrialize if it was to make the most of them. In the later 19th century it acquired a vastly expanded railway system and an impressive heavy industrial sector. Between 1885 and 1914 the Russian economy grew more rapidly than that of any other country. The advances were funded by foreign lenders, especially by the French. Here was a major reason for the initiation and survival of the Franco-Russian alliance, finally signed by Tsar Alexander III in 1894. Industrialization did not at once translate into increased military might and, for the time being at least, Russia needed the prospect of support, diplomatic and conceivably military, from a reliable ally. At the time when the alliance with France was made, Russia's quarrels were most likely to be with Britain. In 1889 Britain's Naval Defence Act laid down that the Royal Navy should be superior to the combined strength of any two other powers. Those which the government had in mind were France and Russia. The attempt to transform the Russian economy placed great strains on Russia's social and political fabric. Many of the professional classes believed the Tsar's absolutism to be an antiquated form of government, while the new industrial workers were hard to control and the heavily taxed peasants were restive. France had tied itself to potentially the greatest, but also the most unstable of the great powers.

Europe now appeared to be divided into two armed camps: the Triple Alliance on the one side, the Franco-Russian Alliance on the other. The Germans did increase the size of their army in 1893 and prepared a new war plan, the Schlieffen Plan, to deal with the prospect of a two-front war. But in fact all the European powers felt more secure. Since the Triple Alliance and the Franco-Russian Alliance were more or less equal in power, neither could attempt anything against the other. Instead, they could concentrate on action against powers not in

1885-1914 growing Russian economy

Franco-Russian Alliance 1894

The Schlieffen Plan 1893

the alliance system. The most important of these was Britain, which had a very uncomfortable time in the later 1890s, when its isolation proved not to be the 'splendid' thing that Joseph Chamberlain claimed it was. In particular, all the powers enjoyed sniping at Britain during the Boer War, though they lacked the naval power to do more than stand at the sidelines and criticize.

By the start of the 20th century, a global power like Britain had to take into account certain powers outside Europe. One of these was the United States of America. Since its Civil War in the early 1860s, the United States had risen, on the back of its agricultural wealth and its vast natural resources, to become the world's foremost industrial power. It had outstripped all other economies by 1890 and every year thereafter its lead increased, with only Russia growing faster. Before the 20th century, the USA had not sought to use its wealth to build up great armies or navies, but what it could do if it wanted was made clear when it humiliated Spain in the Spanish-American War of 1898 and acquired Puerto Rico and the Philippines. The war prompted it to build a huge fleet.

US dominance

Spanish-America War 1898

The defeat of Spain by the USA was a first sign that the domination of the world by Europe might be coming to an end. Another non-European power that was beginning to flex its muscles was Japan. Since the 17th century the Japanese had lived in self-imposed isolation from the rest of the world. A few Chinese and Dutch traders were allowed to use the port of Nagasaki, but otherwise the Japanese and outsiders were not allowed to have anything to do with each other. Nineteenth century Europeans and Americans, however, were unwilling to allow any parts of the world to refuse diplomatic contact or shut out their traders and they had the overwhelming power that enabled them to get their way. Beginning with concessions to the demands and threats of Commodore Perry of the US navy in 1854, Japan was brought into full contact with the western powers. A group of important Japanese leaders, backed by the Emperor, saw that by westernizing Japan could acquire the means to end the series of humiliations which it suffered at

The rise of Meiji Japan

Commodore Perry 'opens' Japan

the hands of the other powers in the mid-19th century. The army and navy were modernized; trade and industry were transformed. By the mid-1890s Japan was able to take on China in war and win, though it was then forced by Russia, France and Germany to give up most of its gains. At the turn of the century, Japan was seeking to end its demeaning subservience to the powers of Europe.

Sino-Japanese War

2. The End of British Isolation

In the 19th century British foreign secretaries had generally avoided alliances with other powers, except for specific and usually short term objects (such as fighting the Crimean War). In the 1890s, when the other major powers had all joined one or other of the alliance systems, this policy had resulted in uncomfortable isolation. After Lord Salisbury's resignation as Foreign Secretary in 1900, his successor, Lord Lansdowne, took it as his priority to end as many of Britain's quarrels with other powers as possible and to reach, if not alliances, then at least understandings with them. For him, the universal animosity shown to Britain during the Boer War showed that Britain had antagonized too many powers and so run into a potentially dangerous situation.

In the 19th century Britain had always aimed to dominate the seas of the world. It adopted the two-power standard, which meant that the Royal Navy had to be at least as large as the navies of any two other powers combined. In the 1890s Britain's priority was to maintain a navy greater than those of France and Russia. The American naval programme after the Spanish-American War posed a problem, since it was impossible for Britain to outbuild the Americans as well. The only solution was to settle all differences with the USA and rely on its continued friendship. Hence, in 1900-1 Britain conceded to the US the right to build and fortify a Panama canal, which would allow the Americans to move their fleet from one ocean to another. There then followed the withdrawal of all military and naval forces from the area

Two-power standard

Panama Canal ceded to US

of the Caribbean and from North America. Future defence planning assumed that Britain would never fight against the US. Ever since the War of 1812, successive British foreign secretaries had settled disputes with the US peacefully, recognizing that Canada could scarcely be defended against determined American attack. Never before, however, had America's primacy, at least in the western hemisphere, been so fully conceded.

Friendship with America was not enough to solve Britain's problems. The world's next flashpoint seemed certain to be in the Far East. The ancient empire of China was rapidly disintegrating and it looked improbable that its carve-up among the powers could be accomplished without war. The power in the best position to profit was Russia, which had contact with China by land since the building of the Trans-Siberian railway. The Admiralty worried that it could not cope if hostilities broke out in the East: in those waters its battleships were outnumbered by those of the Franco-Russian alliance. Anxious about the costs of the Boer War, the Treasury opposed any extra spending on the navy. Plainly, Britain needed an ally which might even up the balance of forces in Far Eastern waters. The only available ally was Japan. Its six battleships and 31 cruisers were more than enough to redress the balance. A five-year treaty of alliance was signed between Britain and Japan in 1902. The two powers agreed to be neutral if either became involved in a defensive war with one other power and to aid the other if such a war drew in a third power. Britain's hope was that the alliance would force the Russians to be cautious in the Far East, with the result that war would be avoided.

The Anglo-Japanese Alliance was profoundly alarming to France, which faced the possibility of having to fight Britain if its ally Russia fought Japan. It seemed essential to Paris to resolve its differences with Britain in order to reduce the chances of this occurring. War between Russia and Japan broke out in February 1904, and it became urgent to reach an understanding with Britain. Two months later the Entente Cordiale was signed. France finally dropped its objections to

Disinteg-
ration of the
ancient
empire of
China

Britain and
Japan allied
1902

Russo-
Japanese war
1904-5

the British occupation of Egypt and Britain accepted French predominance in Morocco. The Entente had been prepared by Edward VII's state visit of 1903 to Paris, which vastly pleased the French public. The King is even supposed to have blown kisses to famous courtesans across the theatres of Paris. The Entente was by no means a military alliance, but simply what its name implies, an agreement to be friends.

Almost at once the French had to act to prevent their ally Russia and their new friend Britain from going to war over an incident at Dogger Bank in the North Sea, when a Russian fleet heading for the east fired upon the Hull fishing fleet and provoked the British public to demand revenge. In the Far East, Russia experienced defeat and humiliation in the course of 1905, when its fleet was destroyed at Tsushima and its army was cut to pieces at Mukden. There then broke out a revolution at home which came within a hair's breadth of destroying the Tsar's government. At a stroke, British anxieties were relieved. The navy now far outweighed the Franco-Russian ones. There was no longer any prospect of the Russians destroying China. The far-flung British Empire was safer than it had been for decades.

Russia humiliated at Tsushima and Mukden

The Germans had hoped that the Russo-Japanese War would force the French to choose between their old ally Russia and their new friend Britain. In fact, Russian defeat made the friendship of France more necessary to Russia and led the British to take advantage of Russian weakness to achieve a settlement of the main issues that remained outstanding between them and Russia. The British had hoped for a settlement with Russia for many years, since it seemed much the cheapest way to defend India, which appeared vulnerable to a southward thrust by the Tsar's forces. The new Liberal Foreign Secretary, Sir Edward Grey, took over at the end of 1905 and began negotiations. Nearly a century of hostility and prejudice on both sides had to be overcome. Many of the Liberals detested the Tsar's authoritarian rule, which the revolution of 1905 had only modified, not ended. Many of the Russians would have preferred an agreement with conservative Germany and feared being pushed forward by France and England against it. Yet finally the many obstacles were surmounted. Neither power was to infringe the territory of Tibet nor interfere in its administration. Afghanistan was to be a British sphere of influence. Persia was to be divided into three spheres: a large northern zone including Tehran was to be under Russian control, while Britain would dominate a smaller area in the south, judged crucial to the defence of India, and there would be a neutral central zone. The protracted negotiations ended at last in 1907. Like the Entente with France, this agreement was simply the resolution of a number of quarrels, not an alliance. It safeguarded the Indian Empire and thereby enabled Britain to focus its attention on European issues.

Britain allies with the Russian bear

3. The German Threat

When Lansdowne became Foreign Secretary in 1900, he said that he had only one aim: 'that we should use every effort to maintain, and if we can to strengthen the good relations which at present exist between the Queen's government and that of the [German] Emperor'. He hoped that it might be possible to gain the Germans as an ally against Russian expansion in the Far East. Germany, though, did not want a war with Russia for the sake of British interests in China and Lansdowne turned to Japan instead.

Hopes for a German alliance were rapidly replaced by fears of a German threat. The rulers of Germany, conscious of Germany's huge and growing economic and military power, believed that Germany should be a world power. Yet in the great share-out of the world in the late 19th century, Germany, as a late-comer on the world stage, had acquired only a small colonial empire, a mere million square miles containing only 15 million people. If Germany was to fulfil its destiny and become a world power, it would have to challenge the status quo (the existing state of affairs) and the powers which benefited from it, above all Britain.

Fear of German threat grow

Admiral Tirpitz had much to do with setting the direction of German policy in the decade after his appointment as State Secretary for the Imperial Navy in 1897. Navy laws were passed in 1898 and 1900 laying down a twenty-year schedule to create a fleet of sixty battleships and battle-cruisers. Tirpitz envisaged that the German fleet would become so strong that Britain could not contemplate taking it on and so would be compelled to make concessions to Germany. In this way Germany would have gained the freedom to alter the status quo in its favour.

Admiral Tirpitz - State Secretary for the Imperial Navy

In adopting Tirpitz's policy, the German rulers had decided that Germany's future as a great power depended on something which Britain could not possibly put up with if it was to remain a great power. For geographical reasons, a huge German fleet in the North Sea threatened completely to remove Britain's freedom of action, not simply to limit it in one part of the world, as the American navy did. Hence Britain and Germany found themselves committed to a naval race. Germany could not reach its goal without outbuilding Britain; Britain could not safeguard its independence without outbuilding the Germans. In such a contest German chances of victory were not good. Tirpitz had banked on Britain's being unable to concentrate its naval forces in the North Sea. He had not supposed it possible that Britain could end its quarrels with France and with Russia. Yet by 1907 Britain had done so and had called back its capital ships from parts of the world where they were no longer needed.

German fleet threatened Britain's freedom of action

The naval race between Britain and Germany entered its most serious phase after 1906. In that year Admiral Fisher achieved his aim of introducing a ship able to out-gun and out-steam any rival. HMS *Dreadnought*, launched in 1906, depended on oil-fired turbines, which were more reliable and faster than the previous coal-burners, and was equipped with ten twelve-inch guns (instead of four). At once, all earlier battleships became obsolete and Germany seemed to have a chance to out-build Britain. Tirpitz took advantage of this opportunity and by 1908 had announced that Germany would construct four

HMS Dreadnought 1906

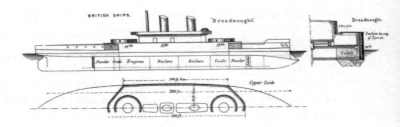

CROSS-SECTION OF A DREADNOUGHT

battleships of the Dreadnought type each year. In Britain there were intense arguments about what the British response should be. The government's radical supporters were anxious to reduce spending on arms and to spend instead on social reforms. They supported an international conference at The Hague, which attempted to reach agreement over arms reduction. The Germans, however, would not accept an agreement which involved their recognition of the existing unfavourable balance of naval power. Despite the arguments, Grey, Haldane, the Minister of War, and Asquith, Prime Minister from 1908, remained resolute in upholding Britain's naval superiority. They were supported by a noisy public opinion crying, 'We want eight and we won't wait' at the height of the crisis in 1909. By 1914 it was clear that Britain had won the naval race: its navy out-numbered the German in Dreadnoughts by 22 to 13 and in battle-cruisers by 9 to 4.

In the course of the naval race Britain had sometimes entered into direct talks with the Germans, who always demanded that Britain should pledge its neutrality in continental affairs. This was not something that Britain dared to do, because German intentions in Europe were not trusted. It seemed to Grey and the leading men in the Foreign Office that the Germans aimed to dominate the continent. Once they had achieved dominance there, they would have no difficulty in outbuilding the British at sea and ending British independence too. This was why Grey said before he became Foreign

Quest to uphold Britain's naval superiority

Secretary: 'Germany is our worst enemy and our greatest danger. Preserving a balance of power against German attempts to upset it was a key British interest'.

Grey's suspicions of Germany were much heightened by the crisis over Morocco, which had broken out in 1905. Relying on the Entente with Britain, a French mission had arrived at Fez, and seemed to be treating this part of Morocco as a French protectorate. The Germans at once protested; the Kaiser went to Tangier and made one of his bellicose speeches. Practically under threat of war, France agreed to submit her Moroccan claim to a European conference; Delcassé, the French Foreign Minister, had to resign. Nothing much came of the conference, held at Algeciras (1906), but throughout it Britain supported France against German bullying. On this occasion Britain had definitely ranged herself - as far as diplomacy went - on the side of France, against Germany, and both countries had become convinced that the Entente was necessary for their security against Germany. Some influential men in the Foreign Office were more certain than ever that Germany was aiming to dominate Europe.

Moroccan crisis 1905

The main result of the Moroccan crisis was to draw France and Britain close together. Sir Henry Campbell-Bannerman authorized 'military conversations' between the British and French General Staffs. These had taken place in a more rudimentary and unofficial way under Lord Lansdowne. These 'conversations' were held to discuss military plans in the event of the two countries becoming allies in war. No undertaking was ever given that they should become allies; nevertheless, the conversations proceeded on that assumption. The British public and Parliament knew nothing of this; the 'conversations' were even kept secret from all but three or four members of the Cabinet. It was judged that publicity might be harmful, and arouse unnecessary alarm, and it is in fact probable that the majority in the Liberal Cabinet would not have sanctioned them. The conversations showed how since the turn of the century imperial issues had declined in importance. Britain was at least contemplating the possibility of

Secret conversations between France and Britain plan military strategies intervening on the near-continent, something it had not done since the days of Napoleon.

The military plans discussed with France made necessary the reorganization of British military forces undertaken by Haldane, Liberal Minister of War. He created the General Staff in charge of all matters to do with military planning and organization. A well equipped and trained Expeditionary Force was created, which could be sent quickly across the Channel to assist the French, should it ever become necessary. Its main deficiency, from the French point of view, was its small size, only six divisions or 160,000 men. At home various defence forces were reorganized as the Territorial Army, while to ensure a supply of volunteers for the army, the corps of schools and universities were taken into the Officers' Training Corps, funded and supervised by the army. As a result of Haldane's reforms, Britain was better prepared for war than it had ever been in the 19th century and the war it was ready for involved a continental commitment.

The Territorial Army

In 1908 another European crisis occurred. Austria-Hungary suddenly proclaimed the annexation of Bosnia and Herzegovina, which had been an Austrian protectorate since 1878. The most significant aspect of the crisis was the German demand in 1909 that Russia should recognize this annexation by their ally. The Germans seemed to be taking advantage of Russian weakness after the defeat and revolution of 1905 and showing their determination to reduce Russia to subservience. More than ever, Britain was determined to stay on close terms with France and Russia and to evade German efforts to get it to promise neutrality in Europe.

Annexation of Bosnia and Herzegovina 1908

A year seldom passed by, in this uneasy period, without at least one fresh crisis. The French were again active in Morocco, and again in 1911 the Germans protested. Their protest this time took the form of sending the gunboat *Panther* to Agadir, a seaport on the Moroccan Atlantic coast where, it was claimed, there were 'German interests'. The German attitude was most menacing; it looked as though France would be compelled to withdraw from Morocco under threat of war.

The Germans took no notice of British protests, and it was this fact that decided Lloyd George, the Chancellor of the Exchequer, to give them to understand that Britain could not, and would not, be ignored. In a speech at the Mansion House, of which the substance had been discussed with Sir Edward Grey, the Chancellor gave this grave warning to the rulers of Germany:

> I believe it is essential in the highest interests not merely of this country, but of the world, that Britain should at all hazards maintain her place and her prestige among the Great Powers of the world. Her potent influence has many a time been in the past, and may yet be in the future, invaluable to the cause of human liberty. . . . I would make great sacrifices to preserve peace. . . . But if a situation were to be forced upon us in which peace could only be preserved by the surrender of the great and beneficent position Britain has won by centuries of heroism and achievement, by allowing Britain to be treated where her interests were vitally affected as if she were of no account in the Cabinet of Nations, then I say emphatically that peace at that price would be a humiliation intolerable for a great country like ours to endure.'

The crisis became so serious that Grey warned the Admiralty that 'The Fleet might be attacked at any moment.' Finally, the German government backed away from a confrontation and the threat of war receded. France had to make concessions to Germany in the Congo area, a gain which Germany could have obtained without a European crisis. The threats employed by the German government seriously weakened the German position. In Britain first Lloyd George, then Churchill moved into the anti-German camp. The Committee of Imperial Defence discussed British strategies to check Germany and came down in favour of an expeditionary force to fight on the Franco-Belgian border. This was still discussion about *how* to aid the French, not about *whether* to aid them, but at least aiding them was becoming

German bullying tactics push Britain and France closer

a realistic option. German hectoring also had an effect in France, where the assertive Poincaré first became Prime Minister and later President in place of the more pliable radicals previously in power.

In 1912 Britain's commitment to France was further strengthened. By a naval agreement of that year the French fleet was to be concentrated in the Mediterranean against Austria and Italy, while the British fleet would guard the North Sea against Germany. Britain was thus able to concentrate its forces against the major foe, but in acquiring this advantage it had taken on a *moral*, if not a binding *treaty* obligation to protect the northern and Atlantic coasts of France in the event of war. The radicals in the Cabinet would not have accepted a stronger commitment than this.

Grey too was anxious to keep a free hand and avoid irrevocable commitment to the Franco-Russian side. His worries about Germany eased somewhat in 1912. The balance of power in Europe, seriously upset by the Russian collapse of 1905, seemed to be righting itself. France made up for its low birth rate by increasing the term of military service for its young men. Russia used French loans to build railways which could transport troops more quickly to the German frontier. The Germans responded by increasing their army, but even so the balance of rival forces looked more even than at any time since 1905. In these circumstances, Grey thought it important to offer friendship to Germany; for example by holding talks to end the disputes over the Baghdad Railway, which the Germans were building.

The value of good relations between Britain and Germany seemed Balkan Crisis to be demonstrated in the Balkan crisis which broke out in 1912. In 1912 a first war, Greece, Serbia and Bulgaria drove the Turks from their European provinces, save the area round Constantinople. In a second war in 1913 the victors quarrelled; the Bulgarians attacked their former allies, but were defeated. When peace was made, the Bulgarians Bulgarians had to surrender to Serbia some of the territory they had surrender won in the first war. Throughout the crisis the powers had united to territory to bring the warring states to a conference of ambassadors in London Serbia chaired by Grey and ensure a settlement which would satisfy them and the rival interests in the area of the great powers. Nonetheless, in two ways the Balkan wars of 1912-13 helped to destabilize European politics. First, the Bulgarians were deeply dissatisfied by the outcome of the wars and awaited an opportunity for revenge on Serbia. Much more important, Austria-Hungary was worried by the new situation in the Balkans. Its enemy Serbia had been greatly enlarged and strengthened by the wars. After taking what it wanted from the Turks, it could now concentrate on prising Bosnia, which contained a large number of Serbs, from Austria's grip. If it succeeded in doing that, it might well initiate the disintegration of the entire multi-national Empire.

Balkan Wars 1912-13

Serbia's growing power

From Grey's point of view, the German threat had receded somewhat by the end of 1913. Britain was winning the naval race; so the failure to secure a naval agreement did not seem to matter too much. The balance of power between the Franco-Russian and Austro-German blocs had been in large measure restored. From the German point of view, these developments were not welcome. The failure to force Britain to terms meant that Germany was still not a world power. The ominous revival of Russian power meant that in Europe Germany was encircled. In the future things were likely to get worse. Russia was destined to become a super-power; Germany's ally Austria-Hungary might disintegrate; in Germany itself the hold of the social and military elite might weaken. Full of gloom about the future, the Germans might decide to cash in on their present military power rather than wait for a future that seemed bound to be less favourable. Some German leaders felt that their country faced a stark choice: *Weltmacht oder Niedergang*, a bid for world power or inevitable decline.

Britain leads the naval race

4. The Crisis of 1914

In May 1914 Sir Arthur Nicolson, Permanent Under-Secretary at the Foreign Office, commented: 'Since I have been at the Foreign Office, I have not seen such calm waters.' Yet by August 1914, all

BALKANS: 1908-13

the great powers of Europe were at war. Between May and August a fateful event had occurred.

Assassination of the Franz Ferdinand and his wife

On 28 June 1914, the Archduke Franz Ferdinand, heir to the Austrian throne, visited Sarajevo, the Bosnian capital. As he and his wife were driven through the town, they were assassinated by Gavrilo

Princip, a youth who, we now know, had been trained as a shot by a Serbian terrorist society known as the 'Black Hand'.

The Austro-Hungarian government was certain that the assassin had acted at the instigation of the Serbian government. They felt that they had to act decisively to cow the Serbs and to discourage any future acts to destabilize the monarchy. They waited a month; then they sent an ultimatum to Belgrade, assuming the guilt of the Serbian government, and demanding the most abject surrender. The German government had already taken the momentous step of declaring that Austria-Hungary could count on German support, and this stiffened the Austrian attitude and made the dispatch of the ultimatum possible. The Serbian offers to give a qualified satisfaction were turned down. At the last moment Germany made an effort in favour of moderation, but on 28 July Austria declared war on Serbia and bombarded Belgrade.

Austria declares war on Serbia

Sir Edward Grey had meanwhile been striving to localize the conflict for several difficult days and as late as 29 July he asserted British neutrality. But that neutrality was already being undermined. Russia was the patron of Serbia and could scarcely permit its client's humiliation if it was to retain any credit or influence in the Balkans. Russia was determined not to bow, as in 1908, to German threats and began to mobilize. Germany gave an evasive reply to the British plea for a conference; and instead, sent an ultimatum to Russia demanding the instant demobilization of the Russian army. This request was refused.

British neutrality undermined by ties to Russia

At this point, German military planning played a crucial role in the way events unfolded. Since the formation of the Franco-Russian Alliance, the Germans had planned, in the event of war, to send the bulk of their forces against France. They assumed that France could be overwhelmed in a few weeks, as effectively it had been in 1870. The Russians would be relatively slow to mobilize and so would not be a serious threat until France had been defeated. This strategic plan, known as the Schlieffen Plan after its inventor, had to be put into operation the moment that Russia mobilized or Schlieffen's timetable

ARCHDUKE FRANZ FERDINAND OF AUSTRIA (1863-1914)

would be thrown out. There was therefore no more time to resolve the situation by diplomacy. Nor was it possible to see whether the French would actually support their ally Russia. Impossible demands had to be put to France to force it into war at once.

Would Britain be involved? Till late in the crisis, a majority of the Cabinet was against intervention, though, as a precautionary measure, the British fleet, which was collected for a test mobilization, was prevented from dispersing on 26 July. On 2 August the Cabinet decided to give an assurance to the French government that 'if the German fleet comes into the Channel or through the North Sea to undertake hostile operations against French coasts or shipping, the British fleet would give all the protection in its power'. This decision was not regarded by the Cabinet as committing England to war, and

British fleet offer the French protection

was subject to the consent of Parliament. One other decision was taken at the meeting of 2 August: that a 'substantial violation' of Belgian neutrality by Germany would be a *casus belli* (an occasion for war).

The success of Schlieffen's plan depended on speed. To attack France in Lorraine over the Franco-German border would bring the Germans up against formidable defences and would not allow a rapid lunge at Paris to knock France out of the war. Schlieffen had therefore proposed to attack France through the flat and weakly defended state of Belgium, even though its neutrality was guaranteed by a treaty of 1839, which Prussia had signed. On 3 August an appeal duly arrived from the King of the Belgians, asking for British help. Germany had sent an ultimatum to Belgium demanding the free passage of the German armies across that country on their way to invade France; the demand had been refused. For many members of the Liberal Cabinet, this new German action made it easier to agree to a declaration of war against Germany. A war for Belgium would be a war on behalf of a small nation and a war for the sanctity of international treaties against a power that regarded the treaty of 1839 as a mere 'scrap of paper'.

Belgium appeals to Britain

The moral cause of Belgium enabled many Liberals to support entry into war with a clear conscience, but it was not the principal reason why Britain fought. Grey and the Prime Minister Asquith took Britain into war because Germany persisted in threatening the independence of France. If it successfully did so, then Germany would be able to achieve domination of Europe, just as Napoleon had in the early 19th century. Britain's independence would not then long survive. Much British opinion was converted to this point of view before the majority of the Cabinet was. It had become clear that the unity of the Liberal Party would not survive a refusal to fight beside France. The liberal Imperialists, such as Grey, Asquith and Haldane, would join with the Conservatives to lead Britain into war. Most Liberals preferred to stay in power and influence the manner in which the war was conducted.

On 20 July 1914 *The Times* argued that intervention in the war brewing in Europe 'is not merely a duty of friendship. It is…an elementary duty of self-preservation…We cannot stand alone in a Europe dominated by any single power.' It was in pursuit of this principle of national security that Britain had fought against Philip II of Spain, Louis XIV and Napoleon of France, and that she was now to fight against William II of Germany. On 4 August Britain sent an ultimatum to Germany requiring an assurance that it would respect Belgian neutrality. No answer came; so from midnight Britain and Germany were at war. On 6 August the British Expeditionary Force (BEF) was sent to France. Almost no one had any idea of what they had committed themselves to.

Britain and
Germany
at war

DATE SUMMARY: THE GREAT WAR
(1914-18)

WESTERN FRONTS	EASTERN FRONTS	NAVAL AND COLONIAL
	1914	
Aug. Germans invade Belgium and France	Aug. ⚔ Tannenberg	
⚔ the frontiers		
⚔ Mons		
		Conquest of German SW Africa and German New Guinea
Sept. ⚔ Marne		
Oct. Fall of Antwerp	Oct. Turkey joins Germany	
Nov.-Dec. 1st ⚔ Ypres		Nov. Capture of Kiao-Chow (Jiaozhon Bay)
		Dec. ⚔ Falkland Isles
	1915	
Feb. ⚔ Neuve-Chapelle	Apr. Gallipoli landing	
May Italy joins Allies	May-Sept. Russian Retreat	May *Lusitania* sunk
	Aug. Suvla Bay landing	
Sept. ⚔ Loos		
	Oct. Bulgaria joins Germany	
	Nov. Germans conquer Serbia	
	Dec. Evacuation of Gallipoli Salonika Front	
	1916	
Feb.-July ⚔ Verdun		Feb. Cameroons conquered
	Apr. Surrender of Kut Lawrence of Arabia	
		May ⚔ Jutland
	June Last Russian offensive	
July-Nov. ⚔ Somme	Nov.-Dec. Germans conquer Rumania (Romania)	
	1917	
		Feb. Unrestricted submarine warfare
	Mar. Baghdad captured First Russian Revolution	
Apr. Submarine peril America joins Allies Nivelle's attack		
⚔ Arras		
June ⚔ Messines	June Greece joins Allies	
July-Nov. ⚔ Passchendaele	Oct. ⚔ Caporetto (Kobarid)	
Nov.-Dec ⚔ Cambrai	Nov. Bolshevik Revolution	
	Dec. Jerusalem captured	Dec. Conquest of German E. Africa
	1918	
Mar. German offensive	Mar. Treaty of Brest-Litovsk	
Apr. ⚔ Lys		
Zeebrugge raid		
Foch Generalissimo		
July Foch's offensive		
Aug.-Nov. Allied advance	Sept. Bulgaria defeated	
	Oct. Turkey "	
Nov. Armistice with Germany	Nov. Austria "	

VI

THE FIRST WORLD WAR, 1914-1918

1. The Character of the War

THE First World War was fought by land, sea and air, and on a scale hitherto unknown in history. On land, four of the original combatants, Germany, Austria, Russia and France, were able, by virtue of their conscription systems, to put in the field armies of several millions of men almost at once; Britain also raised great numbers of men in the course of the war. Such vast numbers could be set in motion and kept supplied only because of the technological advances of the 19th century. The states involved used their rail networks to convey millions of men to the frontiers. These men then had to be fed and provided with ammunition, guns and so forth via a rail system extended behind the front by the construction of hundreds of miles of light railways. Back at home the industrial capacity developed during the previous century was converted or extended to make the huge quantities of munitions which kept the war machines of the various powers in operation.

Memories of the Austro-Prussian war of 1866 and the Franco-Prussian War of 1870 convinced almost everyone that the war would be short. In fact, after the first German effort to overwhelm France had failed, by November 1914, the opposing armies on the Western Front
Trench settled down to conditions of trench warfare. This state of affairs lasted
warfare for four years. It was a little like the siege warfare of former centuries, except that this was a siege extending along hundreds of miles of the Western Front, extending from the Channel coast in Belgium to the Alps in Switzerland. Outflanking the enemy was impossible, but frontal attack offered little hope of success either. The trench systems of the opposing sides were usually three lines deep. A breakthrough could not generally be quickly achieved; the enemy therefore had time

to bring up troops by rail to plug any gap that might have been opened up. But opening up a gap was by no means easy. The attacking infantryman with his rifle was the spearhead of all attacks, but he was a slow-moving target who was vulnerable to the rifle fire of the opposing infantry in their trenches as well as to the hail of bullets pouring from enemy machine guns and the shells of their artillery. He was slowed down further by the weight of equipment he had to carry and by the barbed wire with which the enemy further strengthened their positions. Once ordered 'over the top', the infantry passed out of easy contact with their commanders. The trailing wires of primitive field telephones were often cut by enemy artillery and runners were slow and often killed, with the result that commanders could not adjust their tactics to take account of local successes and failures.

Both sides engaged in an unceasing search for new weapons which might make it possible to break the deadlock. In April 1915 it looked as if the Germans might have discovered such a weapon when they used chlorine gas against the French. Coughing and choking as the gas attacked their lungs, the French fled in panic and a four-mile gap opened up in their line. The Germans were not ready to exploit their opportunity and it never recurred. In all future gas attacks, even with different gases such as mustard gas, the enemy was always furnished with the gas masks which were soon developed. A weapon which turned out to have a greater future in the 20th century was the tank, first used by the British in the later stages of the Battle of the Somme in 1916. Like gas, it had a demoralizing effect on the enemy when it first appeared. It was invulnerable to machine-gun fire and could climb over trenches. Yet in its early form it turned out to have serious limitations. It was extremely slow and cumbersome and very prone to mechanical breakdown.

Gas warfare

Introduction of tanks

The use of the air-arm for the first time in war also pointed the way to its immense possibilities for the future. As an adjunct to the artillery, the aeroplane proved extremely useful; maps of the enemy trenches were always prepared from air photographs. To protect their air-space, both sides developed fighter aircraft and the public back home was kept enthralled by stories of the aerial dogfights of their country's air aces. Men like the 'Red Baron', Manfred von Richthofen, victor in eighty dogfights, became national heroes. By 1918 aeroplanes were beginning to engage in ground attack, but their influence on the clashes of armies was still marginal. Aerial bombing was also only in its primitive stage of development. The Germans sent their airships, called Zeppelins after their inventor, to raid England, and to terrorize the populations of London and other towns. Zeppelins were very likely to be set on fire and to incinerate the crew when attacked and the damage they inflicted was marginal.

The Red
Baron

Zeppelins

It was not aeroplanes, but artillery that proved most destructive in the First World War. Terrible damage was done to towns and villages, and to woods, gardens and orchards, which happened to come within the war zone. The worst places on the British front were the Ypres Salient and the Somme battlefield. On the Somme one could stand on the top of a hill and look for several miles across country without seeing a living thing - not a tree, not a flower, not a blade of grass. All was one vast area of churned-up earth and mud, pitted with innumerable shell-holes, filled with water, broken rifles, abandoned equipment - and the corpses of the slain. Perhaps even more distressing was the townscape of Ypres, where the splendid medieval town, with its medieval cloth hall and cathedral, was reduced to a heap of ruins by the constant shelling throughout the years of war.

Devastating
effects of
artillery
warfare

Within these zones of destruction the soldiers had to live. On most of the Western Front the German infantry expected to remain on the defensive and so built deep, well-constructed dug-outs, often lit by electric light and furnished with simple beds. The French and British infantry, on the other hand, had the prime duty of recapturing the parts of France in German hands. Their accommodation was viewed as temporary and the troops were much less comfortable and more crowded together in the forward trenches. Rats infested the trenches, and the stench in some of the worst ones was horrible. A variety of

'An attack: Moving up a Big Gun' A Daily Mail postcard
FROM *c.* 1915-16.
The reverse carries the following information: 'The toilsome haul of a big British gun
along a muddy hill side on the Western Front by a 12-horse team and the gun crew.'

diseases afflicted both armies: notably, trench foot, which came **The**
of standing in cold, waterlogged boots, and trench fever, which **hardships**
affected men whose clothing was perpetually lice-ridden. The men **of trench**
had also to endure all the severities of winter without any kind of **warfare**
artificial heat (at any rate in the front line) and without fresh food. Of
course, men were not continuously in the front trenches, but were
rotated through forward trenches, reserve trenches and rear areas.

Life in the front trenches was dangerous as well as unpleasant, even
when no attack was planned. Incautious exposure of a head provided
a tempting target for enemy snipers and enemy shells sometimes
landed in the trenches. The effects of shell-fire were among the most
nerve-racking experiences of the war. Already in 1914 British doctors
identified a condition they called shell-shock, which could lead to **Shell-shock**
complete mental breakdown. 80,000 sufferers were identified in the
course of the war, but there were certainly others who were believed

to be malingerers and might be punished accordingly. Poison gas was a further cause of suffering: chlorine and phosgene could wreck men's lungs for life, while mustard gas caused terrible blisters. Perhaps the experience of a gas attack was best conveyed by the poet Wilfred Owen, who fought on the Western Front and died there in 1918. In his poem 'Dulce et Decorum Est' he wrote:

War Poets

> Gas! GAS? Quick, boys! - An ecstasy of fumbling
> Fitting the clumsy helmets just in time,
> But someone still was yelling out and stumbling
> And flound'ring like a man in fire or lime. -
> Dim through the misty panes and thick green light,
> As under a green sea, I saw him drowning.
>
> In all my dreams before my helpless sight
> He plunges at me, guttering, choking, drowning.

The First World War was a struggle between the armed forces of the countries engaged, but it was also thought of as a conflict between whole societies. The armies could not continue to fight without the support of the people from whom they were drawn, great numbers of whom were in one way or another involved in the war economy. Hence there were deliberate attacks on civilian targets, such as those carried out by Zeppelins or by German ships which shelled coastal towns such as Hartlepool and Yarmouth. More likely to succeed in crippling the enemy were the efforts made by each side to undermine the other's economy. The British hoped to cripple Germany by means of their naval blockade, which prevented all of Germany's overseas trade. The most serious effects were on German food supplies. Normally, Germany imported a third of its food and during the war production at home actually declined, partly because of labour shortages, partly because of the cessation of fertilizer imports: the cereal harvest of 1917 was only half that of 1913. Yet the Germans made do. From early on there were measures to cut consumption and rationing was introduced. The people who suffered most were those keenest on the war and least likely to protest, such as civil servants whose wages were frozen at a time of marked inflation. There were strikes and protests, especially in the 'turnip winter' of 1916-17, but there were more strikes in Britain than in Germany, and it was only when it became clear in October 1918 that the people's sacrifices had been in vain that a revolutionary situation developed in Germany. The Germans had the chance fatally to damage the British economy only in 1917, when they had built up their U-boat (submarine) fleet and nerved themselves to risk American intervention against them. The Germans believed that they had the capacity to starve Britain and to cut it off from overseas supplies which kept the war effort going. Though more hesitantly, the British government introduced measures such as rationing which the German government had found efficacious and in any case the adoption of escorted convoys reduced British losses at sea to manageable levels. For neither side did economic warfare prove decisive.

German
U-boats

The First World War was fought also on a psychological level. Partly for this reason, the British government had passed the Defence of the Realm Act, which gave it more or less unlimited power to do whatever was necessary to ensure victory, including censoring the press and all war news. Each side used propaganda to maintain the morale of its own troops and civilian population, to impress neutral powers with the justice of its cause and to undermine the morale of the enemy. Germans at the time and later claimed that their defeat owed much to Allied propaganda. 'We were hypnotized...as rabbit by a snake', Ludendorff was to write, attributing to British propaganda the demoralization of the Germans in 1918. Hitler later referred to the propaganda in the newspapers of Lord Northcliffe as 'an inspired work of genius'. Press lords such as Northcliffe and Beaverbrook endorsed such verdicts on the significance of the British press. Yet all these witnesses were biased. Naturally, the press barons tended to

Defence
of the
Realm Act

Propaganda

overstate their own importance, while the Germans had to find an excuse for their failure. The Germans do seem to have lost the war of words and this failure played at least some role in the decision of the USA to enter the war on the Allied side. Yet this failure had less to do with the brilliance of British journalists than with the propaganda coups presented to them by crass German actions such as the sinking without warning of the *Lusitania**, despite the large number of civilians aboard, or the real atrocities perpetrated in Belgium, which made the exaggerations of British propaganda believable. As to the view of Hitler or Ludendorff that German defeat resulted from a collapse of morale, it seems to put the cart before the horse. If morale among the troops was beginning to fail by the summer of 1918, it was more an effect than a cause of military failures, whilst civilian morale cracked only after Ludendorff had admitted the impossibility of victory.

Sinking of the Lusitinia

For the period after what we now call the First World War, the conflict was simply the Great War. Once another great war had been fought between 1939 and 1945, it had to be renamed. The name chosen, the First World War, seemed to fit a conflict which included non-European powers such as the USA and Japan and saw fighting in Africa and the Middle East. Yet the new label was in some ways inappropriate. In essence, the war was a European war about European issues, especially about the future status of Germany in Europe and whether it was to be the dominant power there. That is why all the big engagements took place in Europe and why Britain was no longer able to make do with the small armies which had sufficed for most of the period since 1815.

---

* The liner carried munitions for the British, but this did not seem to neutrals to excuse German indifference to human life.

2. Recruiting the Army

Before the war, Britain's military plans involved sending a small armed force of regular troops to assist France, if Britain decided to support it in a conflict with Germany. The burden of the early fighting would have to be borne by France, but should the war prove protracted, Britain would have to supply more help, which it could do only by raising fresh armies. Lord Kitchener, the Minister for War, was one of the first to appreciate this necessity. He met it by means of an appeal for volunteers. His mustachioed visage and pointing figure were soon to address the young men of Britain from thousands of posters with the simple assertion, 'Your country needs you.' They responded in their hundreds of thousands. In the first August and September alone three-quarters of a million men joined up.

Three-quarters of a million British men volunteer

No doubt, the response in part reflected the government's successful recruitment techniques. The Parliamentary Recruitment Committee constructed an impressive organization, which organized thousands of meetings and distributed millions of posters and leaflets. Yet it was slow to get off the mark and certainly does not account for the initial rush to enlist. There is a great deal of evidence to suggest that female pressure was significant. Women often handed white feathers symbolizing cowardice to men not in uniform and probably many were shamed into enlisting. Peer group pressure was important too. Groups bound together by locality, occupation or even leisure interest often joined up en masse: frequently they formed pals' battalions who, it was agreed, would all serve together. In some cases, economic factors may have been a factor: recruitment went well in the early months when a financial crisis temporarily led to a rise in unemployment. The middle classes had long been educated to think of death for King and country as a glorious fate. There is danger in basing an argument on what was written by untypical men such as accomplished poets, but it is likely that many shared Rupert Brooke's view that war might provide an escape from triviality and constitute

White feathers

LORD KITCHENER'S 1914 RECRUITMENT CAMPAIGN
Courtesy of The Imperial War Musuem

a great and enobling adventure. No one had any idea what it would be like.

> Now, God be thanked Who matched us with His hour,
> And caught our youth, and wakened us from sleeping,
> With hand made sure, clear eye, and sharpened power,
> To turn, as swimmers into cleanness leaping,
> Glad from a world grown old and cold and weary,
> Leave the sick hearts that honour could not move,
> And half-men, and their dirty songs and dreary,
> And all the little emptiness of love.

By the end of 1915 close on two and a half million men had joined up, but that meant that three million of military age (18 to 41) had not. Nearly half of these were in reserved occupations, that is in jobs essential for the continued functioning of the economy, and another 40 per cent had been rejected as physically unfit for military service. Even so, it was felt to be intolerable that there should be men shirking their manifest duty and besides, the losses of 1915 had to be replaced and reserves created for the planned offensive of 1916. Britain was beginning to run out of men. In the circumstances the scruples of the Liberal members of the Cabinet were overcome and conscription was finally accepted. The effects were disappointing, largely because so many of those not already in the army were unfit for service. The Liberal reforms had not yet succeeded in improving the health of anything like all the poor. Despite conscription, therefore, by 1918 the shortage of manpower was acute and losses caused by Ludendorff's offensive in 1918 came close to exhausting Britain's last reserves. By the autumn, half of the British infantry in France was aged only nineteen or less. *Conscription imposed*

The advent of conscription also created the problem of conscientious objection. Conscientious objectors were men whose consciences forbade them to fight. Quakers and Jehovah's Witnesses *Growth of conscientious objection* had religious grounds for their pacifism and there were groups on the left, especially the Independent Labour Party, who drew on traditional British objections to conscription as 'militarist'. There were 16,000 objectors in all who had to plead their cause before local tribunals, which could decide that their scruples were genuine and grant them exemption from military service. Those granted exemption were assigned to non-combatant duties, usually as ambulance men. A minority of 1500 'absolutists' refused any compulsory service at all and went to prison for the duration of the war. Their cases and those of men whose plea for exemption was rejected were taken up by the No Conscription Fellowship, who lobbied unceasingly on their behalf. Public opinion was not sympathetic to the cause of the 'conchies', who remained a minor problem for the government.

3. Economic Mobilization

The introduction of conscription marked a notable extension of state power in Britain and one which public opinion was willing to accept as essential to success in the fighting on the Western Front. The generals, however, needed not just men, but also munitions on an unprecedented and ever-increasing scale. The week-long bombardment before the Battle of the Somme in 1916 used up one and a half million shells. The Passchendaele offensive required four million in ten days in 1917. In one day in September 1918 the guns fired off not far short of a million shells. Shells were essential, but so too were guns, aeroplanes and tanks. The British Army needed munitions, but so too did those of France, Italy and, later, the USA. Britain was the arsenal of the Allies. In these circumstances, Asquith's hope that his government might be able to conduct 'business as usual' was certain to be proved vain.

The output of the engineering industry had to be raised, at a time when many workers had joined the army. 'Dilution', the use of less skilled workers to do the jobs previously reserved for the skilled, was

Munitions shortages

indispensable. Meeting with the union leaders in March 1915, Lloyd George got the principle of dilution accepted on condition that profits should be restricted and the unions should share in directing the industry. The press was filled with reports of a shortage of shells (the 'Shells Scandal') in the spring of 1915 and partly as a result Asquith had to bring the Conservatives into his government in May. A Ministry of Munitions was set up under Lloyd George to maximize the production of war materials. It fixed their prices and bought up available raw materials at home and abroad. By July 1915 a category of 'controlled establishments' had been created, where manning levels, working conditions and wages were under state control. By the end of the war, the new ministry employed 65,000 officials who supervised 20,000 'controlled establishments' and controlled three and a half million workers. When Lloyd George became Prime Minister in December 1916, the final steps towards state direction of the entire economy were taken. All merchant ships were requisitioned, though they were managed through their owners, while agriculture was controlled by the government through county committees that were dominated by local landowners. State direction of the economy

The government had hoped to leave food prices to be determined by the market, but shortages caused by U-boat sinkings and the insatiable demands of the armed forces led to price controls in 1917 and then to a government takeover of the wholesale meat trade. A panic over the future supply of food in the last winter of the war led the government to impose rationing of certain commodities, such as meat, tea, sugar and butter. There had long been interference in the drink trade for quite different reasons. A report on bad time-keeping in some key industries blamed lost time on the ready availability of alcoholic drink. Opening hours were universally restricted in order to create a long period in the afternoon when pubs were shut. Heavy taxes were imposed upon drink too: by 1919 the price of beer had more than doubled, that of spirits had quintupled. Consumption of beer halved, which had the effect of releasing grain for food. Pub opening hours shortened

Already before the outbreak of war, the Liberal ministry had much increased government intervention in society and the economy. During the First World War, the retreat from *laissez faire* became a headlong flight, as the government was compelled to take responsibility for practically the entire economy. It did so not out of any ideological commitment to collective direction of social and economic affairs, but because it needed to assert the absolute priority of its aim of winning the war against Germany. It remained to be seen how far the British would wish or need to retain so interventionist a government once the defeat of Germany had been achieved.

4. The Campaigns of the First World War

(i) *The Failure of the Schlieffen Plan, 1914*

The Schlieffen Plan, held to by the German General Staff in 1914, was based on attacking and overwhelming France before its Russian ally, hampered by long distances and poor communications, could make an effective entry into the war. Leaving, therefore, only a comparatively small force to hold the Russian frontier, the Germans brought against France one and a half million men, divided into seven armies. It was not expected that the 'contemptible little army' – as the Kaiser was said to have called Sir John French's British Expeditionary (BEF) force of five divisions (90,000 men) – would make any serious difference. Nor was it anticipated that the Belgians would do anything beyond making a formal protest against the violation of their neutrality.

British Expeditionary Force

Ignorant of German intentions, the French planned to attack Germany across the common frontier in Lorraine, despite the immense strength of the German fortifications. French success in Lorraine would, paradoxically have ensured the success of the Schlieffen Plan. Fortunately for the French, their attack failed rapidly and completely. Meanwhile, the German armies invaded Belgium. Their heavy guns destroyed the Belgian fortifications in their way and then the advancing German troops under Kluck and Bülow (1st and 2nd Armies) came up

Germany invades Belgium

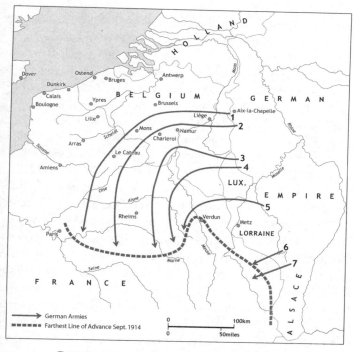

GERMAN ATTACK IN FRANCE AND BELGIUM: 1914

against the French, with the BEF to their left. At Mons and Le Cateau the BEF fought delaying actions (23-25 August). The British Expeditionary Force was a force composed entirely of regular soldiers. Their skills in using to advantage every feature in the semi-urban landscape, their awareness of the utility of deep trenches and their marksmanship had been honed in the war in South Africa. But despite the heavy punishment meted out to the Germans, the Allies could not stem the overwhelming force of the invasion. The German 1st, 2nd and 3rd Armies reached the Marne; the 1st Army was within twenty miles of Paris. About half a million people fled the capital, and the French government moved to Bordeaux. At the front, the French left swung

German army overwhelms British and French forces

back, and the British with it. The British suffered 15,000 casualties, but, at the end of the retreat, they were still a force to be reckoned with.

The Schlieffen Plan was already unravelling. Sclieffen, who originally drew it up, had envisaged the armies of the German right marching to the west of Paris, so surrounding and cutting off the capital. It would then have to surrender and France would be knocked out of the war. Yet the generals on the German right faced far too much opposition from the retreating BEF and French, not to mention the garrison of Paris, to risk splitting from the German armies to their left, which marching west of Paris would have entailed. Instead, they clung to the more easterly armies, effectively forfeiting the chance of dealing France a knockout blow. Worse still for them, the French commander-in-chief Joffre, undismayed by the disasters which had taken place, saw an opportunity to send the Germans reeling back. He used the railways to bring back his armies from the Lorraine border and rallied his men behind the line of the River Marne, protecting Paris. The battle of the Marne (6-13 September), in which the British took part, forced the Germans into retreat. By 13 September the Germans had been thrust back to the line of the Aisne; from there, however, they could be pushed no further back and all efforts to dislodge them failed.

The Battle of the Marne

During the next two months, the two opposing forces attempted to outflank each other in the area between Paris and the Channel coast. The Germans hoped to cut the British off from the Channel ports and the French hoped to force the Germans out of their country. Each side was always able to bring up troops in time to prevent a decisive advance by its opponent. Finally, the two sides were forced to a defensive line, running due north and south from the sea to the Somme, and covering Ypres, Armentières and Arras. The British Army, moved from the Aisne, defended the two former places. The first battle of Ypres, which lasted three weeks (21 Oct.-11 Nov.), saw some of the fiercest fighting of the war. The old British Army practically ceased to exist after Ypres; its casualties were 50,000. But

The first Battle of Ypres

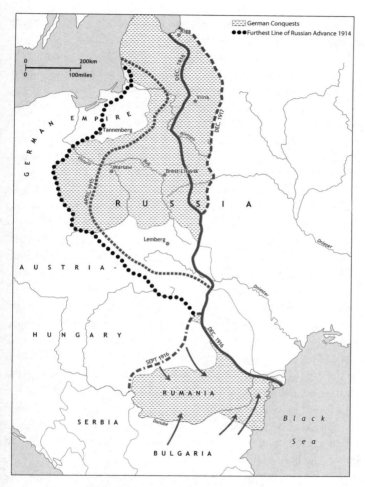

THE DEFEAT OF RUSSIA AND RUMANIA

the Germans, in spite of tremendous attacks made with the utmost commitment, could not break through. The trenches of the Ypres Salient, the grave of tens of thousands of British soldiers, guarded the wrecked city, the sole fragment of Belgium that was still unoccupied. Sentiment made it impossible to give the city up, though doing so might have made good military sense. As winter set in, that first November of the war, the battle came to a standstill in the north as it had already done on the Aisne. The result was that the trenches into which the troops dug themselves that winter became a permanent line, stretching from Switzerland to the sea.

Aisne trench line established

On the Eastern Front too, Schlieffen's expectations had not been borne out. The Russians had mobilized far more rapidly than he had expected and had penetrated far into East Prussia. To stop their advance, a retired German general, and a native of East Prussia, Hindenburg, was put in charge, with Ludendorff as his Chief of Staff. The partnership of Hindenburg and Ludendorff, which lasted till the end of the war, was among the most famous in military annals, and nearly won the war for Germany. It was Ludendorff who brought about on 30 August the encirclement of the second of the two Russian armies at Tannenberg in East Prussia, where 120,000 prisoners were taken. This was by far the greatest victory of 1914, and it was followed by the driving of the other Russian army from East Prussia. Having cleared his native soil of the enemy, Hindenburg then began the invasion of Russian Poland. The Russian casualties in this campaign amounted to 300,000 men. Yet despite these German successes, there remained the chief problem, against which Schlieffen had tried to guard: the need to fight on two fronts.

Russian army driven out of Germany

It was soon clear that in the east the Germans' ally, Austria, would require help rather than give it. Twice it invaded Serbia, and both times it was driven back with losses. Only the intervention of the Germans saved Austria from further defeats. The Germans did, however, acquire a new ally. At the end of October, Turkey declared war on Britain and her allies. Russia was now effectively cut off from

Turkey allies with Germany

132

the Mediterranean and from Western help. Further, Turkish enmity involved a threat to Egypt - which country was forthwith annexed to the British Empire for the duration of the war - and possibly to India, through the Persian Gulf. To counter these threats, the British campaigns in Mesopotamia and Palestine were shortly afterwards begun. Turkey might usefully distract British attention, but it was not otherwise helpful to Germany. Its efforts would be entirely devoted to defending its homeland and its empire.

Mesopotamia and Palestine campaigns launched

At sea, the superiority of the British fleet in the North Sea compelled the Germans to shut themselves up behind their defences at Heligoland, the Kiel Canal and the Baltic. But several German cruisers were on the high seas at the outbreak of the war. The *Emden* steamed about the Pacific and did much damage to British shipping; she was eventually sunk by the *Sydney*, a cruiser of the Australian Navy. Admiral von Spee, with a small squadron, sank two British ships at Coronel, off the coast of Chile, only to meet his fate when he attempted to enter the harbour of Port Stanley in the Falkland Islands, where Admiral Sturdee, with a greatly superior force, was waiting for him. One result of the British command of the sea was that the Germans were unable to send aid to their colonies, all of which, except German East Africa, were captured during the first few months of the war. French and British forces took Togoland and the Cameroons in West Africa; a South African army, led by Generals Botha and Smuts, overran German South-West Africa. Only in East Africa did the Germans put up a stout resistance, which lasted till 1917. A more significant result of British naval dominance was the blockade imposed by Britain on Germany. Only in the Baltic was Germany still able to trade freely. Naval enthusiasts in Britain fondly hoped that the blockade might be decisive in the long run in forcing the Germans to their knees.

German colonies captured

BULGARIA AND TURKEY
(inset: Gallipoli)

(ii) *The Gallipoli Campaign, 1915*

There were many in Britain who argued that fighting a land war on the continent was against British traditions and in any case was bound to be long and costly in lives. Instead, they urged, Britain must seek to make use of its navy to attack Germany and its allies where they were more vulnerable. The British generals were mostly adamant that there was no alternative to slogging it out on the Western Front, but politicians such as Lloyd George and Churchill were on the lookout for a way of minimizing the 'butcher's bill'. The entry of Turkey into the war on the German side gave rise to the notion of seizing

134

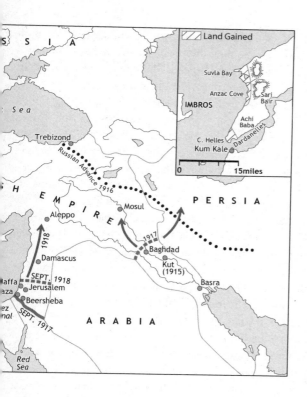

Constantinople. Munitions could then be sent to assist Russia, further allies such as Rumania would join in on the Allies' side and Austria-Hungary could be attacked from the east. Hence in 1915 Britain attempted to open up a route to Russia by way of the Dardanelles. The first attempt to force the entrance to the Straits was made in March from the sea, but the fleet was vulnerable to Turkish mines and shore batteries and was withdrawn after taking severe casualties.

It was decided that the Dardanelles would have to be taken by troops landed on Turkish soil. In April landings were made at the extreme tip of the Gallipoli peninsula by troops under cover of naval artillery fire. Twenty-nine thousand men, under Sir Ian Hamilton's command, were landed on six beaches. The troops were almost all

ANZACs inexperienced ANZACs of the Australia and New Zealand Army Corps or English territorials and the job they had to do, which involved forcing the Turks from their trenches on the ridges overlooking the landing beaches, was a very difficult one. The Turks had ample warning of their enemy's intentions after the naval fiasco in March. The terrain greatly favoured the Turks, who were also close to their capital, from where it was easy to get reinforcements. If

Assault on galvanized by inspiring leadership, the Turks could hardly lose. They
Gallipoli found the right leader in Mustapha Kemal, a divisional commander
1915 who happened to be in the right place at the right time. Despite the heroism of the Allied troops, no decisive advance proved possible.

Suvla Bay Therefore in August a second landing was made at Suvla Bay. The
assault men encountered very similar problems to the earlier wave of troops. They had to advance through difficult country and climb up precipitous cliffs in the face of enemy fire, and they too failed to take the heights above the bay, in spite of great feats of endurance and heroism. The summer heat brought terrible problems, since it was so hard to supply the troops with enough water and the many corpses in no man's land created a plague of flies. Disease, particularly dysentery, spread through the army. By the end of the year, it was clear that

Withdrawal nothing was being achieved and the evacuation of the Allied forces
of Allied was ordered. It was efficiently carried out at the end of December
forces from 1915 and in the first days of the new year.
Gallipoli

The Gallipoli campaign had certainly been a failure which had cost many lives for no gain. Churchill, a major supporter of the venture, got the blame and was driven from office. The military leadership had been ineffectual: Hamilton had cruised up and down the coast, largely out of touch with his subordinates. Yet even if, against the odds, the campaign had been a success, it would have brought little profit to Britain's war effort. There was no quick route from Constantinople to

Vienna, never mind Berlin. A route for Allied supplies to Russia would only have been useful if Britain had possessed surplus supplies to send.

In the First World War opening up new fronts invariably proved disappointing. In May Italy, greedy for Austrian territory, was induced to declare war against the Habsburg Empire. A series of battles on the Isonzo front achieved nothing, failing even to prevent the Austrians and Germans from completely overrunning Serbia later in the year.

On the Western Front the year 1915 saw a continuation of the deadlock. The German effort was concentrated against Russia for the most part, but the German commander-in-chief, Falkenhayn, first experimented with poison gas in a new attempt to break through the Ypres Salient in February. The city was held, though the Salient was narrowed to a radius of less than two miles from the city. The British too were anxious to avoid fighting as far as possible, while they trained the newly recruited 'Kitchener armies'. Occasionally, however, they had to prove their commitment to the French, who had so far taken most of the casualties on the Allied side. In the course of the year, the British launched two unsuccessful attacks on the German line. The first was at Neuve-Chapelle in February; the second at Loos in September. The British losses at Loos were 60,000 men killed and wounded; the gain was a small piece of ground of no value. Shortly afterwards Sir John French was relieved of his command, and his place taken by Sir Douglas Haig.

Sir Douglas Haig assumes command of British Army

Aware that they were no match for the British surface fleet, the Germans largely confined themselves in 1915 to the development of their submarine campaign. British losses of merchant ships varied between fifty and a hundred per month, but the Germans were made aware of the dangers of their policy when in February they sank without warning the large British liner, the *Lusitania*; 1,201 persons, including 128 Americans, were drowned. For a moment it seemed that the USA might enter the war against Germany, but the diplomats managed to prevent that outcome. President Wilson was determined not to abandon his country's traditional neutrality, which had been

The sinking of the Lusitania

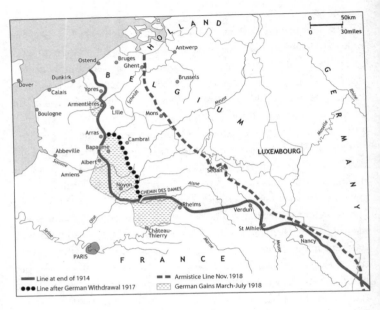

THE WESTERN FRONT (1914-18)

maintained in European wars for a hundred years. Nonetheless, the Germans had to refrain from an all-out campaign against British commerce, which meant that they could not cripple their enemy.

(iii) 1916: The Year of the Great Battles

German
assault on
Verdun

Falkenhayn decided to make a strong German attack on the Western Front early in 1916. He believed that France was nearing the end of its military effort and that a protracted battle on a large scale would finish it off. He selected the fortress at Verdun for this attack, not so much because its capture would assist the German war effort as because it was of great symbolic importance to the French. They would therefore be prepared to be bled white rather than lose it. The attack was launched in February with a bombardment of unprecedented strength. The French commanders were quite

138

prepared to sacrifice the fortress, which was of little military value, but the politicians insisted on resistance. The dogged Pétain was placed in command, resolved to contest every square foot of territory. Though their trenches had been pulverized, French resistance continued from a series of isolated pockets linked by runners. There remained only one road to the resisting troops, now named the *voie sacrée*, along which 3,000 lorries passed every day to maintain supplies. The French repeatedly changed the units engaged, so that most of their soldiers experienced the horrors of a battle in which around a quarter of a million Frenchmen were killed. The Germans did not remain dispassionate about Verdun: it became a place that had to be captured, whatever the losses incurred. As the months went by, the Germans began to lose more men than the French and all for minimal gains. The intensity of the fighting declined after July, when the Germans had another battle to worry about. By the end of the year the Germans were almost back to where they had started. They had achieved something: the French army had been gravely weakened, though it fought on. On the other hand, the Germans had been severely battered too. Falkenhayn had to pay for failure: in August he was replaced as commander-in-chief by Hindenburg.

France's allies did what they could to relieve the pressure. The Russians, who in 1915 had been driven out of most of Poland, managed to organize their production of munitions and by 1916 their armies were adequately supplied with shells. In June General Brusilov renewed the offensive against Austria and, taking the enemy by surprise, made a considerable advance in Galicia, capturing 300,000 prisoners. The Germans had to hurry troops across to the East to the relief of their ally. The Italians, too, made an attack on Austria on the Isonzo Front; they failed to reach Trieste, but took Gorizia.

France looked chiefly, however, to Britain to distract the Germans from their attacks at Verdun. For the first time in the war, Britain took the principal part in the campaign in France. The supply of shells, thanks to Lloyd George's efforts, was now adequate; the New Armies, raised since 1914, had been at least half-trained, though the British commander Haig would have liked more time in which to prepare them. It was decided that the British offensive should be at the River Somme, for no better reason than that the British and French sectors of the Western Front joined there, so that both armies could take part in the offensive. The German positions were strong: they occupied the crests of the hills and had created dugouts as much as forty feet below the surface. The commanders relied above all on a preliminary bombardment, which lasted a week and was supposed to destroy every living thing in the German trenches. In fact, the bombardment failed in many places to achieve its objectives. Up to a third of the shells fired failed to go off. Many of the German dugouts were too deep to be destroyed. Very often the German barbed wire was simply tossed about by the shells and not cut to allow a passage for the attacking British troops. In some ways, the bombardment actually helped the enemy. They were given ample notice of the British intention to attack. No man's land was pitted with craters which were to make the going hard when the British troops went over the top and also provided ideal sites for nests of German machine guns when the bombardment finally stopped.

The offensive began with a daylight attack on 1 July 1916. Heavily laden and advancing upright and in straight lines, the British troops made easy targets for the Germans, who were not supposed to be there. The British artillery was of little help. It was supposed to force the Germans to take cover as the British troops advanced, by shelling the German forward trenches, but for fear of hitting the British, it ceased shelling the enemy trenches long before the troops reached the enemy lines. There are reckoned to have been 20,000 casualties in the first hour and a total of 60,000 on the first day, including 20,000 deaths, making 1 July the most disastrous day which the British Army has ever experienced. Haig was soon compelled to abandon all hopes of achieving a breakthrough, but instead justified the fighting, which continued into November, as subjecting the Germans to a slow

Unparalleled casualties sustained by the British

wearing down, or attrition, as he called it. The problem was that this kind of warfare wore down the Allies just as surely as it wore down the Germans. By November the Germans may have suffered 600,000 casualties; the British Empire and the French had together suffered even more. The ground gained did not weaken the Germans. In the next winter they voluntarily gave up more ground in a retreat to a superior position which became known as the Hindenburg Line.

At sea, the only significant surface battle of the war was fought in 1916. On 31 May Admiral Beatty, with an advance squadron of battle cruisers, sighted the enemy under Admiral Hipper, and engaged him. Beatty suffered heavily, and lost three ships. But behind Beatty was the main British fleet under Admiral Sir John Jellicoe, and behind Hipper the German fleet under Admiral Scheer. Both fleets were drawn into the action off the coast of the Danish peninsula of Jutland; but dusk was falling as the two fleets came into contact, and the Germans made good their escape, aided by a torpedo attack. They had destroyed more ships than they had lost, but many of their surviving ships had sustained heavy damage, with the result that the British were more dominant in the North Sea than ever. The British were disappointed because they had not achieved a new Trafalgar by destroying the enemy fleet. On the other hand, they had done what they needed to do by persuading the Germans finally to give up all hope of challenging the British in an encounter of surface navies. A German journalist summed up the Battle of Jutland well: the Germans had made an assault on their gaoler, but had been forced to return to gaol.

Battle of Jutland 31 May 1916

British fleet reinforces naval supremacy

(iv) *Rival Bids for Victory in 1917*

After the German failure to break the French armies at Verdun, the new commander-in-chief Hindenburg, in partnership with Ludendorff, decided that Germany must seek to gain a decisive advantage elsewhere than on the Western Front. They determined to step up the submarine or U-boat campaign against the British. Attacks on British shipping had been continuous throughout the

Germany launches naval blockade of Britain

war, but on 1 February 1917 it was announced that 'unrestricted' submarine warfare would begin. This meant that the British Isles would be put in a state of blockade, and that any ship, merchant, neutral, or even hospital, would be sunk at sight. It was obvious that this high-handed programme might cause America to declare war, but it was hoped that American intervention would come too late to save Britain from being crippled through loss of crucial imports of food and raw materials. This strategy very nearly succeeded; how nearly, the British public was not, at the time, allowed to know. The first four months of 1917 showed an alarming increase in shipping losses. April was the worst of all; in that month 875,000 tons of shipping were sunk. Only six weeks' corn supply remained in the country, and, though the public did not know it, official circles believed that November would see the absolute limit of British endurance.

Success of the British Naval convoy system

The defeat of the U-boats at this critical point was due above all to the decision that merchant ships should sail in convoy escorted by ships of the Royal Navy. Starting at the end of April, the convoy system was gradually extended to all oceanic sailings and losses began to decline. The merchant ships were found, contrary to expectation, to be quite capable of keeping in touch with their armed escort, without collision; and the escort proved capable of warding off the submarines. The Navy, put to this test, worked wonders; by the end of the war, it had convoyed 88,000 vessels with a loss of only 436. By Christmas 1917, the danger had passed; the figure of sunken ships for the last quarter of the year was little more than half that for April to June. This result was due also in part to other measures. The approaches to the German coast, the Straits of Dover and the North Sea from the Orkneys to Norway were sown with mines, making the activities of the submarines a dangerous and terrible task. 'Q' boats - armed vessels disguised to look like innocent merchant ships - were used to decoy

Rationing

and sink the enemy. Aircraft and airships were used to hunt down U-boats operating near the coast. Finally, the whole population of Britain was put on a strict food ration.

The intensified submarine campaign brought America into the war. In March five American ships were sunk with loss of life. Next month America declared war on Germany. American men-of-war arrived at once, and helped in the mine-sowing, and in the convoy system. They also helped to turn the tables on Germany by tightening the blockade on the German coast. What the USA could not immediately do was to help the allies on the Western Front. The regular army was tiny and it would be well over a year before new recruits could be adequately trained.

America enters the War

America's entry into the war could easily have proved less decisive than Russia's exit from it. In March 1917 a revolution broke out in Petrograd (St Petersburg) and the Tsar was forced to abdicate. The provisional government which was set up tried to continue the war, but the war-weary peasant conscripts wanted to go home and join in the share-out of the landowners' land. The Germans had allowed revolutionaries in exile in Switzerland to go home to Russia in a train that crossed Germany, in the hope that they might persuade the revolutionaries in Petrograd to end Russia's participation in the war. In November Lenin's Communist Party seized power and early in 1918 they withdrew Russia from the war, though they had to hand over vast swathes of the Tsarist Empire to the Germans. Potentially, Russia's withdrawal was a lethal blow to the Allied cause. Germany might be able to utilize the resources of the Russian borderlands and it would certainly be able to transfer troops from the Eastern to the Western Front.

Revolution ends Russian participation in the war 1917

Nor was this the only good news for the Germans. In the autumn of 1917 German troops reinforced the Austrians against Italy. In October the Italian front dissolved in the Battle of Caporetto and the Italians were forced to retreat to the River Piave. Yet they were not forced out of the war. The new frontier was much shorter and, assisted by help from the British and the French, the Italians were able to hold the new line.

Battle of Caporetto 1917

On the Western Front the British and French attempted to use their superiority in numbers to inflict defeat on the Germans, but their efforts proved to be failures. Very nearly ruinous was the offensive near Rheims of a fresh French commander, Robert Nivelle. His offensive caused huge numbers of French casualties and produced a sort of military strike, usually referred to as 'mutinies'. Nivelle had to be relieved of his command and replaced by Pétain, who improved conditions for the men and called off the offensive. These events, fortunately not detected or exploited by the Germans, made it plain that the French had shot their bolt. Henceforth, in this war the initiative on the Allied side was with the British.

'Passchendaele' 1917

The main British effort of 1917 is known as the Third Battle of Ypres, or Passchendaele, which lasted from July to November. The advance began with a very successful opening attack, but as usual the Germans were able to stabilize their position before the British could exploit their success. In Flanders conditions for the troops were even worse than usual. The ground was low-lying; the drainage works had been shelled to pieces; and it happened to be a very wet year. No man's land was a quagmire where men could drown in the mud and rapid progress was impossible. Haig has often been criticized for continuing the offensive long after it had become obvious that the gains were likely to be small and the losses great. As usual, he justified his strategy on the grounds that it was wearing down the Germans. Their losses were indeed heavy, but those of the British, who suffered another 300,000 casualties, were almost certainly considerably greater.

The one striking success on the Western Front was won at the battle of Cambrai in November. There tanks were first used on a large scale. The Germans were taken completely by surprise when 340 tanks suddenly crossed no man's land, and an advance of three miles was made. For the first time in the war church bells in England were rung in celebration. The euphoria was short-lived. There was no way of following up the initial success: the infantry were too slow, the cavalry were too vulnerable to machine guns. The ground gained was soon lost again.

'LAWRENCE OF ARABIA' (1888-1935; second from the left),
Herbert Samuel (1870-1963; centre)
and Abdullah I of Jordan (1882-1951; second from the right)

There was at least good news from the east. General Maude had
been put in command in Mesopotamia, and at the beginning of 1917
he retook Kut, where a British army had been captured by the Turks
in 1916. In March his troops entered Baghdad, and then pursued the
retreating enemy northwards. In Palestine General Allenby assumed
command, with TE Lawrence (Lawrence of Arabia) and his Arabs in
the desert harassing the Turkish communications. Allenby began by
capturing Beersheba in October; then he drove the Turks from Gaza,
and made a general advance. Just before Christmas he entered
Jerusalem, a city which had not been occupied by a Christian army
since the 12th century. Such gains might prove valuable when the war
was over. They helped not at all towards the defeat of Germany.

THE GERMAN
POWER AT ITS
GREATEST EXTENT:
MARCH 1918

(v) *The Ludendorff Offensive and the Allied Counter-Attack, 1918*
In 1918 the Germans were racing against time. They had to take
advantage of the withdrawal of Russia from the war by switching
troops to the west and win the war there quickly before the
Americans could make a decisive difference. By March 1918
General Ludendorff, the planner of the German offensive, had
superiority of numbers on the Western Front and decided to attack
towards the old Somme battlefield, where a great hole was to be
punched in the British front, followed by a drive along the River
Somme and towards the sea. The attack was to begin with a brief
but intense artillery bombardment. Then specially trained forces

were to infiltrate the British position, ignoring pockets of resistance and pushing on at speed. Initial success attended the German push. German success threatened to drive the British and French armies apart and co-ordination had to be achieved by elevation of Marshal Foch to the new position of overall commander. Finally, British morale held up and Ludendorff failed to achieve a decisive victory. In April he tried again to win decisive success, this time in Flanders. Despite the success of the preliminary bombardment, the Germans were unable to compel the evacuation of the Ypres Salient or seriously to threaten the Channel ports. A third attack in May fell on the French, threatening the important railway junction of

Rheims and, more distantly, Paris itself, but once again no breakthrough was achieved.

The effects on the Germans of Ludendorff's failed offensives were highly damaging. The Germans sustained about 800,000 casualties, but they had no manpower reserves apart from the next batch of 18-year-olds. They were running out of men and the men they had lost included many of their most experienced troops. The effects of repeated failure on German morale were perhaps even more serious. When overrunning British positions, they had been amazed to discover how well provisioned their enemies were. This discovery contributed to the growing feeling that victory was not achievable. The German advances also weakened the Germans themselves. They were left in much less good positions holding a longer line.

Second Battle of the Marne 1918

The turning point came in July 1918. Ludendorff's final attack in Champagne failed and at the Second Battle of the Marne the French and Americans were able to launch a successful counter-attack. Haig's attack near Amiens on 8 August showed that the Allied armies had learnt valuable lessons from earlier failures. Surprise was achieved by omitting the preliminary bombardment. Instead, artillery improvements had made it possible to fire over the heads of advancing troops and silence the opposing guns until the infantry got near the enemy line, when the barrage would 'lift' and silence enemy guns behind the front line. The combination of this 'creeping barrage' and surprise gave the infantry a far greater chance of success. So did the use alongside them of masses of tanks, though these continued to be dogged by mechanical failures which meant that they were chiefly of use when offensives started. The Allies also made use of their superiority in the air to strafe and bomb their opponents. German morale began to sag: for the first time in the war, large numbers of surrendering Germans were taken prisoner, 400,000 in the course of 1918. More significantly, Ludendorff's nerve began to crack. He referred to 8 August as the 'black day' of the German army.

Yet though the omens were bad, the German army did not collapse. It fell back slowly in good order and inflicted huge casualties on the advancing Allies. The Hindenburg Line was pierced in the autumn, but the pre-war German frontier had not been reached and Haig had no hope of defeating the Germans in 1918. Yet as they contemplated the future, the German leaders saw no hope of victory. Their allies, Austria-Hungary, Bulgaria and Turkey, were all at their last gasp. The Allied blockade was inflicting great hardships on the home front, especially through the food shortages which it created. The Americans were still at the stage of learning how to fight effectively, but they brought to the Allied cause inexhaustible manpower and material abundance at a time when Germany was running short of everything. On 29 September Ludendorff told the Kaiser that an armistice was essential. Once the news became public, with all hope of victory gone, German morale at home and at the front was shattered. In November, just after the armistice had been agreed, a German revolution began, sweeping away a leadership now blamed for a disastrous defeat. The armistice was signed in a railway carriage in the Forest of Compiègne on the night of 10th-11 November. It came into effect at 11.00 am on the 11 November.

Armistice signed at Compiègne

5. The Legacy of the War

About three quarters of a million men from the British Isles were killed in the First World War. They constituted one in eight of the six million men who had served in the War. The effects of this holocaust on Britain's population figures were not perhaps so very great. Before the War, 300,000 people had been emigrating each year. In largely halting emigration, the War may on balance have raised rather than reduced the total population. But the impact of the War is not to be measured in these crude statistics.

The war claims three quarters of a million British lives

Between the two world wars, men spoke of a 'lost generation'. The losses among the younger men of military age were especially great. Not far short of a third of those who were in their early twenties in 1914 were killed. And those lost included very many who were regarded as the flower of their generation. Almost 20 per cent of Oxbridge graduates who served perished, as did a similar proportion of alumni of the major public schools. Survivors had the impression that Britain had lost much of its next generation of leaders. Those who did survive, men like Clement Attlee, Anthony Eden and Harold Macmillan, were forever haunted by the memory of admired contemporaries prematurely removed by death.

In almost every town and village in England, the war dead were commemorated by memorials erected at enormous expenditure of effort and money. The soldiers were men who had been honoured with no local grave or funeral service attended by relatives or local friends, as Wilfred Owen had pointed out in his 'Anthem for Doomed Youth'.

> What passing-bells for these who die as cattle?
> Only the monstrous anger of the guns.
> Only the stuttering rifles' rapid rattle
> Can patter out their hasty orisons.
> No mockeries now for them; no prayers nor bells,
> Nor any voice of mourning save the choirs,
> The shrill, demented choirs of wailing shells;
> And bugles calling for them from sad shires.

As far as they could, the people of Britain made good whatever had been lacking in the final rite of passage of their young men. Meanwhile, the Imperial War Graves Commission was creating its more than six hundred garden cemeteries in France. Though statues of Haig and Foch were erected in London, the emphasis everywhere was on the sacrifice of ordinary, individual soldiers. This is perhaps best seen in Westminster Abbey. Joining the kings and queens, the great statesmen and literary figures, the Unknown Soldier was laid

Imperial War Graves Commission

finally to rest in the national pantheon. Not far off, in Whitehall, is the simple Cenotaph, where in 1921 King George V inaugurated the tradition of laying a wreath of poppies annually on 11 November, the anniversary of the Armistice.

War memorials, war cemeteries and the Cenotaph testify to the almost unbearable sense of loss which was felt in post-war Britain. Yet the number of the dead was far exceeded by the million and a half serious casualties. Blind and limbless ex-soldiers were living reminders of the cost of war throughout the inter-war years. Less obvious, except to their families, were the thousands who were psychologically crippled by their experiences in the trenches.

The War's artistic legacy

The soldiers of the First World War left to posterity a large body of poetry inspired by their experiences in the war. Less well known is the work of the war artists. Paul Nash was in Flanders in 1917. His most impressive work is empty of people and weaponry. It shows the sun coming up to illuminate a landscape of splintered trees and churned-up earth. The image of murdered nature has become a metaphor for the destructiveness of modern war. One version of this image bears the ironic caption 'We are making a New World.' The artist Stanley Spencer served in Macedonia. He was later commissioned to paint murals for a chapel at Burghclere, Hampshire, in memory of Lieutenant Sandham, who had died of a disease contracted during the Macedonian campaign. The murals are a celebration of the ordinary soldier and the banal routines of military life: kit inspection, ablutions and filling water bottles are depicted rather than scenes of battle. His 'new world' or heaven, shown behind the altar, is not a Valhalla for heroes, but a place where suffering, symbolized by the white crosses, is laid aside and the camaraderie of the soldiers' military service together is renewed.

In some of the later war poetry, the poets sound a note of cynicism about patriotic sentiments. Owen, for example, refers to the motto *dulce et decorum est pro patria mori* (it is sweet and right to die for your

'Dulce et decorum est'

151

'We are making a New World' by Paul Nash (1889-1946)
Courtesy of the Imperial War Museum

country) as 'the old lie'. Siegfried Sassoon seemed critical of the military leaders in his poem 'The General'.

'Good morning! Good morning!' the General said,
When we met him last week on our way to the line.
Now the soldiers he smiled at are most of 'em dead
And we're cursing his staff for incompetent swine.
'He's a cheery old card,' grunted Harry to Jack,
As they slogged up to Arras with rifle and pack.
But he did for them both by his plan of attack.

On the basis of such poems, it is sometimes suggested that by 1917-18 disillusionment had set in and belief in the cause had withered, at least among the troops. Yet Sassoon and Owen were not necessarily

typical. It may be that a more typical voice from the trenches is that John
of John McCrae, whose poem 'In Flanders Fields' became very McCrae
popular.

> In Flanders fields the poppies blow
> Between the crosses, row on row,
>> That mark our place; and in the sky
>> The larks, still bravely singing, fly
> Scarce heard amid the guns below
>> (…)
>> Take up our quarrel with the foe:
>> To you from failing hands we throw
>> The torch; be yours to hold it high.
>> If ye break faith with us who die
> We shall not sleep, though poppies grow
>> In Flanders fields.

McCrae knew the cost of war, but his only concern was that his
countrymen should finish the job which he and his comrades-in-
arms had begun. That the fight was worth fighting he did not doubt.
It seems probable that most soldiers, and civilians for that matter,
were also grimly determined to see it through and that when it was
over, they congratulated themselves on a good job done.

VII

BRITISH SOCIETY BETWEEN THE WARS

1. The British Economy and the Standard of Living

IN the period before the First World War, the British economy was unhealthily dependent on staple industries such as cotton, coal, shipbuilding and iron and steel, all of them exporting much of their production. While stimulating newer industries such as chemicals, motor vehicles and aircraft, the war also encouraged yet more investment in some of the old staple industries, such as shipbuilding and iron and steel. It also caused severe disruption of Britain's export trades, because of a shortage of shipping and the diversion of industrial capacity to the war effort. As a result, much of the Asian market was permanently lost to Japan and much of the Latin American one to the USA.

When the war ended, it was expected that the pre-war demand for British goods would return and there was a rush to invest in shipbuilding and the cotton industry. The boom proved short-lived. By 1922 cotton exports were less than half of the 1913 total and coal exports were down by two thirds: the contraction of the old staple industries had begun. Foreign competition was one factor in this process: even the home market was not safe from the inroads of foreign rivals, as Indian cotton goods were sold in Britain and British shipowners in 1936 bought 15 per cent of their new tonnage abroad. Another factor was the sluggish growth of world trade in the 1920s, followed by actual contraction in the years of the Great Depression, when world trade shrank by a third between 1929 and 1933. There was some recovery in the later 1930s, but only to the level of 1929. Since British staples depended so heavily upon exports, the state of world trade mattered enormously to them. Most seriously hit of all was shipbuilding: by 1932 the order books were almost empty. Great

Contraction of traditional British industries

efforts were made to increase efficiency in the staple industries. Mechanization of the coal industry produced large gains in output per worker and the improvements in iron and steel were greater still, as production was concentrated in new and efficient plants opened in places like Corby. Yet British goods tended to remain internationally uncompetitive. In terms of efficiency, British industry had a lot of ground to make up. In addition, the labour costs of competitors were often very low undercutting British wages, and sometimes they were aided by government subsidies.

British industry overtaken by Continental Europe

The economic history of the inter-war years is, however, not only about the decline of the old mainstays of the British economy. By 1924 Britain had regained the level of production of 1913, despite substantial reductions in working hours. By the later 1930s the index of industrial production was 75 per cent higher than before the war. The average growth rate of the economy between 1924 and 1937 was 1.8 per cent, much better than that achieved in the fifty years before the First World War and comparable to that of the USA. One of the most important areas of growth was the electricity supply industry. In 1926 a Central Electricity Board was set up. It built a new generation of power stations connected through a national grid of high-voltage transmission lines, necessitating the rows of pylons which appeared in the countryside. The significance of this development can hardly be overstated. Industry was no longer dependent on the coalfields and could relocate to areas of the country without them. Homes were transformed. By 1939 two homes in three were connected to mains electricity and a range of electrical equipment became usable: vacuum cleaners, refrigerators, cookers and radios. Life outside the home was changed too. The cinema and many suburban railways depended upon electric power.

Central Electricity Board created

The motor vehicle industry also contributed largely to industrial growth. In 1913, 34,000 vehicles were produced; by 1937 production exceeded half a million. The industry employed nearly 400,000 people. Assembly-line methods were adopted and giant factories at

Growth of the motor vehicle industry

places such as Birmingham, Coventry, Oxford and Luton turned out cheap cars for a mass-market. The Austin Seven of 1921 blazed a trail which was soon followed by the Morris Minor and cheap Ford family cars. Competition helped to drive prices down: they fell by 50 per cent between the mid-1920s and mid-'30s. The engineering industry in general experienced rapid growth: demand for aircraft, motor bikes and consumer durables expanded and after the mid-1930s government orders, especially for aircraft, began to flow in, as the rearmament programme got under way.

There were major developments too in the chemical industry. 'Bakelite', a form of plastic, became a standard material for consumer goods such as radio sets, while 'rayon' and other artificial fibres were increasingly used in the clothing industry. The giant combine Imperial Chemical Industries (ICI) was formed in 1926 and produced a range of products including fertilizers and pharmaceuticals. The chemical industry employed 100,000 people by 1939. More traditional industries also grew, perhaps most notably construction. Huge numbers of houses and public buildings such as schools were constructed by an industry which gave employment to nearly a million workers by 1939.

Imperial Chemical Industries (ICI) formed

People were not employed only in making things. The inter-war period saw a retailing revolution as more and more chain stores appeared on the high streets of Britain. Marks and Spencer was one of the most successful of the new retailers: it opened dozens of stores between the wars. As late as 1929 its turnover was less than two and a half million pounds, but by 1939 it had multiplied tenfold. M&S specialized in clothing, delivering the goods for sale from central warehouses to branches by motor transport. Lipton's and Sainsbury's operated in the same way, but dealt in groceries, while Woolworth's sold a wide range of household goods. Such stores could offer a greater choice of goods than traditional small shops had done. With greater choice came advertising designed to direct people's choices. By 1938, £100 million a year was being spent on advertising through

Domestic appliances and household goods

newspapers and cinemas. Promotional gimmicks made their appearance, with free gifts and special offers at 'sales'. People were encouraged to buy larger items, such as furniture and household durables, through hire-purchase agreements, allowing them to pay much of the cost in small instalments while enjoying use of the item at once. These developments changed the structure of the labour force. The proportion of workers involved in the service industries - shop-workers, clerical staff, managers, transport workers - increased and many of the extra jobs in this sector were taken by women.

Despite setbacks such as the Depression, national income rose in the inter-war period. The evidence shows that wage-earners reaped much of the benefit. After 1922 wages held steady, with a slight fall in the early 1930s and a rise in 1937-8. The trend that most benefited wage-earners was a fall in the cost of living of over a third between 1920 and 1938. At the same time, average family size declined, especially among the working class, so that more money could be spent on each member of the family. The poorer social classes were assisted too by a huge increase in government spending on social services, which redistributed wealth taken in taxes from the more affluent to the beneficiaries of its spending, who were mostly the poorer sections of the community.

In the inter-war years, the living standards of the working class were undoubtedly rising. Per capita food consumption rose by about a third and the food bought was more varied. Fresh fruit and vegetables were sold in hugely increased quantity, which must have brought health benefits. An enormous range of tinned meats, fruits and other foods became available and brand names such as Heinz became universally known. The modern breakfast made its appearance, as American-style cereals, such as Kellogg's cornflakes and Quaker oats, eaten with milk and sugar, became ubiquitous. Sales of potato crisps reached a million for the first time in 1929; the first jar of instant coffee was put on sale by Nestlé in 1932.

Rise in working-class living standards

For all the increased consumption of food, the proportion of their income spent on it by the average family was declining, from around 60 per cent in 1914 to 35 per cent by 1938. Standards of clothing rose too. Barefoot and ragged children ceased in almost all districts to be a common sight. The advent of retailers of cheap clothes enabled even the poor to transform their appearance. In the mid-1930s the writer George Orwell visited Wigan and other northern districts. According to him, a youth in a blind-alley job could 'for two pounds ten [shillings] on the hire-purchase... buy himself a suit which, for a little while and at a little distance, looks as though it had been tailored in Savile Row'. He continued: 'The girl can look like a fashion plate at an even lower price.' Most people's lives became more varied: cheap radios were everywhere, cinema tickets were cheap and cheap transport enabled people to get away from their immediate neighbourhoods during the paid holidays enjoyed by increasing numbers and the increased leisure hours that resulted from reduced hours of work.

Private house-building boom

The majority of the working classes no longer had to limit their ambitions to mere subsistence, but their incomes were too low to enable them to participate fully in the consumer society that was emerging. The middle class – teachers, civil servants, managers, clerks – enjoyed a greater surplus of income over essential expenditure. They were the people who triggered the private house-building boom of the 1930s. Altogether, two and a half million private houses were completed between the wars, by the later 1930s at a rate of 350,000 per year. Low prices and readily available mortgages brought them well within the range of the middle classes and even the better-off working class. The spread of semi-detached houses in the suburbs of the larger towns and along the arterial roads leading out of London and other cities was testimony to the rise of the middle-class owner-occupier. The same people formed the principal market for family cars, available in the 1930s for a little over £100. Increasing numbers of them were even paying public school fees for their children: pupils at public schools increased by about a third between the wars. Domestic service was still an affordable luxury. Fewer households had several servants, for washing machines and gas and electric fires had reduced the amount of labour required in the home, but more people than ever had a single live-in servant to do the cooking and cleaning. Domestic service provided employment for 1.4 million people in 1931, rather more than it had done in 1911. This was still a society which expected a high level of personal service, not only in the home, but in generously staffed shops and on public transport. Such a level of staffing and service was only possible because unskilled labour was still cheap to employ.

2. Unemployment and Poverty

The paradox of the 1930s is that large sections of the community had never had things so good and yet the decade acquired a reputation as the 'devil's decade'. The reason for this evil reputation is the unprecedented mass unemployment from which Britain suffered. Between the end of the post-war boom in 1921 and the outbreak of war in 1939, there were never fewer than a million people, a tenth of the insured population, out of work, and when things were at their worst, in the winter of 1932-3, the total of unemployed workers reached nearly three million.

The 'devil's decade'

It had been clear to 19th-century observers that the level of unemployment in Britain depended heavily on the state of world trade. World trade went through a fairly regular cycle of boom followed by slump. In the booms, British exports rose, investment in new factories at home increased, industrial output went up and more workers were taken on. In the slumps, exports dropped, investment ceased, output fell and workers were laid off. As the purchasing power of these workers diminished, workers in industries producing for the home market also began to be laid off. This cycle continued to operate after the First World War, with the alarming differences that the slumps were more severe and the upturns more limited. The first slump of these years began in 1921, when exports fell to half of the level of 1913 and unemployment reached 17 per cent. There was a recovery in the later 1920s, but exports reached only 80 per cent of the level of 1913 even in 1929. Then came the Wall Street Crash and the Great Depression in the USA, which heavily reduced American demand for British goods and led to a general collapse of world trade. British exports again sank to about half of the level of 1913 and unemployment rose even higher than in 1921, to 22 per cent. The recovery from this slump peaked in 1937 and again proved incomplete, leaving high unemployment and much unused industrial capacity.

Wall Street Crash and the Great Depression

Stubbornly high rates of unemployment, even in the economic upswings, indicated that there had been a permanent fall in demand for the products of certain industries beyond that caused by cyclical fluctuations. These industries were the staple industries of the 19th century: cotton, coal, shipbuilding and, to a degree, iron and steel. The regions where these industries were concentrated became in the 1920s the permanently depressed areas of the country, where unemployment was at two or three times the level experienced in the regions where the new industries were developing, such as the south-east and Midlands. Towns dependent on a single staple industry were often devastated: in Jarrow in the north-east lack of orders for ships in 1934 meant that two thirds of workers were unemployed and coal-mining Merthyr in South Wales was not much better off. In Oxford and Coventry only 5 per cent of workers were unemployed. In addition, most unemployment in the prosperous areas was temporary, whereas in the depressed regions much of it was long-term. Naturally, there was some redistribution of population as people moved to more prosperous regions. The population of the south-east increased by 18 per cent, but that of South Wales declined. The newcomers were not always welcome, especially since they increased the local competition for jobs.

Decline of former staple industries

In the inter-war period the unemployed were eligible for benefits, though these were of bewildering complexity, as successive governments extended and tinkered with the National Insurance Act of 1911, in order to cope with the problem of persistent and long-term mass-unemployment. The economic measures of 1931 included the imposition of the means test on the long-term unemployed. Local Public Assistance Committees were given the duty of assessing the income of claimants to benefit by visiting their homes and prying into their circumstances. The process was regarded by its victims as deeply humiliating and it often led to relief being withheld or reduced. The TUC compiled a dossier of hard-luck cases, especially those which had led to pensioners or the young having to leave a breadwinner's home because otherwise his benefit would have been cut to take account of their pensions or earnings. The means test became a symbol of the heartlessness of the system, but at least the British unemployed were better off than their Victorian predecessors or American contemporaries. Even so, unemployment was a major cause of poverty, which was defined as having insufficient income to maintain health. In 1936 Rowntree made a fresh survey of poverty in York. He found that many fewer people lived in poverty than had in 1899, but that among those who did unemployment was far more important as a cause of their condition. He reckoned that nearly three quarters of the unemployed lived in poverty.

Benefit measures introduced 1931

If unemployment caused poverty as defined by investigators such as Rowntree, it seemed to follow that the health of unemployed workers and their families must have deteriorated, as they were compelled to economize on food. Studies of working-class diets suggested that the families of the unemployed ate more bread and potatoes, but less meat, vegetables, fruit and milk than those of the employed. Yet many enquiries insisted that the evidence showed no significant deterioration in health through malnutrition. It was easy to demonstrate that infant mortality, deaths in childbirth and deaths from a range of common diseases were all higher in the depressed

Effects of unemployment on the populace

areas than in the more prosperous ones, but that had been so even before high unemployment began. The depressed north and Wales had more slums, more overcrowding, worse air pollution and lower wages even for those in work. Unemployment was yet another factor undermining people's well-being in these places and its impact is impossible to separate out.

Unemployment undoubtedly brought a marked deterioration in the victims' material circumstances, but there were other important negative consequences too. Though some men had varied interests which lack of employment gave them time to satisfy, most found idleness a burden. It had what Orwell called a 'deadening, debilitating effect', which might be temporarily relieved by a visit to the cinema or a little gambling. 'Even people on the verge of starvation can buy a few days' hope ("Something to live for", as they call it) by having a penny on a sweepstake,' wrote Orwell. Work did more for workers than simply fill up time. Men out of a job experienced a loss of the status and respectability which went with their work. Money they earned was not the same as money handed out by bureaucratic bodies as a species of charity. Men at work were part of a social group and were sundered from it if they lost their job and could no longer afford to drink with their former workmates at the pub. In some ways, unemployment was easier to bear in those places where whole communities were out of work. Many social investigators of the time feared that unemployment might also place intolerable strains on families, especially where husbands or fathers lost their jobs and wives or children kept them, but in most cases family solidarity held and divorce rates did not increase. 'The family-system has not broken up,' concluded Orwell after his travels through England in the Depression years.

There were fears in the 1930s that mass unemployment might produce a serious threat to social and political stability in Britain. Protests were organized by the National Unemployed Workers Movement (NUWM), which mounted campaigns, including

National Unemployed Workers Movement

hunger marches, to persuade the government to alter its provisions for the unemployed. In the early 1920s demonstrations took place in London: perhaps the most successful in attracting attention were the disruptions of Remembrance Day services by unemployed workers. At that time, the NUWM and the Labour movement were allied, but by the late 1920s official Labour had been alienated by the increasing closeness of the NUWM and the Communist Party. The government branded the movement as subversive, but that did not stop the hunger marches of unemployed workers from Wales, Scotland and the north from arousing sympathy as they passed through more prosperous areas. The hunger march which has become most famous was not organized by the NUWM. It was the Jarrow Crusade, organized on the initiative of the local town council and the Labour MP Ellen Wilkinson. Two hundred men marched on London and presented a petition, which was sympathetically received. Because they presented no kind of threat, they were given extensive press coverage, which made this small hunger march the symbol of the mass-unemployment of the 1930s. The NUWM was too threatening to gain similar sympathy. When its marchers lobbied the TUC holding its conference in Bristol in 1931, there were clashes with the police. NUWM campaigns against the means test in 1932 brought serious disturbances in London and several provincial centres. In 1935 protests in South Wales against the policies of the Unemployment Assistance Board brought perhaps 300,000 people on to the streets. Yet there was no call for revolution, but just for a modification of administrative regulations. Even this cause left most of the unemployed lethargic and apathetic.

The Jarrow Crusade 1936

Apathy induced by idleness may well be one reason why the unemployed did not prove willing foot-soldiers for extremists of the left or the right. In his *Road to Wigan Pier George* Orwell ventured the opinion that; 'It is quite likely that fish-and-chips, tinned salmon, cut-price chocolate... , the movies, the radio, strong tea, and the Football Pools have between them averted revolution.' Orwell's

Orwell's *Road to Wigan Pier*

opinion may perhaps contain much truth, but the 'cheap luxuries' he mentioned still had to be bought. No doubt, British arrangements for the unemployed left much to be desired, but the dole was at least sufficient to enable most of them, with a little ingenuity, just about to make do. That was, after all, what their Edwardian fathers and Victorian grandfathers had also had to do. The people scandalized by mass-unemployment were not so much the people who had to endure it, but the better-off who were shocked by the survival of poverty in a society where so many had begun to enjoy considerable affluence.

3. Leisure and the Media

For people with a job, the tendency towards a reduction in the hours of work, evident from the mid-19th century, continued in the inter-war period. The main gain for workers from the wave of strikes in 1918-21 was a general reduction of the working day from nine to eight hours. Saturday was still a working day, though often the hours of work were shorter. Paid holidays also became more common, though Paid Holiday as late as 1938 only three million people were entitled to them. Finally, Act 1938 the government legislated on the matter: an act of 1938 extended paid holidays, usually of one week, to over eleven million workers.

To cater for the holiday-makers on their annual week off, the major holiday resorts further developed their facilities by building ballrooms, fairgrounds and open-air swimming pools. This was the golden age of the English seaside resort, with Blackpool to the fore, attracting over seven million overnight visitors a year by the later Growth of 1930s, not to mention the half-million day-trippers who came on an British August Bank Holiday Monday. Holidays abroad were growing in holiday popularity, but were still the preserve of the better-off and unable to resorts compete with English resorts for the mass-market.

More dramatic developments took place in the provision of entertainment in people's home neighbourhoods. In the inter-war years cinemas became ubiquitous. There were 5,000 of them by 1939, many of the more recent being purpose-built and some seating huge numbers. A whole series of technical improvements ensured ever-increasing attendances. The first films were silent, but 'talkies' made their appearance by 1927 and then black and white gave way to colour. By 1939 twenty million tickets were sold each week and surveys in Liverpool and York found that 40 per cent of the population went to the cinema at least once a week. Unlike pubs, cinemas offered entertainment suitable for unaccompanied women and for children. With tickets costing only 6d, hardly anyone was excluded on grounds of poverty. Indeed, with their plush seating, wall-to-wall carpeting and exotic décor, cinemas could convey an illusion of luxury as well as the escapist illusions of the films themselves. In the earliest years of the period, some British films were shown, but there was a strong tendency for Hollywood to acquire a virtual monopoly of the British screen.

'Talkies' 1927

American influence was apparent too in the kinds of dance music that became popular. This influence was already evident by 1914, when the foxtrot was introduced to London. When American troops came to Europe in 1917 and American bands came on tour, a craze for American music and dance developed. The more sedate traditional waltzes gave way to what one newspaper described as 'freakish, degenerate, negroid' dances such as the Charleston, introduced in 1925.

Dance crazes

In the inter-war years dancing became an enormously popular pastime. As at the cinema, a small admission fee, of one or two shillings, paid for several hours of entertainment. The new tastes in music and the fame of the big bands that played it were spread through gramophone records and through radio. From 1926 the British Broadcasting Corporation (BBC) had its own house band and in the 1930s a regular nightly feature was devoted to one of the big dance bands.

The growing popularity of cinema and of dance music illustrates two significant trends. One is that a series of entertainment industries

JOSEPHINE BAKER (1906-1975) DANCING THE CHARLESTON

was coming into existence: a film industry, especially that based on Hollywood; a cinema industry, as firms bought up or built chains of cinemas; record companies; and so on. This process of commercialization was evident in sport too, as specialist manufacturers of sports equipment catered for the needs of those who played games increasingly popular among the middle class, such as tennis and golf. The other notable trend was the tendency for leisure pursuits to vary less according to region or class. The same films were shown throughout the country and the influence of the BBC and the

Commercialization of sport and leisure

record companies spread new musical tastes everywhere. Radio, the press and the cinema made the same actors and actresses, footballers and cricketers, band leaders and instrumentalists known to almost everyone in the country.

The beginning of radio broadcasting was one of the most important events of the inter-war years. In 1926 the BBC was set up as a body independent of the government, but responsible to a minister of the Crown, the Paymaster-General. The broadcasts could at first be received only by enthusiasts, but by the 1930s radio sets connected to the mains electricity supply and with built-in speakers had arrived. They cost only a pound or two, with the result that by 1939 over eight million households had licences. Perhaps it was the cost of the licence (10 shillings) which prevented the remaining quarter of households from acquiring one. The first Director-General of the BBC, John Reith, believed that the function of radio was to educate and accordingly classical music and drama figured largely in early broadcasts. It was not long, however, before a wider choice of programmes aimed at a mass market developed. The light music programmes popularized new dances and bands and broadcast performances by the BBC's own orchestras, singers and comedians. The advent of radio was important in broadening the available range of home-based entertainment. It also reinforced the work of the national press in creating a shared national experience. Everyone was encouraged to share in the excitement of sporting events, such as the Oxford and Cambridge Boat Race, the Grand National horse race, the Wimbledon tennis championships and the Wembley Cup Final. Everyone could in a sense be present at the Remembrance Day service or the Christmas service of lessons and carols at King's College, Cambridge, and all could be individually addressed by the King in his Christmas message.

Radio broadcasting had a special immediacy, but the most important form of mass-communication was still the newspapers. This was the heyday of the London press. Between 1910 and 1939,

British Broadcasting Corporation founded 1926

Development of radio entertainment

Heyday of
Fleet Street

sales of the major national dailies rose from 4.5 to 10.5 million, with the *Daily Express* and the Labour-inclined *Daily Herald* leading the pack. The 'popular' press (as opposed to 'quality' papers, like *The Times* and *Daily Telegraph*) was influenced by the layout of American newspapers and tended to banish advertisements from the front page, to use more eye-catching headlines and to sprinkle the pages with photos and cartoons. Competition between newspapers was intense and in the interests of boosting circulation, and hence advertising revenue, newspapers set out to entertain, featuring crosswords and competitions as well as news. Not all could stay the course. The number of national and provincial newspapers tended to decline and ownership became more concentrated. To achieve their colossal circulations the London dailies had to appeal to a wide range of social groups, but there were weekly magazines to meet the requirements of sub-groups in the population such as women and children. The inter-

The *Dandy*
and the *Beano*

war period saw the publication of the first comics, such as the *Dandy*, first published in 1937, and the *Beano*, from 1938 onwards.

More people were reading newspapers than ever before, but then more people were reading books too. The number of books published increased and the numbers sold increased even more dramatically. In part, this was because books were cheaper than they had ever been. Cheap editions made their appearance, the most famous being the 6d paperbacks which Allen Lane began to publish in 1935. The

Peguin
Paperbacks

Pelican range had a marked educational character, while the Penguin Shakespeare made its debut in 1937 and Penguin Specials tackled important social and political issues. Reading was an activity that could be pursued without buying any books at all: public libraries came into being before the Great War and after it they were joined by mobile libraries serving rural areas. Reading was a private, home-based activity and its growing popularity owed much to the greater comfort of the homes of a large swathe of the population and to their greater tranquillity in an age of smaller families.

PORTRAIT OF VIRGINIA WOOLF (1882-1941) *c.* 1902

4. The Arts and Sciences

Every age thinks of itself as modern, but leading figures in the arts after the First World War were so critical of the past and so self-consciously different that the adjective 'modern' came to be applied to their work and is still, a century later, considered appropriate. In Britain 'modern' attitudes were above all associated with a talented group of writers and artists known as the Bloomsbury Set, after the area of London (near the British Museum) where Virginia Woolf lived and ran the Hogarth Press. Later Woolf came to be regarded as the greatest novelist to emerge in the 1920s, but at the time the success of her deeply introspective novels, such as *To the Lighthouse*

Virginia Woolf and the Bloomsbury Set

(1927), was modest. Such experimental work was accessible only to a minority of intellectuals. Also in her circle was Lytton Strachey, whose *Eminent Victorians*, published in 1918, contained iconoclastic studies of such Victorian heroes as General Gordon and Florence Nightingale. The work initiated a less reverent approach to biography, and was important at the time for debunking Victorian values and conventions.

Many of the principal writers of the inter-war period were found both puzzling and deeply shocking. The Irish writer James Joyce's *Ulysses* was published in Paris in 1922, but banned in Britain and the USA for over a decade because of its sexual explicitness. DH Lawrence's *Lady Chatterley's Lover* was banned for even longer (till 1960). One of the central texts of 'modernism' in literature was the
Literary
'modernism'long poem by the American expatriate TS Eliot *The Waste Land*, published in 1922. In it the author abandoned traditional verse forms for free verse and deliberately cultivated incoherence, in that the work is composed of fragments. The result was a 'heap of broken images', meant to convey Europe's broken and sterile spiritual state in the aftermath of the First World War. Aldous Huxley explored the spiritual emptiness of modern European life through a vision of the future developed in his *Brave New World* (1932). Here the economic trends of Huxley's own time - mass-production, consumerism, manipulation through advertising - have produced a version of hell where every artificially induced want is satisfied and every spiritual longing is stifled in the interests of social conformity and stability. Pessimism and literary innovation did not, of course, characterize all, or even most, of the new books published in the 1930s. Some of the books of the period that have lasted best were intended to be simply good fun, such as PG Wodehouse's series on Bertie Wooster and his indispensable manservant Jeeves, published from 1919 onwards, or Evelyn Waugh's comic works, beginning with *Decline and Fall* (1928).

If some writers in English broke new ground, in the visual arts Britain tended to be a backwater, though slowly responding to continental stimuli. This generalization does not, however, hold in the case of sculpture. American-born Jacob Epstein settled in England before the Great War and rapidly acquired notoriety for sculptures which were sexually explicit and rejected the Greek tradition, from which European sculpture had hitherto derived, in favour of primitive and Indian models. His sculpture of 1911 for the tomb of Oscar Wilde in Paris was considered so outrageous that the French police covered it with a tarpaulin for a time. More favourably received were his bronze portrait busts, for example, those of the novelist Joseph Conrad or the composer Vaughan Williams, notable for their expressive modelling. Epstein helped to inspire two much younger British-born sculptors, Henry Moore (*b.* 1898) and Barbara Hepworth (*b.* 1903). Moore in particular was to acquire a worldwide reputation, though after 1945.

In the inter-war period there was a huge expansion in the performance and appreciation of serious music. The 'Proms' had been started under Sir Henry Wood in 1895 and they and increasing numbers of festivals and competitions provided opportunities for composition and performance. Resort bands and orchestras provided openings to talented youngsters such as Malcolm Sargent, who began as a conductor on Llandudno pier. Gramophone records increased the audience for music, while the BBC was even more important in bringing classical music into millions of homes. The BBC and film also provided patronage for composers and performers. William Walton and Vaughan Williams were amongst the significant British composers who wrote film scores.

The 'Proms'

Between the wars, British scientists gained a worldwide reputation for their scientific advances. At Manchester and later at the Cavendish Laboratory in Cambridge, Sir Ernest Rutherford and his team worked on the nuclear theory of the atom and finally succeeded in splitting the atom in 1932. Their work laid the foundation for the development both of the atom bomb and nuclear power. Research into radio, much stimulated by the Great War, also proved fruitful.

Scientific advancement of the inter-war period

John Logie Baird produced the first TV picture, but it was a different system, pioneered by Isaac Shoenberg, that was used when the world's first regular TV service was opened by the BBC at Alexandra Palace in 1936. Radio research also led to the development of radar and, after 1936, to the erection on the Kent and Essex coasts of radar masts for the detection of approaching enemy aircraft.

Alexandra Palace

The First World War led the government to play a bigger role in scientific development. For example, wartime government sponsorship of work on psychology and clinical medicine led to the foundation of the Medical Research council in 1920. The state-sponsored BBC provided some of the driving force behind the development of television. Yet shortage of funds forced the government to leave the bulk of the research in most areas to private firms, such as EMI and Marconi, which were foremost in developing television, and the big aircraft and engineering manufacturers. Sometimes British discoveries could not be developed with inadequate British resources. This was the case with Alexander Fleming's discovery of penicillin, which was developed with American money as the first major antibiotic.

British Medical Research council founded - 1920

The discoveries of the researchers in physics and bacteriology had practical application, but people looked to science also for an understanding of, perhaps even a solution to, the great problems of their time. Some people thought, for example, that the ideas of the Viennese psychiatrist Sigmund Freud might help to explain the discontents of the modern world. His view that human problems were to be explained by the repression of basic human instincts by civilization convinced only a small coterie of disciples, but many of his ideas did enter the mainstream, as the general acceptance of terms such as 'inferiority complex', 'repression', 'sadism' and 'masochism' shows. It was increasingly believed that people could be affected by mental disorders, evidence of which was increasingly made available in courts of law. Whether Freudian insights were scientific in any strict sense, however, was - and still is - a moot point.

VIII

British Politics Between the World Wars

1. The Liberals, the Conservatives and the War

THOUGH they had not yet been able to resolve important problems such as the claim of women to the vote and the future of Ireland, the Liberals seemed in the early summer of 1914 likely to be in a strong position to win the general election that was due in 1915. The outbreak of war, however, was bound to put party unity under strain. Going to war involved a continental military commitment and an alliance with the autocratic regime of the Tsar, which were contrary to the deeply rooted traditions in foreign policy associated with 19th-century Liberal heroes such as Gladstone. War would also inevitably call into question many of the liberties for which the Liberals traditionally stood. The most important of these was freedom from conscription into the army, which was seen as every Briton's birthright. Asquith managed Britain's entry into the war with great skill, so that there were only two not very significant Cabinet resignations. Civil liberties were gradually eroded, but for eighteen months the great symbolic issue of conscription was not raised and the government's Liberal credentials remained more or less intact.

War poses problems for the Liberal Government

Unfortunately for the Liberals, the war proved long and difficult. By 1915 there was increasing criticism of the government. The disasters at Gallipoli were blamed on Churchill, who had to resign from the Admiralty. In the press the government as a whole came under fire over an alleged shortage of shells, which the press believed to be the cause of the failures on the Western Front. In these circumstances, the party truce which had been agreed by all parties after the outbreak of war looked unlikely to hold. Conservative backbenchers were itching to attack the government and might force the hand of their leader, Andrew Bonar Law. If they did, a general election would take place in December. The Liberals by now looked likely to lose, an outcome that did not appeal to Asquith. An election would probably also prove divisive in the country and make it difficult to carry on the war at all, an outcome feared by both main party leaders. In particular, Law did not want to have to conduct the war with a strong Liberal opposition critical of his every move.

It became obvious to Asquith that the war would have to be conducted as a more fully bi-partisan enterprise. In early 1915 he and Lloyd George offered to take the Conservatives into a coalition, which would force the Conservative backbenchers to moderate their criticisms of the government. The Conservatives were very much junior partners in the coalition. The most important offices were still held by Liberals: Law was given only the Colonial Office. The whole arrangement was foisted on the parties by their leaders and neither was very happy with it. The Conservatives did not trust the Liberals to wage war with sufficient vigour and determination. The Liberals suspected that under Conservative influence the war would be fought without regard for traditional liberties. It was not long before Liberal fears appeared to be confirmed. The government's brutal handling of the Easter Rising in Ireland seemed to break with Liberal traditions. It also had the effect of alienating the Irish Home Rulers and then destroying their hold on the Irish electorate. An important constituent of the Liberal majority had thus been removed. Meanwhile, in Britain the government had imposed conscription. Asquith's skilful handling of the issue avoided a crisis over it at Cabinet level, but many Liberal backbenchers and supporters were left alienated from their leaders.

Conservative support for extensions of the life of the parliament enabled Asquith to continue to avoid an election and remain as Prime Minister until December 1916. Lloyd George, however, was beginning to lose confidence in the Prime Minister. He said privately, 'Wait and see [Asquith's characteristic approach to problems] was an excellent precept for peace. But in war it is leading us straight to

Fragile Liberal-Conservative coalition of WW1

destruction.' A crisis arose late in 1916, when Lloyd George, Minister of War since June, sought to reorganize the machinery for running the war. With Conservative support, he put forward proposals for the establishment of a small committee to run the war independently of the Prime Minister and the Cabinet, who he believed were too dilatory. Asquith was unwilling to be sidelined in this way. A deal between him and Lloyd George collapsed and Asquith resigned. Law was not willing to form a ministry, but to Asquith's surprise, Lloyd George was able to find enough support to form a coalition government. The Conservatives were willing to back him, despite the view of many of them that he was a 'little bounder'. They admired his energy and were convinced that only he, not Asquith, could deliver the necessary reorganization of the management of the war and lead the country to victory. Lloyd George also succeeded in winning support from Labour under Arthur Henderson. Yet he needed Liberal support too, and it was soon apparent that a large number of Liberal MPs were ready to serve under him. Asquith was not one of them. It was at this point that the Liberal party split into supporters of Lloyd George as Prime Minister and supporters of Asquith as Leader of the Opposition.

Lloyd George forms new coalition

In theory, Asquith might at this point have reinvented himself as the leader of all who were unhappy about the war. During 1917, yet another year of apparently futile slaughter, this time in Flanders, there were many who wondered whether it might be possible to achieve a negotiated peace. Asquith showed no interest in articulating this point of view. To have done so would have meant going against the policy which he had upheld in government and betraying his own convictions. The only occasion on which he led opposition to the government was when he supported the allegations of General Maurice that ministers had lied about the strength of British forces on the Western Front in order to cover up the serious results of Lloyd George's insistence on sending extra troops to Palestine. In the vote in the subsequent debate, Lloyd George survived easily with

Conservative support, but the Liberals split 98 to 71 in favour of Asquith. The affair deepened the split between the two Liberal factions, but it did nothing to dispel the impression that the split was simply about personalities. Asquith was quite unable to link his quarrel with Lloyd George to any more general concern and as a result his followers among the Liberals wholly failed to engage the interest of the electorate.

Lloyd George's great weakness was his lack of any party organization; his main strength was his position as Prime Minister, which meant that he could dispense government jobs in return for loyalty. He required more than just followers in Parliament, however. He had attracted some Liberals who hoped to achieve something in politics and could see in loyalty to Lloyd George a route to power and the implementation of their policies. Such was Christopher Addison, whose plans could give substance to Lloyd George's rhetoric about 'homes fit for heroes', or Herbert Fisher, who aspired to improve educational provision. There were hopes, then, that a Lloyd George government might be genuinely radical and generate popular appeal.

There was, however, no denying Lloyd George's dependence on the Conservatives. They had been the political beneficiaries of the war. The last nine years of peace had seen them condemned to perpetual opposition, with no certain prospect of regaining power at the next election. War had transformed their prospects, making them an indispensable partner in government in May 1915, thanks to their ability to block extensions of the life of the current parliament and thereby to force an election. Lloyd George needed them even more than Asquith had. Because of the Liberal split, Lloyd George's Commons majority depended on their support, as he recognized by allotting them several of the most important posts in the government. Law, for example, was made Chancellor of the Exchequer and Leader of the House of Commons. Curzon and Milner, men of great influence in the party, were brought into the War Cabinet. With the

Conservatives political beneficiaries of the war

Conservatives providing so much of his support in Parliament, the obvious danger for Lloyd George was that he might become no more than a figurehead for the Conservative party.

Yet if Lloyd George needed the Conservatives, most of the Conservatives believed that they needed him. Law, like the Prime Minister himself, was a man of relatively humble origins. Born in Canada, he had been an iron merchant before he went into politics, and the partnership with Lloyd George helped him to keep the Conservative grandees in check. Men like Balfour and Austen Chamberlain preferred coalition politics to excessive dependence on their own backbenchers and the consequent need to pander to party prejudices. Moreover, the Conservatives had the greatest respect for Lloyd George's ability to win mass-support, a talent which none of the Conservative leaders possessed. The Prime Minister's abilities were expected to be more necessary than ever given the vast expansion of the electorate that was to be implemented under the Representation of the People Act. To go into electoral battle allied to the man who was believed to have won the war would be to give the Conservatives the best possible chance of victory.

Conservative dependence upon Lloyd George

The Conservative leaders were keener on appealing to the electorate as part of a coalition than Lloyd George was. To the last moment Lloyd George considered making an independent appeal to the voters on the basis of Liberal reunification, but in the end time ran out and his only mature plan was for an alliance with the Conservatives. It was agreed that 159 Liberal candidates would receive a letter of approval – the coupon, Asquith called it – from Lloyd George and Bonar Law and in return would pledge to be loyal to the coalition. The vital point was the Conservatives' agreement not to put up candidates against the couponed Liberals.

2. The War and the Labour Party

The First World War divided not only the Liberals, but also the Labour Party. At a conference in 1907 the international socialist movement had committed itself to making every effort to prevent war and, in the event of failure, to intervention to end it. In 1914, however, the continental socialists duly supported their governments and, after some hesitation, the Labour Party in Britain supported the British government's declaration of war. MacDonald, however, felt unable to go with the majority and resigned his position as party chairman. Arthur Henderson was elected in his place. The split in the Labour movement amounted to more than a change of leadership. The majority committed itself wholeheartedly to the war effort. The trade unions declared an industrial truce for the duration of the war and the Labour Party joined the other parties in approving an electoral truce. There was, however, a minority based in the Independent Labour Party, including MacDonald and Hardie, who claimed that the war was the fault of militarists on both sides and worked for a negotiated peace. The ILP tried to prevent the Labour party from joining the Asquith and Lloyd George coalitions, but it was overborne at the party conferences.

Split between the Labour Party and the Independent Labour party (ILP)

The co-operation offered to the government by the bulk of the labour movement brought the latter many advantages. In the spring of 1915 Henderson and the trade unions were consulted over the issue of 'dilution', so that less-skilled labour could be used in jobs hitherto reserved for skilled workers. A body under Henderson as chairman was created to advise the government on labour questions. When conscription was brought in during 1916, key industrial workers had to be exempted and the whole business of granting these exemptions was handed over to the unions. In effect, the government took the unions into partnership. It was a natural further step to bring the political party associated with the trade unions into partnership with the government too. In May 1915 Henderson was offered a

Wartime partnership between government and trade unions

178

post in the government, which finally he accepted with the backing of his party. In December 1916 he was elevated to the small War Cabinet, while other Labour MPs also joined the government. These arrangements were of great importance in enabling Labour leaders to acquire experience in government and to demonstrate their competence. The idea of a Labour government was coming to seem less outlandish.

Labour MPs join Government

Henderson argued that in government he was in the best possible position to look after the interests of the working class. There was a danger, though, that he and the trade union leaders co-operating with the government might come to be seen by ordinary workers as out of touch and even as having sold out to the employers and the government. An unofficial labour movement developed on Clydeside in Scotland in 1915 to organize a strike against employers who had brought in American labour. When the strike was over, the Clydeside Workers' Committee remained to oppose the Munitions of War Act, which had limited the mobility of labour in order to prevent employers from poaching each other's skilled workers. In 1916 several shop stewards had to be deported from their home towns and a few were even sent to prison. There was also trouble in 1915 in the South Wales coalfield. The miners refused to accept a deal over pay agreed between their union and the government and went on strike. The government tried declaring the strike illegal, but the miners had the whip hand, since their strike threatened seriously to disrupt war production. In the end, Lloyd George and Henderson had to capitulate to the miners under their shop stewards. In 1917 there was another wave of industrial unrest when a quarter of a million engineers embarked on unofficial strikes, which were ended by government concessions.

Munitions of War Act

Widespread industrial unrest 1917

Despite its role in government, in the period to mid-1917 the Labour Party did not appear very impressive. There was often a gulf between it and the workers on whose behalf it claimed to speak. It was disunited: some members of the ILP even spoke about pulling out of the party. Yet the final eighteen months of the war proved to be a very significant time in the party's history, when it began to position itself to displace the Liberals as the main alternative to the Conservatives.

It was of the utmost importance that the Labour party ended the war re-united. In June 1917 Henderson went to Russia in order to encourage it to go on fighting for the Allies, but he came to realize that only a rapid negotiated peace could save Russian democracy. He hoped to use a conference of socialists from all the belligerent countries, which met at Stockholm, to achieve peace. When he insisted on speaking in favour of the conference, he quarrelled with the War Cabinet, which was set on military victory, and resigned.

The Labour
Party and
ILP
re-united

Thus it was that Henderson and the members of the ILP found themselves once more in agreement. That the split was then so rapidly mended shows that it had never been deep or bitter. Most members of the party had not so much rejected ILP views on foreign policy as ignored them, preferring to concentrate on practical matters like defence of the workers' interests in wartime. In 1918 the party was able to rally round the principles of foreign policy which had been

Union of
Democratic
Control

worked out during the war by the Union of Democratic Control, a body which had included MacDonald and other members of the ILP. These principles were: democratic control of foreign policy, reduction of armaments and support for an international peace-keeping organization. In acquiring a foreign policy, Labour showed that it aspired to be a party of government. The particular principles it committed itself to had been worked out together with Liberals who were disillusioned by their party's foreign policy record before 1914 and during the war. The principles were essentially those of Gladstone and their adoption showed clearly MacDonald's determination to position his party as the authentic heir of 19th century liberalism, to which all genuine liberals should rally.

The Labour Party was in a strong financial position at the end of the war. Since 1911 MPs had been paid, which removed a significant cause of financial pressure on a party lacking potential representatives with a private income. Much more important was an overhaul of the party's financial basis in 1918. Affiliated bodies, such as trade unions, were to pay twice as much per member as hitherto. The doubling of membership of trade unions affiliated to the TUC from 2.6 to 5.2 million became significant at this point. At the party conference of January 1918, it was decided to set up a local Labour party in every constituency, and it became possible to join the party directly, instead of through an affiliated body. There was no longer any question of the party fighting only a limited number of seats. At the 1918 election, 388 Labour candidates stood, another sign that Labour was a would-be party of government.

Nationaliz-
ation of the
Labour Party

The other sign that Labour had come to view itself as a political party on a par with the Liberals or Conservatives was its adoption in 1918 of a distinctive party programme. This included the famous Clause IV, which committed the party to 'secure for the producers by hand or by brain the full fruits of their industry' and the fairest distribution of those fruits 'upon the basis of the common ownership of the means of production'. What exactly the clause implied was not clear. The trade unions, which were very powerful in the party, did not favour centralized economic planning, and it is probable that the aims of the party leaders included no more than the further development of social welfare to guarantee minimum standards of housing, health and education, together with the nationalization of the mines and the railways, all of them aims included in the manifesto for the election of 1918. Perhaps the clause did no more than define a direction in which the party strove to move. Its importance was to give the party an idealistic appeal and to stress the difference between Labour and the New Liberalism from which virtually all its ideas and policies derived.

Clause IV
and the
Labour Party
programme

3. Lloyd George's Coalition Government, 1918-22

Landslide
coalition
victory
December
1918

In December 1918 the hugely increased electorate of 21 million people gave a resounding election victory to Lloyd George's coalition. It won 526 seats out of 707. The election took place only a few months after the near-defeat in the first half of 1918 and the emotions of wartime still ran high. From this situation the Conservatives and their allies were bound to be the chief beneficiaries, as the party which had been most strident in its hatred of Germans and loudest in its support for military preparation before the war and measures such as conscription during it. The Conservatives stood too for a tough peace and it is likely that many voters, particularly perhaps women, wanted to complete what the troops had begun with their defeat of Germany in the field.

Quite apart from their appeal in the circumstances of 1918, the Conservatives and their allies were bound to do better, especially in terms of seats, than they had in 1910, because the anti-Conservative vote was split between Labour and the Asquithian Liberals, whereas in 1910 the pact between Labour and the Liberals had united it. The Asquithians won only 28 seats and 12 per cent of the vote. This feeble

Labour
emerging as
electoral
contender

performance reflected their poverty and rundown organization, which meant that they could field only 258 candidates. Many former Liberals who disliked the Conservatives were forced to vote Labour: old habits of voting Liberal were broken. That Labour had captured a good slice of the old Liberal vote was evident in the election statistics: Labour won 22 per cent of the vote. It was beginning to appear the Conservatives' main opponent. On the other hand, its tally of 57 seats was disappointing: it was still very largely a party representing mining constituencies.

As Prime Minister after 1918, Lloyd George seemed in a very powerful position, but he could never forget that the Conservatives, with 380 seats, were not only the biggest element in his majority, but were also numerous enough to govern alone if they chose. It seemed to many that he had become nothing but the mouthpiece for the Conservatives when he sanctioned violent reprisals against the IRA in Ireland or put his signature to what appeared a harsh peace settlement at Versailles. But in his dealings with the workers, Lloyd George's government was far from ungenerous. Unemployment insurance was extended to most workers and when mass unemployment became a fact of life in 1921, benefits went on being paid far beyond the period covered by contributions. Yet he could hardly look on benignly as industry was disrupted by waves of strikes on a scale that was unprecedented, except for 1912. There was a showdown with the miners. The government refused to nationalize the mines and hastened to dismantle the controls imposed during the war. In the spring of April 1921 the miners went on strike, but received no support from the other members of the Triple Alliance, the railwaymen and transport workers. By June they had been defeated. Lloyd George appeared as the man who had shattered working-class hopes, though it was the end of the favourable position which labour had enjoyed during the war and post-war boom that was really responsible.

Lloyd George quashes the 1921 miner's strike

By 1921 Lloyd George's Liberal credentials were looking threadbare. Events of 1921-2 destroyed what remained of them. His budget of 1914 had envisaged spending the huge sum of £200 million, but the budget of 1919 exceeded £2,500 million, a level of spending judged insupportable, even taking into account a doubling of prices. Economies had to be made, and the first victim was Addison's programme of house building, under which local authorities had received subsidies to build 170,000 houses. Addison resigned and went on to join the Labour Party. The rate of income tax was reduced and a committee of businessmen under Sir Eric Geddes identified further possible economies. The 'Geddes Axe' cut what was left of the government's social reforms. In these circumstances, there seemed little point to Coalition Liberalism. It lost seats at by-elections. Some of its MPs made overtures to the Asquithians. Half the seats in the Cabinet went to Coalition Liberals and to more and more Conservatives the sacrifice ceased to seem worthwhile.

End of the coalition

By 1922 all that was necessary to destroy the Coalition was a collapse of trust in Lloyd George himself. A miasma of sharp practice had long hung about him and in 1922 it was revealed that honours had been systematically sold in return for contributions to party funds. The practice was not new, but Lloyd George's use of it was especially crude and blatant and, moreover, most of the profits went to him (and were to support his political career for the next twenty years). In October 1922 a meeting of Conservative backbenchers was held. The advice of Bonar Law, returning to politics after a bout of ill health, was that the party should fight the next election independently. The advice was accepted by a two-to-one majority. Lloyd George at once resigned.

4. The Re-Shaping of Politics, 1922-4

In voting to end the coalition with Lloyd George, the Conservatives were voting to restore conventional party politics. In the event, by 1924, a new party system was established in which the main contest was between the Conservatives and the Labour Party and the outcome, more often than not, favoured the Conservatives. In the seventy-six years of the 20th century that remained, they were out of power for only twenty-two.

Liberal Party split

The resignation of Lloyd George and his replacement as Prime Minister by Law led at once to a general election. The Conservatives caught their opponents unprepared and won a clear majority with 344 seats to Labour's 142 and the Liberals' 115. The Liberals were divided more or less evenly between followers of Lloyd George and followers of Asquith. The even split was one of the problems: neither group was the more obvious heir to a great political tradition. Labour was well on its way to picking up the bulk of the working-class seats, though it was also attracting public school men, such as Clement

Attlee (Haileybury) and Hugh Dalton (Eton). These were not men likely to become the generals of the proletariat in a class war. The Conservatives were adapting themselves to a democratic age. When Law's health finally collapsed in 1923, George V called upon Stanley Baldwin to form a government rather than the grand Curzon. Baldwin was a wealthy ironmaster from Worcestershire who had no more fear of Labour MPs than he had of his own employees. In contrast to Lloyd George, whom he loathed, he projected an image of honesty, adherence to Christian morality and sentimental patriotism. 'The domestic war, like the war with Germany, must be fought to a finish,' argued a *Times* leader in the 1920s. Yet Baldwin was no general, but a reassuring, consensual figure, more likely to conciliate than confront. He was to dominate the Conservative party for the next dozen years.

Baldwin appointed to form government 1923

In October 1923 Baldwin decided to seek a mandate for ending free trade on the plea that only the imposition of tariffs to protect British industry could solve the unemployment problem. At the election the Conservatives remained the largest party, but lost their overall majority. The Liberals had reunited round the cause of free trade and won 30 per cent of the vote, almost as much as Labour. Unfortunately for them, their vote was more evenly spread through the country, whereas Labour's was more concentrated in working-class areas. As a result, Labour won considerably more seats (191 as opposed to 158 for the Liberals). When Parliament met, Asquith voted Baldwin out and put MacDonald in, presumably hoping to revive the old co-operation between the Liberals and Labour that had been so successful before the war. He had, however, made the mistake of failing to agree the terms on which the Liberals would give their support. In the event, Ramsay MacDonald, the first Labour Prime Minister, simply ignored the Liberals, taking their support for granted.

First Labour government under MacDonald

MacDonald's key political objective was to replace the Liberals as the main alternative to the Conservatives. An important step on the way was to demonstrate that Labour could form a credible government and this was what he chiefly sought to do in 1923-4. He himself was Prime Minister and Foreign Secretary and certainly looked the part, while there was nothing second rate about Snowden as Chancellor of the Exchequer or Henderson as Home Secretary. MacDonald disappointed many of his own supporters by doing nothing to introduce anything that might be called socialism, but then his purpose was to avoid frightening the voters and show that Labour could run a normal government. His lack of a majority in any case prevented him from pursuing ambitious policies.

Fed up with keeping Labour in power for no reward, the Liberals brought down the Labour government in October 1924. Yet another election followed. The Conservatives ensured that the main issue was socialism. They made much of MacDonald's efforts to normalize relations with the Soviet Union, insinuating that he was aiding and abetting a Communist conspiracy. If he was, then the Liberals were culpable for having kept him in power. Yet the Liberals had lost credit on the left too for having brought Labour down. The result - highly satisfactory to both Labour and the Conservatives - was a disastrous squeezing of the Liberal vote. Their share was reduced to 18 per cent, their seats to a mere 40. Labour went down 40 seats to 151, but since their share of the vote was nearly double that of the Liberals, it was clear that they were now the Conservatives' main rivals. As for the Conservatives, they had 419 seats and eight million votes. A better result than any they had achieved since 1900. The pattern of 20th- century politics had emerged.

Labour and Conservative become the two main parties

5. Baldwin and the General Strike of 1926

Stanley Baldwin was the reassuring presence at the head of the Conservative government of 1924-9. The detailed policy-making was left to others: Austen Chamberlain attended to foreign policy; his half-brother Neville pursued schemes of social reform as Minister of Health, introducing contributory pensions for insured workers or their widows, payable from the age of 65; and Winston Churchill, newly recruited from the Liberals, was Chancellor of the Exchequer.

At the Exchequer, Churchill's most important decision, implemented in 1925, was to return to the gold standard. Just as before 1914, the value of sterling was to be pegged to the value of gold. The hope was that this would assist the return of the economic stability of the late 19th century. Unfortunately, economic stability was not so easily achieved, as the advent of the Great Depression was soon to show. The pound seems also to have been overvalued in terms of gold and therefore of other currencies, such as the dollar, which made life more difficult for British exporters.

Return to the gold standard 1925

In particular, the return to gold made yet more difficult the problems of the coal industry, which before the war had exported nearly a third of its output. The industry, however, suffered from more deep-seated problems, as the Royal Commission of 1925-6 under Sir Herbert Samuel discovered. Some 2,500 coal mines were divided among 1,400 owners. Many of the mines were too small to be efficient and many of the owners lacked the will or the capital to modernize. The Samuel Report advised in favour of a reorganization of the industry into larger, more viable units in order to bring down costs and recapture export markets. The Mining Association (of owners) was utterly opposed to this remedy and argued instead for wage cuts, which were wholly unacceptable to the miners. Hence the Samuel Report, which the government had hoped might bring a compromise solution, brought only further conflict.

Failure of the Samuel Report

At the end of April 1926 the owners began to lock the miners out of the pits. The government proclaimed a state of emergency and activated its machinery for maintaining essential supplies and services during strikes. A conference of trade union executives was meeting and voted by an overwhelming majority to call a general strike in sympathy with the miners. The General Strike polarized the nation. Most manual workers felt a bond with the miners, as the huge scale

General Strike 1926

of the response to the call for the General Strike showed. They believed that the miners' dirty and dangerous job should be adequately rewarded and they feared that, as after the miners' strike of 1921, a defeat and wage-cuts for the miners would be followed by wage-cuts for everyone else. For other people, the calling of the General Strike displaced the miners from the centre of attention. Instead of considering the plight of the miners, people were concerned with the legitimacy of the General Strike itself. Almost everyone was affected as the transport, power and printing industries closed down. Baldwin's argument that the unions had no right to attack the whole community was accepted by many people. Some agreed with the bellicose Churchill that there was a danger of 'a Soviet of Trade Unions' taking over the country. The menace of Russian-style revolution haunted the nightmares of many in the 1920s and the *Daily Mail*, printed in Paris, vigorously stoked their fears. Hence thousands of people from professional backgrounds volunteered to man services disrupted by the strike or serve as special constables in keeping order.

General
Strike
called off

Yet the unions were not interested in revolution. Everything in the experience of their officials inclined them to seek moderate and limited gains through established procedures. They did not see the General Strike as an opportunity to overthrow capitalism, but undertook it unwillingly as a gesture of solidarity with the miners. As soon as they could, they called it off. The straw they clutched at was a proposal for a settlement by Sir Herbert Samuel to which none of those involved was actually committed. The General Strike was called off on 12 May, but the miners fought on alone for another six months and finally had to give way on every point at issue, accepting longer hours, lower wages and district rather than national agreements with the owners.

Largely because of the miners' strike rather than the General Strike, the year 1926 was the worst year for strikes of the entire 20th century. It was, however, the last of the run of bad years since the

Great War. Belief in the efficacy of strikes declined among union leaders such as Ernest Bevin of the Transport Workers and talk of a general strike faded away for the next forty years. The unions were in any case under pressure. Union membership steadily declined from a high point at the start of the 1920s of 8.5 million to a low point of under 5 million by 1927 and mass unemployment forced the unions on to the defensive.

Baldwin had been deeply unhappy about the events of 1926. He disliked the mine-owners, whom he considered 'stupid and discourteous', but when his pleas for decency and common sense did not prevail, there was little he could do, given that he believed in the right of employers to be masters of their own enterprises. Nationalization of the mines was ruled out, but so was forced reorganization, which left only wage-cuts as a means to reduce the industry's costs. The rapid end to the General Strike brought Baldwin enormous prestige, but it ebbed away again when he was unable to settle the miners' strike. He was compelled to allow his followers to pass the spiteful Trade Disputes Act, which made sympathetic strikes illegal and banned civil servants from membership of a union affiliated to the TUC. Baldwin also failed to make progress in reducing unemployment, a cause which Lloyd George tried to put at the top of the political agenda. In the Yellow Book of 1928 the Liberals put forward ideas to revitalize the British economy, drawing on the ideas of the economist JM Keynes. They proposed that the government should borrow money and spend it on matters such as transport infrastructure in order to create jobs. Lloyd George did not restore Liberal fortunes, but perhaps he helped to damage Baldwin. In the election of 1929 the Conservatives lost 159 seats and finished 28 seats behind Labour.

Trade
Disputes Act

6. The Second Labour Government, 1929-31

When Ramsay MacDonald assumed the role of Prime Minister for the second time, at the head of another minority Labour government, it was already clear that the main task of his government would have to be tackling the problem of unemployment. Yet MacDonald had no economic strategy. His commitment to socialism meant no more than waiting for and welcoming the transformation of society which would come in due time through the evolution of the present order of society. What he was not prepared for was economic crises along the way which might expose the Labour Party's supporters to intolerable hardship. Yet he was to be faced not only with the stubbornly high unemployment that had existed since 1921, but also with unemployment resulting from the world economic crisis which began in 1929.

Wall Street Crash 1929

MacDonald was offered advice from several quarters. Lloyd George, now Liberal leader, could offer the ideas of his Yellow Book and the votes of his supporters in the House of Commons. MacDonald was not keen to be dominated by Lloyd George, who in any case ceased to be able to offer substantial support in the Commons, as his party shattered into fragments. MacDonald kept Lloyd George in play with interminable negotiations, in order to prevent him from allying with anyone else, but the Prime Minister seems to have had no real intention of making a deal. In Labour's own ranks was Sir Oswald Mosley. Like Lloyd George, he had derived ideas from the economist JM Keynes and in February 1930 he produced a memorandum in which he advocated restrictions on imports as well as public control of banking in order to finance industrial development. The Cabinet rejected Mosley's ideas and they were (narrowly) rejected again when he brought them before the party conference in October. Acceptance of Mosley's ideas would have meant abandoning free trade, which would have broken up the government and removed all hope of Liberal support. In disgust, Mosley went on to found his New Party.

Sir Oswald Mosley founds the New Party

By 1931 MacDonald and the British economy were suffering what the Prime Minister called 'an economic blizzard'. In the summer of 1931 the international banking system began to collapse. The Treasury and the Chancellor of the Exchequer, Philip Snowden, thought it essential to restore confidence in the pound and to avoid devaluing it in terms of gold. That, they assumed, meant balancing the budget at a time of heavy social spending, especially on unemployment benefit. Snowden drew up a list of cuts, which included a 10 per cent cut in unemployment benefit. The Cabinet agreed reluctantly by 12 votes to 9, but when the General Council of the TUC rejected the cuts, several of the ministers, including Henderson, changed their minds. On August 23rd the government broke up.

Government disintegrates over cuts

Yet MacDonald did not cease to be Prime Minister. After the collapse of his Labour ministry, he accepted George V's commission to form a National Government. MacDonald brought with him four members of his government, including the Chancellor, Snowden. Four Conservatives joined, under the leadership of Baldwin, who was content to serve under MacDonald, as did two Liberals including Sir Herbert Samuel, who was leading the party during the illness of Lloyd George. The immediate task of the new government was to carry out the cuts. Unemployment benefit was cut by 10 per cent and all public salaries were reduced. The reductions produced a mutiny at the naval base of Invergordon, which led the government to limit all cuts to 10 per cent. That limit, together with the general decline of prices in the depression, ensured public acquiescence in the government's measures.

National Government formed

The cuts did not save the pound, as they were supposed to do. The mutiny at Invergordon finally shattered confidence in sterling. The Bank of England was forced to abandon the gold standard and allow the pound to depreciate to the point where a pound was worth only $3.40 instead of $4.86. Interest rates were allowed to drift downwards to 2 per cent by mid-1932. It turned out that the conditions were in place for a modest economic recovery.

Bank of England abandons the gold standard

7. Politics under the National Government, 1931-9

When the National Government was formed, it was envisaged as a temporary expedient that would allow unpopular measures to be taken to balance the budget and restore confidence. Yet in October 1931 a general election was held in which the members of the government and their followers fought as a coalition against Labour, the only party outside it. Labour claimed to have been a victim of speculation by bankers in the summer of 1931. Few beyond those committed to the party believed this account and the coalition partners successfully pinned on Labour the charge that it had run away from difficulties.

Labour loses support in 1931 elections The election proved disastrous for Labour. It lost 6 per cent of the vote and ended with only around 50 MPs, most of them representing mining areas. The government counted 554 supporters in the Commons, including 473 Conservatives. After selling itself to the public in the election as the National Government, the government had no alternative but to remain a multi-party coalition.

The politicians consolidated the National Government by means of an election in part because they expected the economic crisis to be more prolonged and severe than proved to be the case and it seemed prudent to augment the government's authority by keeping the National label. The most significant decision, to abandon the gold standard, had already been taken. Neville Chamberlain became *Neville Chamberlain adopts protectionist measures* Chancellor of the Exchequer after the election. He abandoned free trade and adopted import duties on manufactures and imperial preference, which allowed in imports from the Empire at lower rates of duty. These policies probably helped less than low interest rates to bring about recovery. From early in 1933 unemployment figures began to tumble and a housing boom stimulated the economy. Such a happy outcome had not been predictable in 1931.

The politicians also had their individual reasons for maintaining the National Government. MacDonald and his small band of Labour followers were expelled from the Labour Party, which meant that if

MacDonald were to have a political role at all, it had to be as part of an alliance with other party leaders. It seems at first sight odd that Baldwin should have agreed to serve under MacDonald, since after the election the Conservatives could have governed with a comfortable majority on their own. Yet Baldwin had no wish to lead a party dominated by right-wing die-hards. Participation in the National Government helped to check them, and not only at Cabinet level. Many of the Conservatives newly elected in 1931 were aware of their dependence on the votes of people who had previously voted Labour or Liberal and knew that they could keep their seats only if they conducted themselves as 'National' rather than partisan representatives. Consequently, Baldwin found his party much easier to manage in the 1930s than it had been in the later '20s.

Baldwin was a conciliatory, centrist politician. His and MacDonald's government was conducted on pragmatic lines. Thus it had no absolute commitment to private enterprise if state intervention seemed more appropriate. In 1933 the National Government accepted without significant amendment the Labour politician Herbert Morrison's plan for a London Passenger Transport Board. The private companies were bought out and London transport was henceforth managed by a body of experts and businessmen. In 1939 the government merged the private airlines into a public body, British Overseas Airways Corporation (BOAC). The government accepted the principle of helping the areas hardest hit by the decline of their industries when it passed the Depressed Areas Act of 1934, but its commitment to economy restricted spending under it to a mere £2 million.

Baldwin was no doctrinaire imperialist either. He had been unconnected with the Conservatives' stand over Ireland and dropped the label 'Unionist' from his party's title. He pursued a policy of conciliation in India, which provoked criticism in his party. Churchill resigned from Baldwin's Shadow Cabinet in 1931, so that he could freely attack the leader's Indian policy. The critics could attract only

Centralization of London Transport

Criticism of Baldwin's foreign policy.

40-50 votes in the Commons, but were more powerful at party conferences. In this respect too Baldwin was more easily able to hold to his liberal Conservative policy because he was part of a national coalition. Foreign policy was also affected. The keynote of the National Government's foreign policy till 1936 was support for the League of Nations, a stance which was attacked by Conservative right-wingers, who preferred to rely on British rearmament.

The Labour Party acquired a reputation for irresponsibility and socialism after the crisis of 1931, partly because it remained outside the National Government, partly because some socialists admired the miracles that socialist planning was said to be achieving in the Soviet Union. The unions, however, led by Ernest Bevin, remained uninterested in socialism, in that they had no wish to wait for or bring about a fundamental re-shaping of society. They were more interested in practical measures to create jobs, such as public works financed by government borrowing and a maximum working week of 40 hours. They derived more inspiration from Roosevelt's patching up of the capitalist system in the USA than from Stalin's creation of a wholly different economic system in the USSR. The economic planning envisaged in Labour manifestos of the 1930s owed more to the ideas of Keynes than to the practice of the Soviets. They recommended the nationalization of public utilities, such as power and transport, on the model of Herbert Morrison's London Transport, and some ailing industries, such as iron and steel and shipping, but there was no suggestion that this would be extended to the economy as a whole. It suited the National Government to paint Labour as an extreme left-wing party. The reality was very different.

In the 1930s the moderate Conservatism of Baldwin and the moderate 'socialism' of the Labour party almost monopolized serious political debate in Britain. Left-wing bodies such as the Socialist League and the Communist Party attracted some middle class support - the latter had some 18,000 members by 1939 - because they appeared the most reliable bulwark against the fascist

British politics monopolizsed by moderate parties

movements of Europe. Their appeal to the working class was negligible. The Communists tried to ally with the NUWM, but the latter was never particularly strong and was certainly not revolutionary. The lack of a credible threat from the Communists was probably a major factor in the failure of Sir Oswald Mosley's British Union of Fascists.

Mosley's New Party unsuccessfully fought the general election of 1931 with a programme based on keeping out foreign goods and government borrowing to finance public works, which would create employment. In the course of the next year, Mosley visited Italy and was impressed by many aspects of Mussolini's fascist regime. He now proposed to scrap British democracy and replace Parliament with a body representative of various industries and professions. He was proclaimed leader of the movement and his followers wore black shirts, a garment which gave them their popular name, the Blackshirts. Mosley's vigorous leadership led some on the right, such as Lord Rothermere, proprietor of the *Daily Mail*, and some on the left, such as Aneurin Bevan, a rising socialist politician, at first to prefer him to apparently ineffectual leaders such as Baldwin and MacDonald. The extent of his ability to mobilize popular support was never properly tested, for he was unready for the election of 1935 and had to call on his followers to abstain. Probably, by then his chances of mobilizing decisive levels of support were receding. By 1933 Britain was beginning to climb out of recession and the popular appetite for radical change, never perhaps very great, was reduced.

Failure of the New Party

8. The Twentieth-Century Monarchy

One of the factors making for stability in early 20th-century Britain was the survival and continued popularity of the monarchy. The ancient institution survived by adapting to new times. Queen Victoria and Edward VII were members of an international guild of monarchs, but George V domesticated the monarchy. Though his

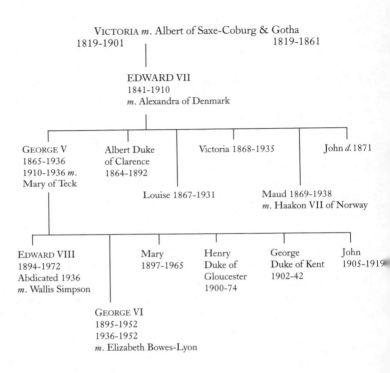

VICTORIA *m.* Albert of Saxe-Coburg & Gotha
1819-1901   1819-1861

EDWARD VII
1841-1910
m. Alexandra of Denmark

GEORGE V   Albert Duke   Victoria 1868-1935   John *d.* 1871
1865-1936   of Clarence
1910-1936 *m.*   1864-1892
Mary of Teck

Louise 1867-1931   Maud 1869-1938
                                         m. Haakon VII of Norway

EDWARD VIII   Mary   Henry   George   John
1894-1972   1897-1965   Duke of   Duke of Kent   1905-1919
Abdicated 1936   Gloucester   1902-42
m. Wallis Simpson   1900-74

GEORGE VI
1895-1952
1936-1952
m. Elizabeth Bowes-Lyon

wife, Queen Mary, was descended from the Kings of Württemberg,
she had been brought up in Britain and her father bore a British
title. Appreciating the damage which its German links had done to
the Russian monarchy, in 1917 George changed the name of
the royal family from Saxe-Coburg-Gotha to Windsor. Though he
looked like the last Tsar, George unheroically distanced himself from
his Imperial cousin when he found that offering him a refuge in
Britain after the Russian Revolution was likely to prove unpopular
with his subjects.

Royal family
adopts new
name

George V also by his practice redefined the role of a
constitutional monarch in Britain. His grandmother had expected
her ministers to take into account her views about policy, though she

could not enforce her will. She had also had strong prejudices in favour of and against certain ministers. George V followed expert advice on occasions when it was unclear who the ministers should be: in 1922 he took Balfour's advice that it was inappropriate for a peer to be Prime Minister when he asked Bonar Law rather than Lord Curzon to form a government. Policy-making he left to ministers. He took an active role in politics only when a crisis could not be resolved by the normal processes of politics. Hence in 1911 he agreed to create peers if necessary to end the deadlock between the Houses of Parliament; in 1914 he took initiatives in the hope of ending the Irish crisis; and in 1931 he assisted in the formation of the National Government. George made no difficulty about receiving MacDonald as the first Labour Prime Minister and relations between the two men became very warm.

George V projected the image of a dutiful monarch who was faithful to his wife, unlike his father, and whose family life was a model for his subjects to follow. In the name of duty he pledged total abstention from alcohol for the duration of the war and he spent the war years in a round of visits to the frontline, to hospitals, factories and dockyards. In the age of broadcasting, he became better known to his subjects than any previous monarch: from 1932 his Christmas broadcasts gave millions of his subjects an opportunity to hear their sovereign's voice. Rather to his own surprise, this 'ordinary sort of bloke' became very popular with his subjects. His Silver Jubilee of 1935 was intended to revive memories of his grandmother's great pageants of 1887 and 1897 and to suggest Britain's continued greatness. It certainly provided a chance for the King's subjects to demonstrate their affection for him.

George V's Christmas broadcasts

In January 1936 George's eldest son succeeded as Edward VIII. He had an image as a playboy prince very different from that of the dutiful monarch cultivated by his father. By 1936 his constant companion was Wallis Simpson, an American who already had one divorce behind her and was seeking a second. When she had it, so

Edward VIII accedes the throne 1936

Edward VIII (1894-1972) and Wallis Simpson (1896-1986)

Edward VIII
and Wallis
Simpson

Edward told Baldwin in November, he was determined to marry her. There were grave difficulties with the King's plans. As King, Edward was Supreme Governor of the Church of England. But members of the Church were not then permitted to marry a divorcee. Hence it was questionable whether a man who broke this prohibition could be head of the Church or King. Till December 1936 the British press contained nothing about the King's affair or the significance of Wallis' divorce hearing. Suddenly the news broke on 1 December. Baldwin had meanwhile consulted the Dominions and most respectable opinion there and in Britain thought that if the King continued with his plans, then he would have to abdicate. Such was the advice which Baldwin offered the King. Faced with a choice between his crown and his lover, Edward chose his lover and abdicated on 5 December.

Baldwin had overcome the crisis with great dispatch, before the King's various supporters, who included Churchill, could combine into a party.

In place of Edward, his younger brother Bertie, Duke of York, became King as George VI. He was already married to Elizabeth Bowes-Lyon, a strong woman whose support enabled her shy husband, afflicted with a crippling stammer, to become a much loved monarch whose conception of his royal office was very similar to that of his father. The new King and Queen were to prove admirable figureheads for a nation under siege in the dark days of the Second World War.

Edward VIII abdicates

George VI succeeds his brother

IX

THE RE-SHAPING OF THE UNITED KINGDOM

1. Ireland: The First World War
and the Easter Rising of 1916

BEFORE the war, the Ulster Unionists had asserted their loyalty to the Crown while practising disloyalty. The outbreak of war in 1914 gave them an opportunity to align their words and their deeds by volunteering for the army. Kitchener was grateful for the services of a well-organized force like the Ulster Volunteer Force (UVF) and he agreed that it should serve in the army as a unit, the 36th Ulster Division, with its own insignia and officers. Pride in the exploits of their Division reinforced the Ulster Unionists' sense that they were different and special. The role of the Division on the first day of the Somme offensive was especially noteworthy. They took more ground than any other unit in the army, though because of the lesser success of other divisions most of it could not be held. Their sacrifice was heroic: two thousand died, three thousand more were wounded. In a sense, this was payment up front for the ultimate reward of a Northern Ireland exempted from Home Rule.

Ulster Volunteer Force at the Somme

The Irish Home Rule leader, John Redmond, pledged his support for Britain's war effort too. His reward was the immediate passage into law of the Home Rule Bill, though it would actually come into operation only when the war was over. Redmond opened the way to the mass recruitment of Irishmen into the British Army: by the end of 1915, 81,000 had volunteered. Redmond's own son was to die in the course of the conflict. The leader's policy was not approved by all Irish nationalists. Some wanted nothing to do with a war for the preservation of the British Empire: notably, Sinn Féin (Gaelic for 'Ourselves alone'), a political party founded in 1905, dedicated to total independence for the whole of Ireland; and the

Home Rule Bill passed

Irish Republican Brotherhood (IRB), a secret organization prepared to use physical force, biding its time till a favourable moment for armed revolt should occur. The split in the nationalist movement was reflected in a split of the Irish Volunteers, formed before the war to uphold the Home Rule cause: 150,000 followed Redmond's line; 13,500 rejected it.

Division among Irish nationalists

To begin with, Redmond carried the bulk of Irish opinion with him. There were a number of by-elections in 1915 and his party won them all. Yet the war turned out not to be the short conflict he had envisaged. The sacrifices of Irish lives in the war mounted up, but Home Rule remained only a future prospect. In contrast to the Ulster Unionists, other Irishmen were not allowed to wear any national emblem on their uniforms (they had hoped to wear the harp) and they were always referred to as 'British'. Such treatment hardly helped them to feel that the war was theirs. Political changes in Britain were not reassuring. In June 1915 Asquith became leader of a coalition government which included Unionists such as Bonar Law and Edward Carson. Redmond was offered a seat in the Cabinet, but he refused it. By 1916 there were signs that Redmond was losing his hold on the loyalties of his compatriots. Membership of his local party organization began to fall away. As yet, however, there was no popular alternative to his programme and his leadership. That alternative Irish extremists now set themselves to supply.

Extremism gathers support in Ireland

Plans for a rebellion had begun to germinate as early as the summer of 1914. It was recalled that war with France had provided an opportunity for revolt in the later 18th century, and it was hoped that Britain's war with Germany might do likewise in the 20th century. An American Irish group arranged for Sir Roger Casement to travel to Germany to procure arms and support for a rebellion in Ireland. The Germans were not enthusiastic, but finally offered support and dispatched 20,000 rifles to the Kerry coast in April 1916. There they would be met by Casement, who would have travelled there by U-boat, and by Irish rebels. Meanwhile, the Military

Council of the IRB had decided that the spring of 1916 was a good time for a rebellion and had adopted a plan to seize the major strategic buildings in Dublin on Easter Day. Almost everything went wrong. No one was there to meet the ship carrying the German rifles, which was finally intercepted by a British warship and was scuttled by its captain. Casement attempted to land, but was arrested before he could contact any of the conspirators. Lacking arms, some of the leaders tried to call the rising off, but the IRB decided to start it on Easter Monday.

Easter Rising

Around 1500 people were involved in the insurgency on Easter Monday. Outside Dublin, very little happened. Inside the city, the poorly organized rebels seized a few important buildings, above all the General Post Office. From the steps of the GPO they read the Proclamation of the Provisional Government of the Irish Republic, effectively a statement of the kind of regime that they hoped to set up in Ireland. The revolt lasted for several days, until Patrick Pearse surrendered on the following Saturday. In the intervening days about 450 people were killed, 2,600 were injured and British artillery attacks on rebel strongholds destroyed parts of the city. At no time was British control seriously endangered: the rebels failed to take either Dublin Castle or Trinity College. In military terms, the Easter Rising was a dismal failure.

2. Ireland's War of Independence

What mattered about the Easter Rising was not so much the events in Dublin of that Easter week, but the British reaction to them. The rebels sent to prison in Britain were spat at when they were marched to the waiting ships, an indication of how little support they originally had. Badly rattled by a revolt in the middle of a desperate war, however, the British authorities over-reacted. Martial law was proclaimed throughout Ireland and there were mass arrests, of nearly 3,500 people, more than had taken part in the rising. The whole

Martial law declared in Ireland

population began to acquire a sense of grievance. The government was warned by Redmond not to turn the rebels into martyrs by executing them, but he was ignored. In early May fifteen rebels were shot; Casement was convicted of treason and later hanged.

The authorities in Dublin Castle knew nothing of the IRB or of the socialist Irish Citizen Army, the groups which had participated in the rising. They blamed Sinn Féin, which they did know about, and most of the arrests fell on this political group. Ironically, the authorities' mistake did more than anything else to raise the profile of what had been an insignificant group. Its nationalist credentials were now impeccable. Once released, its leader Arthur Griffith improved its organization and resumed publishing a newspaper. Support for the party began to increase as the war became ever more unpopular. A turning point was the defeat of Redmond's Home Rulers in a by-election in early 1917 and the election instead of a Sinn Féin candidate. This was the first of a number of by-election victories for Sinn Féin. One of them was won by Éamon de Valera, who soon after was elected president of the party. The party gained too from the death after a hunger strike in prison of Thomas Ashe, a survivor of the Easter Rising. His funeral became a massive exhibition of support for Sinn Féin. Over 30,000 people gathered to hear a speech by Michael Collins, a member of the IRB. A volley of shots was fired at the graveside. Nonetheless, Redmond still had substantial support in Ireland, as by-election results in early 1918 proved. Sinn Féin did not yet control Ireland.

Sinn Féin blamed for the Easter Rising

The transformation of Irish politics was completed by the re-emergence of the issue of conscription. Ireland had been exempted from the imposition of conscription in the rest of the United Kingdom in 1916, for fear of an adverse public reaction. In March 1918, however, stemming Ludendorff's offensive on the Western Front cost the British Army about 300,000 casualties, leaving it very short of troops. In these desperate circumstances, Parliament passed the Military Service Bill giving the government power to extend

Military Service Bill 1918

conscription to Ireland when it needed to do so. Not a single Irishman was ever conscripted, but the new act was enough to provoke an unprecedented display of Irish unity in opposition to it. The Home Rulers, led by John Dillon since Redmond's recent death, pulled out of Parliament and joined with churchmen, Sinn Féin and labour leaders in agreeing to obstruct the implementation of conscription in Ireland. There remained the divisive issue of what might follow a campaign against the threat of conscription: Home Rule or independence? Lloyd George's government at this point intervened again in such a way as to undermine Dillon's moderates. They decided to appoint Field Marshal Lord French as Viceroy, which seemed to suggest that Ireland was to be brought under military rule. French proceeded to confirm that suggestion. There had been some desultory contacts between some Irish nationalists and the Germans, and fearing a German plot, French ordered the arrest of nationalist leaders such as Griffith and de Valera. They were only too pleased to be arrested, since they knew that their arrests would help to turn Irish opinion away from any compromise with Britain. Everywhere, except in Protestant Ulster, Sinn Féin clubs were founded, 110,000 of them by the end of 1918. A national network of volunteer organizers was established and money poured in from membership dues. The general election of December 1918 marked the triumph of Sinn Féin. It won 73 seats, whereas the Home Rule party could manage only seven. The remainder, mostly in the north, were taken by the Unionists.

Growth of Irish nationalist parties

Success for Sinn Féin in general election 1918

The Sinn Féin MPs refused to attend at Westminster and instead formed their alternative parliament in Dublin, Dáil Éireann. There they accepted the Proclamation of the Republic of 1916 and pledged to work for its establishment by any possible means. They sent representatives to the peace conference at Versailles to argue in favour of Irish independence, but they wholly failed to arouse the interest of the American President Woodrow Wilson, the only statesman who might have taken up their cause. Independence would not be won in Paris; it would have to be won in Ireland.

Proclamation of the Republic accepted

In the course of 1919-20 the nationalists began to establish some of the structures of an alternative Irish state. The machinery of British justice was gradually supplanted by a hierarchy of Dáil courts. The Dáil Ministry of Local Government developed contacts with the local government bodies, which became especially strong when Sinn Féin won control of so many county and local district councils in 1920. The Dáil and its ministries were, from the British point of view, illegal and the Irish nationalists were bound to find themselves in conflict with the agencies of law and order, the Royal Irish Constabulary (RIC) and the magistrates. Attacks on the RIC were also the most obvious means by which the nationalists could equip themselves with arms. From early in 1919 the Irish nationalists began to think of themselves as being at war with the police, even though the policemen were Irish and often had good relations with their communities. The key figure in this war was Michael Collins, who directed the actions of the Irish Republican Army (IRA), which he had been building up since 1916, and used the elite IRB in the struggle with British intelligence. The war was not a matter of regular battles, but of ambushes and assassinations. It involved terrorizing Irishmen, if they were suspected of being informants, or of fraternizing with the enemy, or simply of being insufficiently enthusiastic for the cause. *IRA engages in war of terrorism with the Irish police*

The British only gradually came to think of the struggle as a war rather than a not wholly unusual spate of crimes of violence against the police. As they did wake up to what was going on, IRA violence began to be followed by counter-violence and that again by yet more violence. It became necessary for the British to help out the army and the police by recruiting an auxiliary force. There were plenty of young men available who could not settle to civilian life after the war and were used to a career of adventure and bloodshed. Such men were added to the RIC and became known as the Black and Tans, because a shortage of equipment obliged them to wear khaki uniform with the black-green caps and belts of the police. They were not used to showing much respect for life or property, and in any case, the *Black and Tans sent to reinforce the RIC* conditions of service in Ireland imposed a severe strain on any self-discipline they had. They were liable to sudden attack by bomb or gun and enemies rapidly melted back into the general population. Not surprisingly, the Black and Tans tended to see the whole population as hostile and had little compunction about subjecting it to a reign of terror.

The problem of countering IRA violence was difficult. The Restoration of Order in Ireland Act of 1920 gave power to the military commander General Macready to arrest and hold without trial anyone suspected of connections with Sinn Féin and then to try them by court martial. One of the main duties of the Black and Tans was to arrest these suspects. The military hankered also after a policy of official reprisals after attacks by the IRA (by destroying the houses of known adherents of Sinn Féin, for example), but when these were tried, the IRA simply attacked government sympathizers. The Black and Tans undertook many unauthorized reprisals: whole towns were terrorised and partially destroyed in retaliation for IRA attacks; after eleven presumed British intelligence officers were killed in November 1920, the Black and Tans fired randomly into a crowd at a football match, killing twelve and injuring sixty more. The British had lost control of their own forces.

Despite some horrific incidents, violence never spread over the whole country, partly because the forces engaged were quite small: a total of perhaps 40,000 on the British side; and according to Collins, no more than 3,000 IRA operatives at any one time. Deaths among police and troops during the whole of the war amounted to about 230; among the IRA and civilians the best estimate is 750. By 1921 there were in London signs of mounting public disquiet concerning the war in Ireland. Churchmen, some of the press, a Labour Party commission of inquiry, all condemned the methods being used to repress the Irish, which seemed ineffectual and were blackening Britain's name in the world. The pressure on Lloyd George to start talks to secure a truce was becoming irresistible. The initial efforts

Restoration of Order in Ireland Act 1920

Suppression of the populace by Black and Tans

Britain seeks peaceful resolution to war in Ireland

BUST OF MICHAEL COLLINS (1890-1922)

were unproductive, but continuation of the war looked a bleak prospect for both sides. Lloyd George feared the public response in England should he have to increase the number of troops in Ireland and meet the cost. George V made a speech in Belfast appealing 'to all Irishmen to pause, to stretch out the hand of forbearance and conciliation, to forgive and forget and to join in making for the land which they love a new era of peace, contentment and goodwill'. His speech was at once followed by Lloyd George's offer to de Valera of a conference to consider the Irish problem. If the Irish leadership was receptive, it was perhaps because outright victory in the near future looked improbable. Death and imprisonment had taken a fearful toll of members of the IRA, and it was even shorter of materials than of men.

A truce came into operation on 11 July 1921. It was followed by a long period of negotiations, the final result of which was the Anglo-Irish Treaty of December 1921. The Treaty gave Ireland Dominion status within the Empire, similar to that enjoyed by Canada or Australia. A Northern Ireland Parliament would exercise power in the six counties of the north which had a Protestant majority, though the boundaries were to be reviewed by a future commission. All members of the Dáil were to pledge their primary allegiance to the King, not the Free State. Finally, Britain would retain key defensive naval ports round the coast. This treaty settled the quarrel between Britain and Ireland. It was, however, deeply controversial within Ireland. War between Britain and Ireland was therefore replaced by civil war within Ireland.

Anglo-Irish Treaty 1921

Northern Ireland created

3. Ireland Partitioned, 1920-39

The Anglo-Irish Treaty was finally ratified by the Dáil by 64 votes to 57. The slender margin of victory for the supporters of the Treaty indicates how controversial it was. The division of Ireland did not seem the crucial stumbling block at the time, since everyone assumed that the division would prove temporary. Debate instead centred on whether the Irish state recognized in the Treaty would actually be free. The oath of allegiance to the King seemed to some to betray the very notion of an independent Irish nation.

The split in the Dáil was followed by a split in the country and civil war. On one side the pro-Treaty men formed the first government of the Irish Free State. They were headed by Griffith and Collins. The latter headed the Free State Army, which included the bulk of the old IRA. At first, it was probably outnumbered by its opponents, but energetic recruiting drew in many from the

Institution of the Treaty provokes Irish Civil War

unemployed and those demobilized from the British Army. Soon the government had an army of 60,000 equipped with artillery. It also increasingly won the support of the property-owners of Ireland, since it alone held out any prospect of a return to law and order under a settled government. The anti-Treaty forces served under the figurehead of de Valera, but in reality a junta of military men was in control. They tried to hold a line from Waterford to Limerick, since their main forces were in the south and west, but no town could resist for long artillery bombardments from the pro-Treaty forces. By late July 1922, after two months of fighting, the pro-Treaty government had won the first phase of the war, when the two sides directly confronted each other. Thereafter, the anti-Treaty forces resorted to the same tactics of guerrilla warfare which had served against the British. The familiar round of violence and reprisals recurred. Rumours abounded of torture of guerrillas by government troops; it was even said that guerrillas were dispatched by being chained to landmines. Even so, public opinion hardened against the guerrillas, influenced perhaps by the condemnation of the Catholic Church. At last, in May 1923 there was a ceasefire, though the guerrillas did not hand over their arms, but hid them where they could be recovered later. The Civil War had cost more lives and done more damage to property than had the revolutionary struggle against the British of 1916-21. It had also created long-lasting feuds and enmities which affected the new Ireland for decades to come.

Regression to guerrilla warfare

Ceasefire May 1923

In the Irish Free State WT Cosgrave and his pro-Treaty party won the election of 1923 and dominated politics until 1932. Their main achievement was to establish a democratic society, with governmental, legal and administrative systems based on the British model. An unarmed police force, the Garda Síochána, succeeded in maintaining law and order despite the number of guns that circulated in the post-Civil War period. Within the new state the Catholic Church held a central place and its norms were reflected in the legal prohibition of divorce. What disappointed some nationalists was the failure to deliver prosperity. The economy continued to be based upon agriculture, and even that was not very efficient.

Perhaps the greatest achievement of Cosgrave's government was to induce de Valera and the losing side in the Civil War to participate in democratic politics from 1927 onwards. De Valera founded a political party called Fianna Fáil, thereby turning the Free State into a functioning multi-party democracy. There were always elements within Ireland which looked to the gun as the ultimate arbiter in politics, but from the late 1920s most people were committed to pursuing their political goals through the democratic process. In 1932 de Valera won the general election and entered upon a period in power that lasted until 1948.

In power, de Valera sought above all to modify the terms of the Anglo-Irish Treaty of 1921. He abolished the oath of allegiance to the British monarch and fought an economic war with Britain rather than meet the payments due under the Treaty. Irish agricultural exports to Britain suffered when the British retaliated by imposing tariffs on them, and eventually in 1938 the matter was settled by a one-off payment of £10 million. At the same time the Irish ports that remained British naval bases were transferred to Irish control. In 1937 de Valera drew up a new constitution, which stressed the sovereign right of the Irish people to direct their own affairs. Irish jurisdiction was said to extend across all 32 counties of Ireland, though it would only be applied to 26 of them until the North was reintegrated.

De Valera found it much easier to achieve his political goals than his economic ones. He tried to nurture Irish industry by imposing duties on many imports, but in a country lacking crucial raw materials such as coal and a large home market it was difficult to develop industries which could compete in world markets. Ireland remained dependent on agriculture, but agricultural exports struggled in the adverse trading conditions of the 1930s. Irish incomes did slowly

Democratic politics start to prevail in the Free State

De Valera comes to power 1932

De Valera campaigns for greater independence

Irish economy suffers

increase, but the gap between them and British ones widened: in 1931 average Irish incomes per head were 61 per cent of the British average; in 1939 the figure was 49 per cent. Inevitably, emigration began to increase again.

Northern Ireland had been created as a political entity by the Government of Ireland Act of 1920. Sinn Féin had opted out of any discussions concerning it and had therefore been in no position to insist on protection for the rights of the large Catholic minority, consisting of about one third of the total population of the province of 1,250,000. The Treaty negotiations of 1921 had also largely ignored the internal structure of the North. Believing that it was only a matter of time before Ireland was reunited, the northern Catholics at first refused to sit in Parliament, or to serve on school boards or in local government. As a result, the state created in the North was wholly in the Protestant image. The Ulster Unionist Party (UUP) exercised unchallenged political dominance. Sir James Craig, veteran of the anti-Home Rule campaign, became Prime Minister, a post he retained until his death in 1940. His cabinet hardly changed in two decades: when he died, five of his seven cabinet ministers had been continuously in office since 1921. Measures were taken to entrench the UUP even more securely in power. Originally, a system of proportional representation was used in parliamentary elections, but in 1929 it was replaced by a first-past-the-post system, which tended to ensure that the Catholic minority could not achieve representation. In local government, most notoriously in Derry, constituency boundaries were drawn and qualifications for the vote determined in such a way as virtually to ensure the powerlessness of Catholic voters.

Exclusion of Catholics from power in Northern Ireland

Northern Ireland had originally been born in a time of widespread Catholic refusal to co-operate and difficulties all along the borders with the South. The government had therefore passed the Special Powers Act allowing the Home Secretary to do whatever seemed necessary for preserving the peace, including imposition of a curfew, prohibition of drilling and special uniforms and arrest and

Special Powers Act 1922

detention of anyone suspected of planning an act disruptive of peace and order. In the early 1920s Northern Ireland had lacked full control of the police and had recruited its own special constables. Later they were retained on a part-time basis. Usually fervent Protestants, they conducted a covert war against the IRA. There was persistent low-level inter-communal violence in the North, with the IRA taking the lead on the Catholic side, the Specials on the Protestant. The violence helped to keep Catholics and Protestants in fear of each other.

Education Act for Northern Ireland 1923

In 1923 an Education Act for Northern Ireland attempted to create an inclusive and secular educational system in the hope that adherents of the two religions might gradually grow closer together. Catholic clergy and Protestant groups campaigned against the policy and largely got their way. Secular schools remained few; most children were educated in specifically Catholic or Protestant schools. Evidently, the two groups wanted to remain as distinct from each other as possible.

Before 1914 the north of Ireland had differed from the rest of the island in that it had a significant industrial sector: a textile industry, chiefly linen, and shipbuilding and engineering. These industries depended heavily on exports, but after the First World War they operated in a difficult environment. World trade was in the doldrums most of the time, with shipping particularly badly hit. The linen industry was hit by the increasing use of man-made fibres in textiles.

High unemployment in Northern Ireland

The result in Northern Ireland was a stubbornly high rate of unemployment, usually of about a quarter of the insured workforce. The Northern Irish government lacked resources and was not generously treated by the United Kingdom government. Housing in town and country was of the poorest standard. The death rate was the worst in the British Isles apart from the Irish Free State: infant mortality was getting worse and tuberculosis was a terrible scourge of the young adult population. Catholics suffered disproportionately from every ill. Most of them were unskilled manual labourers who were among the first to lose their jobs in a downturn. Poverty ensured that they left school as early as possible: they therefore lacked the education to compete for jobs in the public service. They lived in the worst housing in the province. It is not surprising that every now and again religious war broke out. Riots in Belfast in 1935 left eleven dead and almost 600 injured and a trail of damage to property. Britain might have reduced the scale of its Irish problem, but it had by no means got rid of it altogether.

Catholics
disadvant-
aged

4. The Status of Wales and Scotland

In the years before the First World War, the Liberals discussed the possibility of granting Home Rule to Ireland as part of a re-modelling of the United Kingdom as a federal state, with England, Wales and Scotland as well as Ireland responsible for their internal affairs, while an imperial Parliament at Westminster dealt with foreign policy, defence and the economy. Home Rule for Scotland became Liberal policy and the Welsh Liberal Council declared for Home Rule for Wales in 1911, though the attention of most Welsh Liberals was concentrated on disestablishing the Anglican Church in Wales.

Movements
for Home
Rule in
Scotland
and Wales

The issue of Home Rule in Ireland absorbed Liberal attention till the early 1920s and thereafter the Liberals were no longer in a position to deliver any of their schemes. The Conservatives were not keen on such a drastic change as 'Home Rule All-Round', while in the thirty years after the Great War Labour was more concerned with establishing itself in the United Kingdom as a whole than with schemes for devolved governments in Wales and Scotland.

No doubt, things might have been different had there been obvious and fervent support for Home Rule in Wales and Scotland, but of this there was little sign. In 1925 Plaid Cymru (the party of Wales) was founded, but its main concern was the preservation of the Welsh language at a time when only 37 per cent of Welshmen were Welsh-speakers. This issue was not the central one between the wars, when the Principality's main industries were under pressure.

Plaid Cymru
founded

Scottish
National
Party
founded
1928

A Scottish National Party was founded in 1928, but before 1939 it had little impact beyond the confines of the Scottish universities. Events in Ireland did not initiate a general re-shaping of the United Kingdom.

X

THE BRITISH COMMONWEALTH AND EMPIRE BETWEEN THE WORLD WARS

1. The Impact of the First World War

THE First World War seemed to show that everything which imperialists like Chamberlain had said about the value to Britain of the Empire was true. Britain called upon the manpower of the Empire to supplement its own: about two and a half million colonials fought in Britain's armies and over 200,000 of them were killed. Imports from the Empire also poured into Britain to keep the population fed and the war industries supplied with raw materials. Imports from Canada tripled; those from Africa, Asia and Australia nearly doubled. It was therefore fitting that the imperialists of Chamberlain's day should have returned to power. Joseph Chamberlain himself had died in 1914, but once the Coalition Government was established in 1915, the imperialists made a comeback. Milner and Curzon were both members of Lloyd George's five-man inner cabinet, which ruled after December 1916. Men such as John Buchan and Leopold Amery held significant advisory positions. The conditions looked favourable for realizing their hopes of expanding and consolidating the Empire.

Resurgence of Imperialism in British government

It was clear that provided that Britain won the war, there would be opportunities for imperial expansion. Britain had not fought in order to expand the Empire, but the opportunity to undo the work of Bismarck, who had intruded the Germans into Africa and the Pacific, was too good to miss. In any case, South Africa, Australia and New Zealand had their own shopping lists of desirable German territories and deserved a reward for their contribution to the war. The other area outside Europe where the war had made a difference was the Middle East. The Ottoman Empire had thrown its lot in with

Opportunity for Imperialist expansion in the Middle East

Germany, which encouraged the British to undermine its hold over Arabia, Mesopotamia and Syria. By 1918 the Turks' Asian empire was in ruins. What happened to the area was of deep concern to Britain. Loose Turkish control had in many ways suited Britain well, which is why Britain had lent Turkey support for much of the 19th century. Its demise might create a power vacuum in an area of great interest to the Empire. The Suez Canal and Red Sea route was important to imperial communications. Oil was beginning to be an important commodity. It seemed vital to prevent any other great power from replacing the weak Ottomans and extension of British control appeared the surest way of attaining that objective.

In 1919, the international situation looked benign. In some ways, the good old days of the mid-Victorian period seemed to have returned, in that France was once again the only serious colonial rival in most of the world. At the end of the war, British power still seemed to bestride the world. Germany was defeated. Russia had temporarily collapsed into revolution and civil war, leaving Britain free of anxiety that it might expand into the Middle East, or India or China. The United States seemed uninterested in claiming the global power to which its economic weight entitled it, and once the war was over, it retreated into isolation.

However promising the international situation seemed at the end of the war, there had been moments during the conflict when defeat had seemed all too possible. Britain's vulnerability had been noted by subject peoples and British rule would never again seem so unshakable. Moreover, Britain had been compelled to concentrate its forces on the Western Front. At one point, there were only 15,000 British troops in India, fewer than half the number stationed there at the time of the Mutiny. In these circumstances, reliance on force was out of the question. Britain could retain control only by winning the goodwill of its colonial subjects. In India promises about the future had to be made, but promises aroused hopes that could not later be dashed with impunity and they whetted appetites for yet more concessions. In Egypt too it seemed wise to buy off potential opposition by offering promises concerning the country's future system of government, but this promise, like the Indian ones, was incompatible with the consolidation which imperialists envisaged.

The First World War affected the British Empire in contradictory ways. Initially, it created a more favourable international situation for British interests for at least the following decade. On the other hand, in some areas it helped to strengthen separatist forces and nationalist sentiments within the Empire, which were to become the principal factors thwarting imperialist ambitions.

2. Towards Indian Independence

In the first years of the Great War, India was remarkably peaceful. Some officials, like the outgoing Viceroy Hardinge (1912-16) and the incoming Chelmsford (1916-21), urged that concessions should be made while they could appear as the product of generosity rather than fear. In the event, nothing happened until opposition to British rule began to look formidable. The moderates and extremists in India at last made up their quarrel in 1916 and at the end of the same year the Muslim League and the Congress Party patched up their differences. The revived nationalist movement began to set up Home Rule Leagues. At the same time, there was growing popular unrest, caused by trade disruption, inflation and the endless demands of the British for money and manpower. In these circumstances, it appeared to the leading British officials that it was essential to make a big conciliatory gesture. The new Secretary of State for India, Edwin Montagu, therefore made in the House of Commons in 1917 a radical declaration of policy. He announced that the aim of British policy in India was 'the progressive realization of responsible government in India as an integral part of the Empire'. In other words, India was to follow the path earlier trodden by the 'white Dominions' such as Australia and Canada towards self-government.

Indian self-government a stated aim of British policy 1917

Montagu's idea was not novel, but in ordinary circumstances so radical an initiative would probably have been blocked by inertia in London and the entrenched conservatism and suspicion of Indians characteristic of the Indian Civil Service (ICS). After three years of war, however, a mixture of appreciation of the large contribution of Indians to the war effort and fear of what Montagu called 'a seething, boiling, political flood raging across the country' swept caution aside, despite resignations in the ICS and the consternation of the House of Lords. Montagu toured India in 1917-18 and with the Viceroy Chelmsford produced a report that became the basis of a new constitution for India, enacted in December 1919. At the provincial level there was to be 'dyarchy' or double government. The governor and his council were to control matters such as revenue, justice and police; ministers responsible to elected assemblies were to deal with education, public health and agriculture. The electorate was determined by a property qualification, satisfied nationwide by about five million people. At the centre there was less change, but the principle of consultation with representatives of (usually moderate) Indian opinion was extended.

New Indian constitution enacted 1919

The Montagu-Chelmsford reforms were of greater interest to the educated elite than to the masses, but as the war ended the masses were in ferment in several places, particularly in the Punjab. The Muslims of the province were roused by British attacks on Turkey, the Sultan of which was still regarded as the Caliph or representative of the Prophet. The Rowlatt Acts were therefore passed in 1918 to give the government additional weapons against insurgents. They permitted imprisonment without trial and allowed judges to try political cases without juries. These powers were never actually used, but the mere passage of the acts inflamed opinion. It was at this point that the lawyer Mohandas Gandhi, former champion of the Indians of South Africa, first came to prominence in India itself by proposing a *hartal*, a traditional method of protest involving the cessation of all activity for a day. Riots spread and the government became

Rowlatt Acts 1918

Gandhi rises to prominence

increasingly jumpy. There was fear of a general collapse of British authority. Against this background, General Dyer proclaimed martial law in the Punjab and banned public meetings. On 13 April 1919, the day of a Sikh festival, there were thousands of people in Amritsar, a city holy to the Sikhs. When large numbers gathered in a city park, Dyer resolved to show that the law could not be flouted with impunity. He seems to have thought that a good way of teaching the people a lesson and stemming the tide of insurgency was to order his troops to fire without warning on the unarmed crowd. They ceased only when ammunition ran out. By then between 379 (British figures) and 1,000 (Congress Party figures) lay dead, some not shot but crushed in the panic. The governor of the Punjab approved Dyer's action, but a committee of inquiry decided that he had acted on a mistaken idea of his duty and relieved him of his post. The repercussions of the affair included a great wave of unrest in India and a non-co-operation movement led by Gandhi, but the Indians were not united and eventually the storm abated. *Martial Law declared in the Punjab 1919*

Amritsar massacre

For most of the 1920s things went quiet in India. The new provincial governments worked, despite being boycotted by the Congress Party. Yet much of the former British self-assurance was gone. The morale of the British rulers of India seems gradually to have dropped. Indians began to be taken into the Indian Army as officers and into the ICS, which came to seem a less attractive career for the ambitious Briton. If the writer George Orwell, who served in Burma in the 1920s, is to be believed, many British officials had doubts about the morality and effectiveness of the regime they were part of. The Anglo-Indian establishment was subjected to corrosive criticism in works such as EM Forster's novel *A Passage to India*, published in 1924. *British rule in India criticized*

The act embodying the Montagu-Chelmsford reforms had provided for a review of their operation after ten years. The review, undertaken by the Simon Commission, began early. The Commission outraged Indian opinion, because it had on it not a single Indian. As *The Simon Commission* it went round India on its fact-finding tour, the Commission attracted demonstrations and riots. The nationalist movement revived. In 1928 it produced its own constitution for an independent India. There was a clear danger of a breach between Britain and impatient Indian nationalists, but the Labour government of Ramsay MacDonald, which governed from 1929 to 1931, and the new Viceroy, Lord Irwin, were determined to avoid one. Effectively, the Simon Commission's report was set aside and a Round Table Conference was proposed to discuss the future of India, but the Congress Party refused to co-operate. Men like Jawarharlal Nehru demanded a showdown with the British government. At this juncture Gandhi took over the protest movement.

Gandhi leads the protest movement 1928

Mohandas Gandhi came of a high caste Hindu family and was trained in Britain as a lawyer. He first made his name as a champion of the rights of the Indians in Natal, but returned to India in 1914. By the 1920s he was coming to be known as *Mahatma* or Great Soul. He cultivated the traditional image of the holy man, clad only in the garments of the peasant, the *dhoti* (loincloth) and shawl, and living the life of an ascetic, with frequent fasts and a vegetarian diet. He lived in a simple *ashram* (hermitage), where he made his own clothes using a spinning wheel. This activity dramatized his rejection of Britain and its machine-made textile exports and associated him with simple manual labour. He appeared quite unlike the other nationalist politicians who often found it hard to reach beyond the ranks of the educated elites to which most of them belonged. By birth and training Gandhi belonged to these elites too, but the image he presented embodied the cause and enabled him to appeal to the Indian masses. Above all, he had a capacity for investing the Indian cause with an aura of moral superiority. His determination to occupy the moral high ground underlay his rejection of violence and adherence to non-violent methods of protest.

In 1930 Gandhi demonstrated his rejection of British rule by undertaking a well-advertised march to the sea at Dandi, where he

MOHANDAS GANDHI (1869-1948)

proceeded to make salt, an illegal act, because it evaded the salt tax, one of the pillars of government finance. Gandhi was joined on his march by huge multitudes. He and tens of thousands besides were arrested. Having shown that he was an Indian patriot and had mass support, Gandhi was eager to compromise, eager because he was constant in his rejection of violence, which would certainly have resulted if no agreement with the British had been reached. He took part in a second Round Table Conference, though his policy made him the target of many hostile demonstrations in India. In 1932 he began yet another campaign of civil disobedience, but the resolute

The Salt Satyagraha 1930

National Government in Britain insisted on a crackdown: Congress leaders were arrested and public meetings forbidden. The movement collapsed. Even so, the Government of India Act of 1935 extended responsible government in the provinces, leaving governors with only a very limited ability to act independently. A new two-house parliament was created at the centre. This measure in effect made India a unitary federal state by bringing it all under one supreme legislative body. On the other hand, nationalists saw much to object to, in that the princely states were over-represented and their representatives were chosen by the princes, not elected by the people. It was also the case that important matters were reserved for the Viceroy, such as defence, foreign affairs, protection of minorities and tariffs on trade.

Government of India Act 1935

The Act of 1935 did not, then, win universal acclaim. Imperialists in Britain thought that it gave away far too much. Indian nationalists suspected that they had not won very much: perhaps, wrote the nationalist Bose, this was a design 'not for self-government, but for maintaining British rule in the new political conditions'. In retrospect, it is clear that an important precedent had been set: the British and the Indians had settled their quarrels more or less peacefully. They would continue to do so. Unfortunately, Indians of different religions would not be able to do the same.

3. The Problems of the Middle East

In 1914 Britain was supposed to be merely in temporary occupation of Egypt, which was still in theory part of the Ottoman Empire. Once Turkey declared war on Britain, the British felt bound to reject the Sultan's theoretical authority and they declared Egypt a protectorate. This was not the kind of clarification of their status which most Egyptians wanted, for it seemed to block any prospect of escape from the British Empire. In the hope of quietening them, the British government made a vague and cautious promise that at the end of the

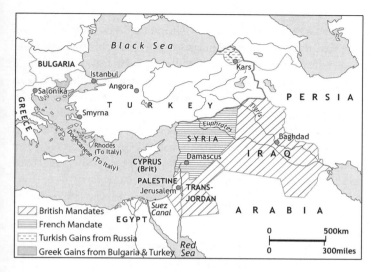

THE NEAR EAST: 1923
After the Treaties with Bulgaria and Turkey

war the issue of Egyptian self-government would be considered. When this time came, the British showed every sign of forgetting their promise. The Egyptians were not allowed to put their case to the peace conference and many nationalist leaders were arrested or exiled. Not unnaturally, the Egyptians forced the British to remember their pledges by demonstrations, riots, assassinations and sabotage. At the very same time, Britain was faced with unrest in India and Ireland, violence in Palestine and war in Afghanistan.

Egyptian self-government

Britain's forces were far too few to cope with enemies in so many places at once. Some of them had to be bought off. In Egypt it seemed that something that could be called independence was most likely to calm the people. Therefore, in 1922 the country was given full powers to manage its internal affairs. Foreign and military affairs were to continue to be run by Britain, however, and a British garrison remained to guard the Suez Canal. Britain kept what mattered to it,

Egypt granted government of internal matters 1922

and without the expenses involved in running the country as a colony. Egyptian nationalists were not so happy with this arrangement, unilaterally imposed by Britain, and Britain had occasionally to bring them into line by dispatching gunboats to Alexandria. The Egyptians preferred the presence of the British to the prospect of domination by Mussolini's Italy, however, and in the shadow of the Italian threat from Libya and then Abyssinia (Ethiopia), the Egyptians and British signed a treaty in 1936, which removed all restrictions on Egyptian independence, apart from a continued British military presence at the Canal and their shared control of the Sudan.

Egyptian Independence Treaty 1936

The war with the Ottoman Empire which the war with Germany had brought in its train compelled Britain to develop new policies not only for Egypt, but for the entire Middle East. It had to find ways of safeguarding its essential interests, which were twofold: to prevent any strategic threat to the security of the Canal, which was vital to imperial communications; and to safeguard access to oil, which was already in production in the states round the Persian Gulf and powered the Royal Navy.

In the earlier stages of the First World War, Britain's frontal assault on the hostile Ottomans at the Dardanelles was unsuccessful and peripheral attacks from the Persian Gulf or from Egypt achieved little with the small forces at the disposal of the British. In fact, the only way of undermining the hold of the Turks on the Middle East was to incite their Arab subjects to fight their masters, which they would do only if there was something in it for them. Hence promises of independence were made to Arab leaders and the British at last began to make military progress. The most colourful figure associated with the Arab revolt against the Turks was TE Lawrence, a historian and archaeologist, who was signed up during the war as an intelligence officer with expert knowledge of Arab culture. He attached himself to the Arab leader Sheikh Faisal and played a significant role in mobilizing Arab guerrilla forces against the Turks. In the summer of 1917 he took the port of Aqaba and later used the

Lawrence of Arabia

guerrilla forces to distract the Turks while the regular troops under Allenby advanced into Palestine and Syria.

British advances at the expense of the Turks reignited the ancient rivalry in the region between the British and the French, which the British sought to defuse by means of a promised partition of the region between the two powers. This agreement was not wholly compatible with the promises made to the Arabs. Yet no one supposed that the Arabs would be able to establish a stable political settlement in the Middle East, which would therefore have to be divided into spheres of influence assigned to the major powers, in practice, France and Britain.

France and Britain share authority over Middle East

The British made one other commitment as they contemplated the future of the Middle East without Turkish control. It was to be even more fraught with important consequences than their other promises. In November 1917 the Balfour Declaration gave the blessing of the British government to 'the establishment in Palestine of a national home for the Jewish people'. This Declaration fulfilled the hopes of the Zionists among the Jews. Partly in reaction to outbreaks of anti-semitism (hostility to Jews) in Europe, especially in the Tsarist Empire, many Jews had concluded that they needed a national home of their own. Their reading of the Bible convinced them that this home should be in Palestine, centred on the holy city of Jerusalem or Zion. By no means all Jews shared these views. Edwin Montagu, the only Jew in the British cabinet, believed that the future of the Jews was bound up with that of their host societies in Europe and America. He also foresaw that encouragement to Jews to emigrate to Palestine was likely to upset the existing inhabitants of the land, who were mostly Arab.

Balfour Declaration 1917

British motives for supporting the Zionist cause seem to have been mixed. Genuine sympathy for the Jews seems to have been one. For many years British statesmen had from time to time contemplated setting up a homeland for the Jews: Joseph Chamberlain had suggested Uganda as a possible site. If Britain actually acted in 1917, it was partly because it hoped to win over the Jewish lobby in Russia and the USA. Jewish pressure might help to keep the two countries in the war, which was believed to be essential to victory. Jewish businessmen such as Dr Chaim Weizmann had helped Lloyd George make up the shortage of shells in 1915, which put the future Prime Minister in his debt. Not least important, perhaps, was the assumption typical of the period that the immigration of European settlers into the area was bound to be good for everyone, including the Arabs, since the settlers would inevitably act as a civilizing and modernizing presence.

Scramble for the Middle East

In some ways the end of the First World War represented the high noon of imperialism. The war was immediately followed by scramble for the Middle East, a little like the late-19th-century scramble for Africa, except that this time there were only Britain and France to do the scrambling. The Arabs were allotted the Arabian Desert, but Britain and France divided up the rest of the area. France took Syria and the Lebanon; Britain gained Palestine, Transjordan, Iraq and the states of the Persian Gulf. These acquisitions were called 'mandates', territories entrusted to Britain by the League of Nations, to be ruled in the interests of their inhabitants. The British considered that they did this anyway, so that the new label made little difference in practice, other than making President Wilson feel better about the fact that Britain now held sway over not just a fifth, but a quarter of the land mass of the globe.

Iraq & Persia successfully resist Imperial control

Unfortunately for Britain, international recognition was not a sufficient basis for the exercise of power. The Middle East contained relatively sophisticated and in many places urban populations who were not prepared to be subjected to a colonial administration. In Iraq the British had soon to step back and rest content with the kind of military guarantees that they had in Egypt. An effort to bring Persia (Iran) fully within their orbit had to be abandoned altogether. These retreats turned out not to matter. Control of the Suez Canal, Aden and the Gulf states secured Britain's immediate interests. All that mattered otherwise was that other great powers should keep out of the area. The main threat was the Soviet Union and Britain was fortunate that regimes came to power in Turkey and Iran that were powerful enough to keep it at bay.

The only part of the Middle East to give serious trouble between the wars was Palestine. As Edwin Montagu had foreseen, from the start it proved difficult to reconcile Jewish and Arab claims upon the land, though the British authorities tried hard in the 1920s. There was a great deal of sympathy for the Jews in British governing circles, but the British could not wholly ignore the duty imposed on them under the terms of the mandate to safeguard the 'civil and religious rights of non-Jewish communities'. The problem was Jewish immigration, at first from Russia and then from intolerant Poland and Hungary. The resulting displacement of Arabs brought about an Arab uprising, beginning in 1929, and then Jewish retaliation. The British government threatened to restrict Jewish immigration and the sale of Palestinian lands to Jews, but a storm of protest led it to back down.

Start of the Palestinian Conflict 1929

Even had the British government been more resolute in 1930, it could probably not have prevented the decisive torrent of immigration in the 1930s. Between 1931 and 1936 the number of Jews in Palestine more than doubled to become really formidable for the first time. Most of the immigrants were fleeing from Hitler and, finding most other doors closed to them, including those of Britain and the USA, they made for Palestine. Their growing numbers encouraged the Jews of Palestine to become ever more assertive. The task of reconciling the Jewish and Arab communities became impossible, but the British had no idea how to get rid of their irksome duty. Some of them had once hoped that a Jewish presence might buttress their position in the Middle East, but by the 1930s it had become an embarrassment.

4. The White Dominions

Nothing encouraged those who hoped that Britain might find in its Empire a source of strength to counteract its slow relative economic decline and maintain its power in the world so much as the way in which all the white Dominions had rallied round the mother country in her hour of need during the First World War. It was the aim of imperialists like Leo Amery, Colonial Secretary from 1924 to 1929, to build on this precedent and bind Britain and the Dominions together in a federal structure in which the centre and the periphery would offer each other mutual economic and military support.

The results of the First World War were not all helpful to Amery's plans. The War had brought a demonstration of loyalty from the Dominions, but it had also strengthened their sense of nationhood. This was particularly so in the case of Australia and New Zealand. There, 25 April 1915, the day when the Anzacs had landed at Gallipoli, became the proudest day in their history. The troops had not defeated the enemy, but they had given an inspiring example of courage and endurance. In Australia 25 April became a national holiday and the occasion for patriotic marches and ceremonies. The war produced heroes like Sir John Monash, the Melbourne engineer who was promoted to the command of 200,000 soldiers and was important in rolling up the German defences in France in 1918. Many Australians convinced themselves that, man for man, they had displayed more energy and courage than the British. The statesmen too came to see themselves in a different light. The political leaders of the Dominions were all granted the right to attend the peace conference which ended the War and most of them received handsome territorial acquisitions. They signed the peace treaty as if they were entirely independent nations. Finally, their countries became full members of the new League of Nations.

Even if the war had not lessened the deference of the Dominions towards Britain, it is unlikely that their willingness to co-ordinate

Growing nationalism in British Dominions

their policies with Britain's would have survived the end of the great crisis that gave rise to it. The Dominions were soon insisting that Britain could not make international agreements affecting them without their explicit consent. When the Treaty of Washington limited the navies of major powers, which affected the balance of power in the Pacific, Australia insisted that it must sign independently. Any hope that the Dominions and Britain might pursue a joint foreign policy was dashed in 1922, when Canada and South Africa made it clear that if Britain got involved in a war with the revamped Turkey of Mustapha Kemal over the Straits, then it would not be able to count on their help. In 1923 Canada again demonstrated its independence in foreign policy by signing a treaty with the USA over fisheries without any reference to Britain. By the mid-1920s, it was clear that Britain's relationship with the Dominions had altered. A series of imperial conferences debated how the partnership between Britain and the Dominions was to be defined. In 1926 it was declared that Britain and the Dominions were

Treaty of Washington

> autonomous Communities within the British Empire, equal in status, in no way subordinate one to another in any aspect of their domestic or external affairs, though united by a common allegiance to the Crown, and freely associated as members of the British Commonwealth of Nations.

An imperial conference in 1930 accepted this definition and it became the basis of the Statute of Westminster of 1931, which formally gave to the Dominions the independence which they already in practice enjoyed. As far as the Dominions were concerned, the Empire had now metamorphosed into the Commonwealth. This new concept had a satisfyingly modern ring to it: it seemed like a mini-League of Nations. The question was whether it could ever be more than a talking shop.

Statute of Westminster 1931

Emergence of the Commonwealth

One little success that the imperialists had was to procure in 1922 the Empire Settlement Act to assist emigration from Britain to the Empire. In the 1920s 400,000 people were helped to emigrate from Britain to the colonies, which must have tightened the ties between them and somewhat alleviated the problems of unemployment in Britain (though it certainly did not cure them). The imperialists were anxious also to achieve Joseph Chamberlain's old aim of turning the Empire into a trading bloc. In the 1920s Britain continued to adhere to the Victorian policy of free trade. When the Conservatives proposed abandoning it in 1923, they suffered electoral defeat. The collapse of world trade in the great depression after 1929, however, reduced the appeal of free trade. In 1932 a tariff was levied on most imports, which made it possible to set up preferential arrangements for imports from the Empire. This was then done at the Imperial Economic Conference at Ottawa. As a result, the Dominions faced less competition in selling their agricultural surpluses and raw materials to Britain at a time when world markets were glutted, and there was less competition for British manufactures in the markets of the Dominions. In the 1930s, British trade certainly became more Empire-orientated, partly perhaps as a result of the new tariff policy. How good it was for the long-term health of British industry to take shelter in protected markets is another question.

As apprehensions about Germany mounted in the 1930s, the attitude of the Dominions was yet another pressure acting on British ministers to incline them to seek a peaceful way out of their problems. In the Czech crisis of 1938 the High Commissioners of the Dominions were very active in pressing for a peaceful outcome. They seemed to expect to influence British policy, while also expecting Britain to meet the costs of their defence. While Britain spent 5.6 per cent of its national income on defence, Australia spent 1 per cent and New Zealand even less. In the years before the Second World War it was open to question whether the ties to the Dominions were worth their cost (chiefly the cost of keeping up their defences).

Margin notes:

Empire Settlement Act 1922

Imperial Economic Conference 1932

High Commissions press for peaceful solution to Czech crisis 1938

5. The African Colonies

Britain's power to shape the future of the white Dominions, India or the Middle East turned out to be very limited. In many of its African colonies, however, it appeared to have almost unlimited power to shape the future in the absence of any organized or articulate African public opinion that might have different ideas about the destiny of these countries. The possible economic advantages for Britain of exploiting their resources were enticing too. Amery thought Kenya and Rhodesia (Zimbabwe) especially promising candidates for development.

What made Kenya and Rhodesia special was the number of white settlers already attracted to them even by 1914. Encouraging white settlement seemed much the speediest way of effecting a transition from African subsistence agriculture to the cultivation of cash crops. Cash crops, sold on the world market, would generate the tax revenue that could finance the general development of the colony. Such desirable changes could occur only if the settlers secured some of the best lands for themselves, as they did, in Kenya with government help. A few settlers were wealthy men who sought to finance their leisured lifestyle, but most were hard-working small farmers, described thus by Churchill in 1921:

> They have mostly sunk every penny they possess in their holdings, and they are engaged in a struggle, comparable only to actual war, to keep themselves alive and to make a home; fighting against the wilderness, the wild beasts, the loneliness, and the difficulties of these new, wild lands.

Since the settlers brought or borrowed their own capital, from the government's point of view, this was development on the cheap. What men like Amery hoped was that from the nuclei in existence in 1918 new white dominions would develop, tied to the mother-country by

White settlers in Kenya and Rhodesia encouraged

Whites dominate Southern Rhodesian legislative 1923

kinship and sentiment. In Southern Rhodesia the whites were relatively numerous and well entrenched and from 1923 a legislative assembly dominated by them assumed responsibility for the government of the colony, in line with the precedents set long before in the case of Canada and the Australian colonies. The Kenyan whites were not so fortunate. There were far fewer of them in a much larger black population, which in the 1920s and 1930s was beginning to organize itself politically. Still quicker off the mark in organizing

Kenya intolerant of British rule

themselves to oppose schemes for white domination were the Kenyan Indians. Opposition within Kenya was successful, because many people in Britain had doubts about handing over the destinies of millions of non-whites to a few thousand white settlers. In 1923 a White Paper declared that 'Primarily, Kenya is an African territory... The interests of the African natives must be paramount.' Later, in 1929, a Royal Commission affirmed that African policy should not be entrusted to the white settlers. The latter would be important in the colony for some decades yet, but it was already certain that Kenya would never be a white dominion.

Creating white dominions in black Africa had turned out to be controversial. Much less so was development by other means. It was agreed on all sides, by Labour ministers as well as Conservatives, that Britain had a duty to promote the moral and educational progress of the peoples in its charge and to exploit the natural resources of the lands they inhabited. Such exploitation would help Britain, of course, but it would also enrich the inhabitants and stimulate world trade. The problem was paying for this desirable development. The British were accustomed to the idea that colonies should be self-supporting and, particularly in the 1920s, were difficult to persuade of the need to spend money on them. In the 1930s the case for spending money was more widely accepted, but Britain was not believed to have the money to spend. As Colonial Secretary, Amery did get railways built in East Africa, roads in Nigeria and harbours in several places. He improved research facilities for tropical medicine and agriculture.

His Empire Marketing Board encouraged people to buy imperial products. What all these activities had in common was that they cost the government little. The infrastructure projects might at most receive a government loan. The Colonial Development Act of 1929 envisaged outright grants to colonial projects, but in practice gave little money away, only £1 million in its first three years.

His Empire Marketing Board encouraged people to buy imperial products. *Empire Marketing Board*

Colonial Development Act - 1929

It is not surprising that efforts to promote the economic development of the Empire in the inter-war years achieved little. World trade was in the doldrums and the prices of the primary products which the Empire produced fell dramatically. That is why private enterprise did not do more to help where the government hung back. Their revenues static, the colonial governments were rarely able to achieve more than marginal improvements in such matters as provision of hospitals and schools. The grand imperial vision of Leo Amery was not realized. The economic climate of the inter-war years perhaps did most to ensure stagnation in the Empire, but Amery had enjoyed little support from his ministerial colleagues and the Treasury had been particularly obstructive.

The years between the two world wars were years of intensive imperial propaganda. Empire Day was celebrated, Empire songs were sung, Empire essay competitions were held, but all that was achieved was a widespread feeling of pride in the sheer extent of the Empire. Some people, chiefly among the working class, were impervious even to that, but those who were susceptible were not won over to any kind of programme. The Empire did not seem to touch their vital interests, nor was it easy to represent it as a great moral cause. Imperialists like Amery never had a great popular movement at their backs. Yet there was no great drive for change either. There were already some people who wanted to turn the Empire into a free and equal association of peoples of many colours and races, but racial stereotypes were ingrained and most people had difficulty in accepting that Indians might be capable of self-government, never mind the Africans. In these circumstances, there

Empire Day

was little chance that the peoples of the Empire would be offered self-government and as yet, outside India and the Middle East, those peoples were not organized to demand it. In India the end of British rule was already in prospect in the 1930s, but elsewhere the British Empire still seemed a fixture.

XI

BRITISH FOREIGN POLICY, 1919-39

1. The Peace Treaties of 1919

THE conference charged with the huge task of remodelling the world after the First World War met at Paris in the first half of 1919. The main decisions were taken by the Big Three: President Wilson of the USA, the French Premier, Georges Clemenceau and Lloyd George. Germany was not a participant: the terms of peace were imposed upon it under threat of renewed war. Russia, in the middle of a civil war, was not represented either.

Versailles Peace Conference 1919

Lloyd George's first objective was to eliminate the German fleet as a menace to British security. It was interned at Scapa Flow and the German skeleton crews scuttled it. He could also agree with France and the Dominion premiers to share out the German colonial empire. Wilson was not keen on empires, and it was agreed to describe the new colonies as 'mandates', which implied that the new owners were entrusted with them for the good of the inhabitants. Lloyd George also had to take notice of popular demands for financial compensation from Germany, which had surfaced in the election of 1918. The French were also determined on 'reparations', since much of northern France had to be reconstructed after its use as a battlefield.

Reparations

On such issues as reparations and the fate of the German colonies and the Turkish Empire in the Middle East, Lloyd George tended to side with Clemenceau against Wilson. When it came to deciding what to do about Germany within Europe, however, Lloyd George often sided with Wilson against the French. Clemenceau wanted security against any fresh German invasion like those of 1870 and 1914. This goal was hard to achieve, given that the French population was only two thirds that of Germany and its heavy industry only a quarter as productive. Clemenceau wanted Germany wholly disarmed: in the end,

EUROPE: 1914

it was allowed 100,000 men to keep internal order. He also demanded Alsace-Lorraine, the Saar and the Rhineland. He succeeded in regaining Alsace-Lorraine, lost in 1871, but achieved only a temporary occupation and permanent demilitarization of the Rhineland and the exploitation of the Saar coalfields for fifteen years. The French did not regard this as sufficient to guarantee their security. They hoped that perhaps the League of Nations could be given an army to enforce the peace and when this hope was dashed, they sought an Anglo-American guarantee of their security. The American guarantee did not survive the American refusal to ratify the peace treaty and the British then refused to accept that their guarantee was binding either.

EUROPE: 1924

France's position had deteriorated since 1914, because it could no longer ally with Russia to keep Germany in check. The Communists, who had seized power in Russia in 1917, regarded themselves as the enemy of all capitalist states. France tried to find a substitute for the old Russian alliance by making alliances instead with the new states of eastern Europe, which had been carved out of the east European empires. Most of them were economically and militarily feeble; some, like Yugoslavia and Czechoslovakia, were uneasy unions of different linguistic groups; and some, like Poland and Czechoslovakia, had significant German minorities. Alliances with them did not solve France's security problem.

France allies with new Eastern European nations

237

German outrage at Versailles terms

The Germans were very resentful of the peace terms contained in what was called the Treaty of Versailles, signed in June 1919 in the Hall of Mirrors of Louis XIV's Palace of Versailles. They regarded as false the declaration that the rulers of Germany and Austria were responsible for the outbreak of the war. They regarded the reparations it imposed as certain to destroy the German economy. They were shocked by the limitations placed on their armed forces when powers such as France remained armed to the teeth. Of all the territorial losses, they resented above all those to the newly re-created state of Poland. The making of the new Poland cut off East Prussia from the rest of Germany in order to restore to the Poles a corridor to the sea. The Polish Corridor contained a large minority of Germans and allowed the Poles access to Danzig (now Gdansk), which, though German in population, became a separately governed Free City. The entire peace was seen as a Diktat, an unjust peace imposed on the Germans. Yet only a year earlier, in 1918, the Germans had been prepared to impose upon Russia a much more savage peace. If in 1919 and after they complained so bitterly, it was because the Germans did not really believe that they had been defeated. At the moment of the Armistice, none of the European territory of Germany was occupied by its enemies; instead, German armies stood everywhere beyond the Reich frontiers.

German resentments and French fears were obvious and disturbing factors in international relations in 1919, but President Wilson hoped to make his League of Nations the cornerstone of a new world order. All nations were invited to join the League. Their representatives were to be members of the League Assembly and to meet once a year to discuss matters of common concern and vote funds. Decisions, which could include the imposition of economic or military sanctions against an aggressor, were to be taken by a smaller body, the Council of the League, including Britain, France, Japan and Italy as permanent members. The machinery of the League was set up in neutral Switzerland at Geneva, where a

Wilson proposes League of Nations

permanent staff was soon at work, dealing with problems of international relations and of the general welfare of the world.

As it turned out, the most valuable work of the League was humanitarian in nature, carried on by committees established to deal with the urgent post-war problems of hundreds of thousands of refugees and prisoners of war and with more permanent issues of health and working conditions. The most important task of the League, however, was intended to be the prevention of another great war. That was why the Covenant of the League was included in the peace treaty. A 'covenant' means a list of promises. The signatories of the peace treaties and all states joining the League made a number of pledges designed to banish war. They pledged to encourage co-operation in trade and to promote disarmament. They promised too to respect the frontiers and independence of all members.

Covenant of the League incorporated in Peace Treaty

It was soon clear that making progress towards the banishment of war might be difficult. Agreement about disarmament was generally seen as an important step towards peace. Germany was compulsorily disarmed. Britain and the USA, anxious to save money, rapidly demobilized most of their enormous armies. The problem was France. Its chief security against Germany was its army of 600,000 men and it was adamant in its refusal to reduce its armed forces significantly. Protected from Germany by distance, Britain and the USA could take risks which no French statesman dared to run. Perhaps things might have been different had the French felt able to rely on collective security. 'Collective security' meant all countries clubbing together to protect any weak member of the League against aggression. In theory, this was what members of the League were supposed to do. Yet the most the Assembly could do was to vote for a resolution, and that had to be unanimous. The founders of the League supposed that usually states would give way before the moral force of world opinion. If aggressors did not give way, then the Council might act by imposing economic or military sanctions. Yet the League had no forces of its own; its ability to act depended on the

France resists call to disarm

'Collective security'

willingness and ability of the major powers of the Council to act in its
name. In short, the only military, as opposed to moral, force behind
collective security was the power of France and a Britain which
consistently refused any binding pledge to France.

Trust in the League was all the more surely doomed to
frustration because of the non-membership of two of the greatest
powers in the world. It was an American, President Wilson, who had
insisted on setting it up, but he mishandled the Senate (the upper
house of Congress, the American parliament) and failed to persuade
it to ratify the Treaty of Versailles and accept membership of the
League. Its inability to rely on the enormous economic power of the
USA was a very serious weakness of the League. The new Union of
Soviet Socialist Republics (USSR), as Russia was called after the
early 1920s, was also not a member, largely because it was committed
to undermining other states, if they were capitalist. This too weakened
the ability of the League to make an impact in certain areas of the
world, until Stalin decided to join the organization in 1934.

The peace-makers of Versailles were loudly denounced by the
Germans for treating them vindictively and unfairly, and the German
point of view has often been accepted. Yet consideration had to be
paid to France, which had made enormous sacrifices to defeat the
Germans. Its security had to be improved, but all the measures
which improved French security – disarmament of Germany,
demilitarization of the Rhineland, etc. – were bound to be regarded
by the Germans as punitive and unjust, because they all involved
treating Germany differently from other states. The underlying
problem was the collapse of the balance of power in Europe,
especially with the withdrawal of Russia during its long period of
internal reorganization, and there was little the peace-makers could
have done about that.

Limitations of the League of Nations

League hampered by absence of USA and USSR

Balance of power in Europe collapses

2. Britain's Defence Problems

In the 1920s Britain seemed to occupy a pre-eminent position in world politics, thanks largely to temporary factors, such as revolutionary upheaval in Russia, the results of defeat in Germany and the retreat of the USA into isolation. Yet in significant ways the First World War had weakened Britain. The British trading position had been undermined as the USA penetrated British markets in Latin America and the Japanese in China and India, while British industry concentrated on war production. Britain's share of global commerce had been 14 per cent in 1913 and after the war it continued to decline, to under 11 per cent in 1929 and under 10 per cent by 1937. 15 per cent of Britain's overseas assets had been sold and earnings from them had been proportionately reduced. The USA had been converted from a net debtor nation to a great creditor nation, with the result that New York rivalled London as a financial centre. The consequence of these developments was a tendency for Britain to earn less abroad than it spent. The British government was often in financial difficulties. The war had increased the national debt elevenfold and interest payments on it in the late 1920s took a far higher proportion of central government spending than in 1913. Financing a huge debt was not the only additional call on government funds. The arrival of full democracy and the competition of the political parties for votes forced the government enormously to increase social expenditure. The sum spent in 1933 was about five times higher than it had been in 1913, and by the later date social spending accounted for almost half of all government expenditure.

British post-war economic turmoil

New York emerges as rival financial centre

Given the vastly increased costs of servicing the debt and providing social services, something had to give and that something was defence spending. By 1924 the defence budget had been stabilized at about £130 million a year, about an eighth of all spending, whereas its traditional share had been about a quarter. These cuts forced the abandonment of the ambitious policies of the

Costs of servicing national debt and welfare provision

immediate post-war period, when Britain had intervened in Russia, Persia and Afghanistan and contemplated intervening against Turkey. Britain had also scaled back in another way. From 1920 conscription, so recently introduced, was phased out. Concern about popular feeling and the efforts of the political opposition to exploit it overrode the argument of the War Office that conscription was essential if Britain was to meet its worldwide responsibilities. In fact, the only responsibility that necessitated conscription was a commitment to Europe. The end of conscription heralded an attempt to retreat again into splendid isolation, like that of the 1890s, and to concentrate on Britain's imperial destiny.

Britain reduces military spending

Behind the reduction of military spending and manpower lay an assessment of Britain's strategic position. As early as August 1919 the War Cabinet instructed the armed services to operate on the assumption 'that the British Empire will not be engaged in any great war during the next ten years, and that no Expeditionary Force is required for this purpose'. The Treasury made use of this Ten-Year Rule to compel the defence chiefs to justify all that they asked for on grounds of immediate need. Since in the 1920s the world was generally peaceful, they could rarely make a convincing case for heavy defence expenditure and military spending went on falling. Even the navy, so favoured before 1914, was now seriously neglected. Battleships were not replaced; numbers of cruisers and destroyers were reduced; overseas bases were run down. The army concerned itself chiefly with the garrisons of India and Egypt. It wholly lacked the means to intervene in Europe.

The War Cabinet of 1919 ruled out the dispatch to the continent of another British Expeditionary Force (BEF). This made clear the wide difference between the French and British attitudes to the Peace of Versailles. For the French, Versailles was not an ideal settlement, since it did not give them all the security against Germany that they needed, but they were determined not to give up any advantage it did give them, since then they would be even less secure. If necessary, they were ready to use force against Germany, as they did in 1923. At the start of the year, the Germans failed to meet their obligation to pay reparations to France. In response, the French invaded the Ruhr industrial area to take by force the products which the Germans were not delivering as reparations. The British, by contrast, regarded the Peace as a settlement which could and should be renegotiated. The British tended to make a distinction between the militaristic and aggressive Germans who had been in the ascendant before and during the First World War and the moderates who had prevailed earlier and who, it was believed, had recovered control since the overthrow of the Kaiser in 1918. The British looked to revise the terms of Versailles in favour of the Germans, because they were sure that a reasonable, freely negotiated peace would produce political and economic stability in Europe from which everyone would benefit. For the British, the French occupation of the Ruhr set back this desirable outcome, triggering the collapse of the German currency, the mark, in 1923, an outbreak of violence between German Communists and the new Nazi Party and an explosion of hostility between invading French troops and German inhabitants.

France invades the Ruhr 1923

Collapse of German currency 1923

The British helped to ensure that French schemes to establish separate German states in the Rhineland came to nothing and that the occupation of the Ruhr soon ended. A different approach to reparations was tried thereafter. The Dawes Plan of 1924 and later the Young Plan of 1929 scaled payments down. Agreement on the controversial issue of reparations made possible the Peace of Locarno in 1925, which, unlike the Peace of Versailles, was freely accepted by the Germans. They, the French and the Belgians agreed to respect the borders between them fixed at Versailles, and Britain and Italy acted as guarantors. The French lost by the Treaty in that they could not again invade the Ruhr without falling foul of it and yet the British guarantee meant nothing in the absence of any plans to send a BEF to Europe. The British still evaded all but the most minimal commitment to France. Austen Chamberlain (son of the famous

Peace of Locarno - 1925

Joseph), Foreign Secretary from 1924 to 1929, declared that the maintenance of the Entente with France was 'the cardinal object of our policy', but he did not propose to assist any of France's eastern allies, should they be attacked. Less Francophile Foreign Office officials suspected that France's network of alliances was part of a plan for European domination.

Only in 1931 did British complacency about the state of the world come into question. Doubts about the Ten-Year Rule were raised, as evidence of secret German rearmament came to light, and the Rule was finally cancelled in 1932 after a Japanese attack on China. Even then British hopes for a positive outcome of the Geneva Disarmament Conference in 1932-4 postponed any action to remedy the deficiencies of the armed forces till 1934. Meanwhile, in January 1933, Adolf Hitler had come to power in Germany. Hitler was leader of the National Socialist or Nazi Party. He aimed to unite all Germans in one great national community, which would exclude those who were not Germans by blood, such as Jews and gypsies. Once in power, he established himself as dictator and worked to revive German power in Europe. He sought first to end all limits on German freedom of action and then to establish a New Order in Europe, based on German dominance of the continent. He expected the achievement of his aims to involve war and in preparation he began to rearm at breakneck speed as soon as he assumed power. Britain's slowness to act enabled the Germans to get ahead and put Britain in the demoralizing position of always playing catch-up. Even when the British began to rearm, British industry could not easily respond, since the relevant industries had run down during the years of disarmament. In certain crucial areas, Britain lagged far behind Germany. In the 1920s the Germans had developed a significant domestic aircraft industry on the basis of which the production of military aircraft could readily be set in train. Britain lacked this advantage.

In 1933-4 the Defence Requirements Committee (DRC) considered the shortcomings of Britain's armed forces and outlined a

Marginal notes: Ten Year Rule abolished 1931 · Adolf Hitler comes to power in Germany 1933 · German industrial superiority · Defence Requirements Committee (DRC)

programme to remedy them. The politicians insisted on revising the DRC's recommendations, partly to save money, but also to meet what Baldwin described in 1934 as 'semi-panic conditions' among the public about the control of the skies. In the early 1930s there seemed no prospect of effective defence against the German bomber. In theory, bombers could be destroyed by fighter aircraft, but hardly by the slow, poorly armed biplanes in service at the start of the '30s. Hence, in 1932 Baldwin had predicted that 'the bomber will always get through'. It seemed likely that in any war with Germany the Luftwaffe (German air force) would at once seek to knock Britain out by aerial bombardment that would probably, according to an official estimate, cause 150,000 casualties in London in the first week. The only hope was for Britain to get its blow in first. Therefore, the Cabinet, led by Neville Chamberlain, the Chancellor of the Exchequer, centred their defence plan on the rapid creation of a bomber force to rival that of Germany. They hoped that such a force would also have a deterrent effect which might assist the efforts of British diplomats. The casualty of this change in the DRC's plans was the Army's plan for an expeditionary force to be sent to the continent in the event of war. It was argued that the public, besotted by the League of Nations and ideas of collective security, as it was to show in the Peace Ballot held by the League of Nations Union in 1934-5, would never stand for a continental commitment. Ironically, the surest way of stopping the Luftwaffe was to deny it bases in Western Europe by fighting there, since its aircraft lacked the range to attack from Germany proper.

'Semi-panic conditions' in Britain 1934

Chamberlain launches bomber production programme

Britain's rearmament lagged behind that of Germany largely because for a long time Britain spent so much less on it. In 1933 the defence spending of the two countries was roughly equal, but in 1933-8 as a whole Britain spent only about a third as much as Germany. Only in 1939 did Britain again spend more or less the same as Germany. Throughout the 1930s the Treasury took the line that 'today financial and economic risks are by far the most serious and urgent the country has to face' and the Treasury achieved a remarkable dominance in the government. It was concerned that imports and exports should balance, a goal that would be threatened by rapid rearmament, which would suck in imports to make weapons, and till 1937 it resisted borrowing to finance rearmament for fear of the effects on confidence in the pound and on inflation. Hitler, by contrast, had absolutely no interest in a balanced economy or avoidance of a budget deficit and forged ahead with his rearmament programme regardless. Essentially, the Treasury envisaged doing what Britain had always done before: conserving Britain's strength for a long war. The strategy was risky. It assumed that the enemy would not become overwhelmingly powerful by winning a short war.

Treasury
concerns
delay
rearmament

The National Government under MacDonald (1931-5) and Baldwin (1935-7) had certainly not decided that Hitler would have to be fought. Indeed, their policies were confused and confusing. In April 1935 they tried a joint approach alongside France and Italy in condemning German rearmament, but then they resorted to unilateral negotiations and signed an Anglo-German naval pact in June, whereby the Germans agreed to limit their navy to 35 per cent of the Royal Navy's strength. The French complained that Britain had undermined the joint condemnation, but the British were trying to avoid any division of Europe into power blocs, which was supposed to have led to war in 1914. They had not decided that Hitler was irreconcilable and his occupation of the demilitarized Rhineland in 1936 did not change their minds. 'I suppose Jerry can do what he likes in his own back garden,' said the politician Anthony Eden's taxi-driver on 9 March 1936, and the Cabinet's view was not essentially different. It continued to be supposed that the aims of the Nazi regime were moderate and that the wild men could be counterbalanced by sane and rational figures such as Hjalmar Schacht, President of the Reichsbank. It was also hard to focus clearly on the German threat when so many dangers were looming in other quarters.

Anglo-
German
naval pact

3. The Danger from Japan and Italy

Before the First World War Britain had been able to resolve its difficulties with its other international rivals, France and Russia, and then to concentrate on checking Germany, identified as the most serious threat. In the 1930s Britain failed to achieve compromises with other potential enemies, Japan and Italy. This failure greatly impaired its ability to respond to the new German threat represented by Hitler.

In 1921 the US President Warren Harding (1920-23) invited the naval powers to confer in Washington about an agreement to limit the size of their navies and thus to prevent a new naval race, such as was believed to have brought about the First World War. The conference imposed limits of a total of 525,000 tons on US and British capital ships, 315,000 tons on Japan and 175,000 tons on France and Italy. All construction work would stop and there would be a ten-year 'naval holiday' during which no replacements would be built. The Admiralty was very unhappy with most of this. After ten years the fleet would be obsolescent and the shipbuilding industry would have decayed, so that making replacements would be difficult. The limit set would make it hard for Britain to uphold its interests in the Atlantic, Mediterranean and Pacific. The Anglo-Japanese alliance had helped to protect Britain's Pacific interests, but the USA, which saw Japan as a future potential enemy, insisted that this alliance must be ended. Britain was in no position to hold out against US pressure, since the alternative seemed to be a naval race with the USA, which Britain could not win, given the Treasury's insistence on massive cuts in the defence budget. The Washington Treaty had weakened Britain's ability to uphold the stability of the Far East and yet the USA had assumed no responsibility for enforcing the peace of the region itself.

America forces Britain to abandon Anglo-Japanese alliance

During the 1920s the peace of the Far East was not seriously disturbed, but at the end of the decade the Japanese economy suffered

ADOLF HITLER (1889-1945) AND BENITO MUSSOLINI (1883-1945)

Collapse of Japanese silk exports to USA

badly in the Great Depression. In 1930 the slump in the USA caused silk exports to collapse, with devastating consequences for millions of small farmers. Extreme nationalist and anti-Western views had already made progress in the army and economic troubles among the peasantry from which much of the army was recruited increased their appeal. Extremist elements came to believe that Japan could solve its problems by acquiring a sphere of influence in South-East Asia. As a first step, the Japanese army stationed in southern Manchuria staged an incident on the railway it protected, blamed the Chinese and proceeded to occupy the whole province. It set up the last Chinese Emperor, deposed in 1911, as a puppet ruler. More directly threatening to British interests in the form of huge investments was the fighting that broke out in Shanghai in 1932 between a Chinese army and the Japanese. Britain wholly lacked the military power to

Marco-Polo Bridge Incident

object to Japan's aggressions and the Admiralty urged that it was now imperative to build up British naval and air forces in the Far East in order to deter further Japanese attacks. This policy was thought to be beyond Britain's means at a time when there was a growing threat from Germany. The obvious alternative was to try appeasement. In 1934 Neville Chamberlain urged that Britain must seek agreement with the Japanese by offering a commercial agreement in China in return for a new naval understanding. It may be that the Japanese were already too far committed to empire-building to accept any compromise, but in any case the policy was not seriously pursued for fear of alienating the Americans. Britain ended up with no workable policy at all, merely, as its ambassador to Japan said, 'alienating one party [the Japanese] without assisting the other [the Chinese]'.

Negotiations with Japan fail 1934

The incoherence of Britain's policy in the Far East was partly due to the emergence of yet another enemy which distracted attention from the Far East after 1934. That enemy was Italy. Benito Mussolini had become ruler of Italy as early as 1922. His Fascist regime was in some ways similar to Hitler's: anti-Communist, anti-democratic and based on the person of the Leader (*Führer* in German, *Duce* in Italian). His ambitions too centred on a glorious foreign policy, though it lacked the racial overtones of Hitler's: he hoped to found a new Roman Empire which would dominate the Mediterranean. By the 1930s Britain had long since learnt to live with Mussolini and it was felt that he could be useful in keeping Hitler in check: he had helped to prevent a German takeover in Austria in 1934, for example. Both France and Britain were anxious not to alienate him.

Emergence of Fascist Italy as a threat

Italy, which already had colonial possessions in the Horn of Africa, had long coveted Abyssinia, partly to avenge a defeat suffered there in 1896. Though the area was not valuable, Mussolini hoped to enhance his prestige by a rapid conquest. No important French or British interests were at stake, but Abyssinia was a member of the League of Nations and the British electorate believed in the League. Pandering to pro-League sentiment, the British government followed

Economic sanctions on Italy

the League's condemnation of Italy by imposing a number of economic sanctions. They did not include vital commodities such as oil and were merely to keep public opinion in Britain happy while the diplomats discussed a scheme to give Mussolini the bulk of Abyssinia, which would avoid any breach with him. This plan, the

Hoare-Laval Pact

Hoare-Laval Pact, concocted by the foreign ministers of Britain and France, was leaked to the press and then disowned, Hoare being forced from office. Britain, then, had not succeeded in keeping Mussolini as an ally. Instead, he developed economic links with

Mussolini allies with Germany

Germany to overcome the sanctions imposed on Italy. Yet Britain had not done anything either to deter Italy or any other aggressor in the future. Mussolini was able to crow about his victory over the League and over Britain.

In 1936 civil war broke out in Spain. Mussolini became involved

Outbreak of Spanish Civil War 1936

on the side of conservative and monarchist generals such as Franco in order to strengthen Italy's strategic position in the Mediterranean and to prevent a victory for the socialist (and in part Communist) republicans. Once committed, he had to see his side through to victory or his prestige would have suffered. Over Spain too Britain failed to commit itself wholeheartedly to deterrence or appeasement of Mussolini. British and, still more, French opinion was deeply split and the two powers proposed a Non-Intervention Agreement. Other powers accepted the Agreement, but almost nothing was done to enforce it. Italy and Germany on Franco's side and the Soviet Union on the Republican side intervened with impunity. Mussolini was given little reason to fear Britain and France, nor was he offered any prospect of gain from their friendship. In the circumstances, it was not surprising that there was increasing talk of a Rome-Berlin Axis.

Anschluss March 1938

Mussolini's acquiescence in the Anschluss (the union of Austria and Germany) in March 1938 was a clear indication that he had moved into the German orbit. Britain's position now looked weaker than ever, with its hold on the Mediterranean under threat and imperial communications through Egypt and the Canal liable to be disrupted.

4. The Crisis over Czechoslovakia

In May 1937 Neville Chamberlain became Prime Minister. He had a big impact on British foreign policy, not so much by altering its direction as by pursuing established lines of policy with more energy and conviction. He hoped to achieve the elusive goal of a settlement with Germany.

Neville Chamberlain Prime Minister May 1937

After the Anschluss or absorption by Germany of Austria in March 1938, it was obvious that Hitler would next raise the issue of Czechoslovakia. This state had been created out of the Habsburg Empire after the First World War. It was the most industrialized of the new states of Eastern Europe, which made it a useful prize for Hitler – and the only functioning democracy – which made it an object of the Führer's hatred. Militarily, it was relatively formidable, possessed of strong fortifications and a large, efficient army. It was allied to France. While it survived, it restricted German freedom of action in eastern Europe. The principal weakness of the state was its multinational composition. The Czechs and Slovaks made up about two thirds of the population of 15 million, but the relations between them were uneasy. There were substantial minorities of Hungarians, Poles and Germans. The last group were the most numerous (over 3 million) and vocal. They lived mostly round the mountainous western rim of the country, known as the Sudetenland, and many were inclined to sympathize with the local Nazi Party and to demand autonomy. Hitler encouraged the Sudeten Germans in their demands and made the most of any incidents between them and the Czech police. At the end of May, he determined to invade the country by 1 October at the latest. German troop movements, riots in the Sudeten area in early September and a bellicose speech by Hitler convinced Chamberlain that war was imminent and that he must act.

Hitler incites unrest in the Sudetenland

In acting Chamberlain was not concerned for the Czechs. He had no affection for them or their makeshift, artificial state. At the height of the crisis, he was to say on the radio, 'How horrible, fantastic, incredible, it is that we should be digging trenches and trying on gas-masks here because of a quarrel in a far-away country between people of whom we know nothing.' Chamberlain was convinced that war would probably be suicidal. In March 1938 the Chiefs of Staff reported their calculation that in a war the Germans would outnumber the Czechs, French and British by 90 divisions to about 50 and they warned that Italy and Japan would probably seize the opportunity to launch attacks on the British Empire. Germany was also thought to have nearly twice as many front-line aircraft as Britain, able to inflict 50,000 casualties in the first 24 hours of war. All these calculations and predictions assumed a worst-case scenario: for example, that the Germans would be able to spare the Luftwaffe to bomb Britain when they were fighting the Czechs and French.

Germany's military superiority

Ironically, Chamberlain's desperate efforts to avoid war very nearly brought it about. He assumed that Hitler preferred a peaceful solution if he could get what he wanted by diplomacy. On 15 September he flew to meet Hitler to discover Hitler's peace terms and Hitler indicated that he wanted the cession to Germany of the Sudetenland. This aim seemed reasonable to Chamberlain, since the inhabitants of the Sudetenland were German. It did not seem so reasonable to the Czechs, since the cession of the area would leave them defenceless and would certainly encourage the Poles, Hungarians and Slovaks to make demands that would break up the state entirely. Yet the French were prepared to follow Chamberlain in accepting Hitler's terms, which left the Czechs with no alternative but to agree to them too. When Chamberlain met Hitler for the second time on 22 September, however, Hitler made difficulties about accepting the terms that had seemed acceptable the previous week. He appeared determined to fight the Czechs after all, but the British Cabinet could not agree that his new position was a reasonable one. It began to look as if all that Chamberlain had achieved by his intervention was to ensure that Hitler's war was with Britain as well as with the Czechs and their French allies. In the next few days the

Chamberlain fails to reach peace terms with Hitler

French mobilized their army and Britain mobilized the fleet. If finally war was avoided, it was thanks to a last-minute change of mind on the part of Hitler.

It now seems certain that Hitler was not bluffing in the crisis of September 1938. Until the last moment, he wanted to destroy Czechoslovakia by war because he believed that there was no better way of demonstrating Germany's determination and irresistible might. Yet on 28 September he drew back from the brink, impressed perhaps by the doubts of henchmen such as Hermann Goering, the head of the Luftwaffe, and by the evident lack of enthusiasm among Berliners as they watched a military parade through the city. Mussolini offered his services as a mediator, which made it easier for Hitler to give up his war without loss of face. The result of Mussolini's offer and Hitler's decision was a meeting at Munich on 29 September of the two dictators together with Daladier of France and Chamberlain. It was decided that Germany was to have the Sudetenland, Polish and Hungarian claims were to be resolved, and the remainder of Czechoslovakia was guaranteed by all four powers present. Hitler had achieved very cheaply a quite remarkable increase in German power, but it was noted by observers at the time that he seemed depressed rather than exhilarated. He was fêted in Munich, but so was Chamberlain, and for the same reason, that peace had been preserved, whereas what he needed to do, Hitler believed, was to make his people enthusiasts for war.

Munich Talks 29 September 1938

For Chamberlain, the most important fruit of the talks at Munich was not the agreement over the Sudetenland, but the Anglo-German Declaration of 30 September. This Declaration resulted from a private meeting of the Prime Minister and the Führer, which occurred just before Chamberlain left Munich for England. The two countries, they affirmed, would 'never... go to war with one another again' and were determined 'that the method of consultation shall be the method adopted to deal with any other questions that may concern the two countries.' This Declaration was the piece of paper which

Anglo-German Declaration 30 September 1938

Chamberlain famously waved after his plane touched down on his return to England. It marked, he hoped, the taming of Hitler, his agreement to proceed in foreign affairs by negotiation with Britain and France. Yet Hitler was determined not to accept an Anglo-French veto on his foreign policy, nor to confine himself to the moderate goals which the Western powers might accept. For him the Anglo-German Declaration was no more than a form of words which would become irrelevant as soon as Germany was strong enough to ignore the views of France and Britain.

5. The Undermining of Appeasement

Though Chamberlain was hailed as the saviour of peace when he returned home, his Cabinet and their advisors had been shocked by the revelation of the country's vulnerability during the crisis before Munich. Though the Treasury still worried about the economic consequences, rearmament was at last pushed vigorously ahead. In **New air programme approved 1938** November 1938 a new air programme was approved. Production of the fast monoplane fighters, the Hurricanes and Spitfires, was stepped up; the building of radar stations, to give early warning of aerial attack, was pressed forward; and the airfields and Fighter Command were linked by 'phone. It was beginning to be possible to stop the German bomber. Even greater changes occurred in the spring of 1939. Rumours of possible German aggression in the west drew attention to the vulnerability of France, especially now that its **Creation of European Field Force** eastern allies were gone, and led to the decision to create a European Field Force of six divisions. The Territorial Army was to be greatly expanded to provide reserves for the Field Force and conscription was introduced.

Though Britain was now preparing more busily for the worst, underlying difficulties had not gone away. Rearmament sucked in imports which were not balanced by exports. Government expenditure rose rapidly and could be met only by massive borrowing. The country's future economic stability was very seriously at risk. Hence there remained a strong case for appeasement in order to avoid war. Germany was offered economic inducements, such as an increase of credits so that it could purchase British colonial produce, in the hope of persuading it of the value of economic co-operation. If the policy did not work and Germany was not persuaded, then it would be all the stronger in war for having stockpiled important raw materials.

Economic case for appeasement

What was beginning to develop, in the months after the Munich Conference, was an increasing awareness of the risks of appeasement, combined with a decline of the hope that it might produce benefits. Hope declined chiefly because of what the dictators did in the six months after Munich. There was detailed press coverage of the attack on the German Jews on the night of 9/10 November, when synagogues were set on fire, Jewish-owned businesses attacked and individual Jews beaten up and arrested. Peaceful agreement with so violent and brutal a regime began to seem a chimera. Much more damaging to the prospect of peaceful relations with Hitler, however, was his treatment of Czechoslovakia in March 1939. Slovakia was forced to declare its independence and the Czech President was terrified into committing his country to German protection, whereupon the German army occupied Prague. All this was done without consulting Britain and France: the piece of paper which Chamberlain had brought home from Munich containing the Anglo-German Declaration was shown to be worthless. The Treaty of Munich, signed by Hitler himself, guaranteeing Czech independence, had been torn up as soon as it suited the Fuhrer. Since the area invaded by the German army contained hardly any Germans, it was now obvious that Hitler's ambitions went far beyond merely reuniting all Germans in an extended Reich. As further illustration of the insatiable appetites of the dictators, the next month Mussolini attacked Albania.

Post Munich Conference

Kristallnacht

Germany occupies Czecho-slovakia

Even before the occupation of Prague, public opinion in Britain was changing. The Labour Party, for so long attracted by pacifism, urged that assistance should be given to any states willing to stand up against the dictators. Conservative rebels such as Churchill ceased to be lone voices crying in the wilderness and a section of the press called for their entry into the Cabinet. Suspicion of Hitler's intentions was mounting in the Foreign Office and the Foreign Secretary, Lord Halifax, was sensitive to the changed mood. This shift of opinion was strengthened by the events of March 1939. The government increasingly felt that it must be seen to be doing something to stop Hitler. That is why guarantees were given to Poland, Greece and Rumania (Romania), rumoured to be Hitler's next targets. This is also a major reason why in April the re-imposition of conscription was announced.

Conscription announced

Within six months of what seemed their greatest triumph, the salvaging of peace at Munich, the advocates of appeasement were already on the back foot. Chamberlain still hoped to deliver peace, if not with Hitler, then perhaps with some moderate who might replace him. Yet more and more of those who formed public opinion in Britain no longer shared his hope. If Chamberlain failed to deliver what he had promised, then he and his henchmen would stand condemned as 'guilty men', who had strengthened Hitler by their concessions and who had only ever brought temporary peace with dishonour, since it had been purchased by the sacrifice of people such as the Czechs.

CONCLUSION

After the extraordinary run of successes of the 18th and 19th centuries in British history, the earlier decades of the 20th century appear an anti-climax. Britain still had the trappings of greatness, especially the possession of the largest empire ever known, but it lacked the economic and military might necessary to sustain its foremost position in the world. This was especially true after 1918, when Britain remained the global superpower only because the USA did not yet want the position and Russia had collapsed in revolution. It was only a matter of time before Britain's bluff was called. The difficulties of the 1930s arose from the simultaneous emergence of three serious external challenges, many more than Britain could cope with.

Too much concentration on Britain's decline as a world power, however, obscures important achievements during the first four decades of the 20th century. One of these was economic in nature. For all the technological achievements of 18th- and 19th-century Britons and the astonishing development of trade and industry, the British economy in the Victorian era was very narrowly based on a few staple industries, such as coal, cotton goods and shipbuilding. It was one of the often overlooked achievements of Britain in the inter-war years that the economy was diversified, even if the process was not rapid or complete enough to remove the scourge of mass unemployment from South Wales, Scotland and northern England. On the back of economic change, many inhabitants of Britain began to enjoy an unprecedentedly high standard of living. Far more people lived decisively above subsistence level than in Victoria's day. Perhaps the most obvious sign of this spread of wealth was the appearance of millions of owner-occupied semi-detached homes ringing the cities of England and lining the main roads.

Not everyone shared in the prosperity of the inter-war years, but those who did not were no longer subjected to the indignities of the

257

Poor Law. Bit by bit the foundations of what would later be called the Welfare State were being laid. It was increasingly accepted that it was the job of the state to relieve those suffering poverty caused by old age, sickness and unemployment. The New Liberals in power in the years before the First World War blazed the trail, but in the 1920s the Conservatives very greatly extended what the pre-war Liberals had done. The means-tested unemployment benefit of the 1930s has become a symbol of the niggardliness of the state, but it was generous by comparison with benefits offered in Germany and the USA and it was high enough to take some of the sting out of unemployment and ensure social peace. Those with jobs got used to paying far more in taxes than had been thought acceptable in Gladstone's day.

Perhaps the greatest achievement of the earlier decades of the 20th century was the relatively trouble-free absorption into parliamentary politics of huge sections of the population previously excluded. In the Edwardian period the omens for the peaceful evolution of the British political system were not particularly good. The Liberals under Asquith seemed incapable of dealing with the demand of women for the vote, while the Conservatives seemed unwilling to accept the loss of the political veto which the powers of the House of Lords had formerly given them and came close to encouraging civil war in Ireland. Yet in the end the electorate was tripled in 1918 and no great crisis ensued. Under the emollient leadership of Baldwin after 1922 the Conservatives learnt to play the game of politics under the new rules with considerable success. They displayed a talent for winning elections and for ruling without exciting serious extra-parliamentary protests. The replacement of the Liberals by the Labour Party as the main opposition to the Conservatives made surprisingly little difference. Most Labour ideas and quite a lot of their personnel came from the Liberals and the attraction of radical socialist thinkers like Marx for the hard-bitten pragmatists of the trade unions was always small. For all the talk of socialism, Labour in the 1930s under Attlee was committed to parliamentary politics and to a mixed economy in which private firms would continue to play the major role. Perhaps too the role of the King was significant. George V adapted the monarchy to the new democratic age. He did what he could to make the system of government work and in his unshowy way this modest and conventional family man provided a unifying symbol to which people of most views could feel loyalty.

Peaceful political evolution characterized this period of British history, but as usual, things were different in Ireland, where self-government was achieved only after a violent confrontation with Britain. A civil war within southern Ireland then followed over the terms of the country's future relationship with Britain. Developments in India, however, indicated a different possible route towards self-government. The Government of India Act of 1935 largely pacified the nationalists and envisaged Indian progress towards Dominion status as enjoyed by Canada and Australia. A path towards decolonization avoiding violent confrontation with the colonial power had been sketched out and was to prove of the greatest importance later in the century. Moreover, it had been sketched out when the party of Empire, the Conservatives, was in power as the mainstay of the National Government. This suggested that decolonization beyond the British Isles would prove much less traumatic than the issue of Ireland had done.

Britain's foreign policy in the early decades of the 20th century has often been considered a failure. Yet in many ways Britain enjoyed great success in the period between the death of Queen Victoria and the peace treaties after the First World War. Germany, the state identified as the most serious enemy, was kept isolated and unable effectively to challenge Britain's world power. When it made a bid to dominate Europe, it was defeated in part by a military effort unparalleled in British history. British military achievements in the First World War have often been denigrated, but the British did eventually learn how to defeat the best army in the world, that of Germany, which by late 1918 saw no possible route to victory.

Yet the sequel to the success of 1918 did not turn out well. The unfortunate outcome had little to do with the allegedly punitive terms of the Versailles Treaty, which in any case Britain always intended to revise in Germany's favour. The heart of the problem was that Britain ended the war even more grossly overextended than when the war had started. In Europe the old balance of power disappeared with the demise of the Austrian and Russian monarchies. Only a firm alliance of Britain and France could in the long run prevent German domination of Europe. Yet Britain would not commit itself in Europe, as the French desired, because of its commitments elsewhere. Since the collapse of the Ottoman Empire, it had assumed responsibility for the stability of most of the Middle East. In the Far East Britain had since 1902 relied on its alliance with Japan to protect its interests in the area, but the Americans insisted on Britain's ending the alliance. The British built up their power in Singapore, but they lacked the ships that might have made their power effective. All these commitments had to be borne by a country that no longer far outdistanced economically all possible rivals. It is not surprising that British power was increasingly a hollow façade, unsupported by armed might. In such circumstances, Britain was bound to appear feeble in the face of any serious challenge, especially if challenges came from more than one source at a time. No doubt, many valid criticisms of British foreign policy in the 1930s can be offered, but the statesmen of the period sat down to the game of international politics with a very poor hand of cards.

INDEX

INDEX

Tillett, Benjamin 27

Tirpitz, Alfred, Admiral 102-4

trade and commerce: alcohol 42-3, 127; colonial trade 78-9; foreign competition 154-5; free trade 39-40, 79-80; imperial preference 78, 192, 230; import tariffs 38-40, 76-7

trade unions: General Strike 1926 187-9; growth in number 17; legal rights increased 43; legality questioned 24, 26; 'new unionists' 21-4; pay and conditions strikes 28-9; political representation 25, 30-1, 181; Trade Union Congress (TUC) 22-3, 25, 28; Triple Alliance 30; war production 179

transport 26, 28, 30, 45, 193

TREATIES: Entente Cordiale (1903) 86; Anglo-Japanese Alliance (1902) 100; Entente Cordiale (1903) 100-1; Anglo-Irish Treaty (1921) 208; Egyptian Independence Treaty (1936) 224; Washington Naval Treaty (1921) 229; Treaty of Versailles (1919) 238; Anglo-Japanese Alliance (1902) 247; Washington Naval Treaty (1921) 247

Triple Alliance 95, 97-8

Triple Alliance (unions) 30

Ulster Unionists 50, 200, 211

Ulster Volunteer Force (UVF) 50, 200

UNITED STATES 98, 99-100, 137-8, 143, 160, 247

Versailles Peace Conference 1919 235-8

Victoria, Queen 73

voting rights 62-3, 71

WALES 52, 213

Webb, Sidney 20

Wells, H G 35

Wilhelm II, Kaiser 96, 105

Wilson, Woodrow 235, 238

women:.anti-suffragism 63-4; campaign for voting rights 62-71; divorce rights 57-8; domestic service 18, 61, 159; employment opportunities 18, 59-60; higher education 58-9; political support groups 57, 62; role in local politics 64-5; upper and middle classes 55-6; voluntary work 57; war effort 70; working class 60-1

Women's Social and Political Union 66-8

Woolf, Virginia *169*, 169-70

working class: indoor entertainment 33; political representation 21, 23-6; religious organizations 20; sport 32; standard of living 18, 29, 43, 157-8; state benefits 44, 48; trade union growth 22-4

World War I: aircraft, use of 117-8, 142-3; Armistice signed 149; artistic remembrance 151-3; Belgium's appeal for help 113-4; Eastern Front *131*, *134-5*, 139; economic hardships 120-1; economic mobilization 126-8; Gallipoli Campaign 1915 134-7, *135*; gas warfare 117, 120, 137; German invasion begins 128-9, *129*; legacy of 149-53; *Lusitania*, sinking of 122, 137; Middle Eastern campaigns 133, 145, 145; post-war British Empire 214-7; press propaganda 121-2; tanks 144; trench warfare 116-7, 118-20, *119*; U-boats and shipping losses 121, 137, 141-2; Western Front 129-30, 132, 137, *138*, 140, 144-5, *146-7*, 146-9